'A' IS FOR ALASKA:
TEACHER to the TERRITORY

NAOMI GAEDE-PENNER

The Story of Anna Bortel Church

'A' IS FOR ALASKA:
TEACHER to the TERRITORY

*To Mickey!
My dear friend and
former neighbor.
Anna Bortel Church*

TATE PUBLISHING & *Enterprises*

Published by Tate Publishing & Enterprises, LLC
127 E. Trade Center Terrace | Mustang, Oklahoma 73064 USA
1.888.361.9473 | www.tatepublishing.com

Tate Publishing is committed to excellence in the publishing industry. The company reflects the philosophy established by the founders, based on Psalm 68:11,
"The Lord gave the word and great was the company of those who published it."

Book design copyright © 2011 by Tate Publishing, LLC. All rights reserved.
Cover design by Amber Gulilat
Interior design by Blake Brasor
Alaska map by Barbara Spohn-Lillo
Front cover photo from Anna Bortel Church collection.
Photos within book are from the collections of Anna Bortel Church, Elmer E. Gaede, and Naomi Gaede-Penner
Songs are copy written by Anna Bortel Church

Published in the United States of America

ISBN: 978-1-61777-756-1
1. History, United States, State & Local, West (Ak, Ca, Co, Hi, Id, Mt
2. Biography & Autobiography, Educators
11.07.19

DEDICATION

· ·

To the pioneer school teachers who considered it worthy to leave the comforts of home and teach Alaskan children.

APPRECIATION

Comprehensive details, facts, and context of this book would not have been possible without the contributions of Alaska peers in the 1950s and 1960s. Appreciation goes to notes written by Margie Gronning, and letters shared by Dr. Elmer and Ruby Gaede.

Transforming the story into quality book form was made possible by Sarah Pat Quigley's first edit; Sally Dolan's painstaking read for flow, accuracy, and congruency; and Marianna Gaede, Nicole Penner Clark, and Jack Neff's thoughtful responses as typical readers.

RECOGNITION
AND REAL NAMES

Not everyone can write, yet everyone does have a story. With due diligence to accurately portraying the characters in the book, and the people with whom Anna overlapped in activities and mission, except when unknown, real names have been used, with the distinct purpose of providing these characters with clear identities, and subsequently, recognition. Apologies are extended for errors that can occur due to erosion of facts or perceptions over time.

These characters include, but are not limited to, the first Free Methodist ministry workers in Alaska; school staff and orphanage workers in Valdez; Public Health Services employees Dr. Elmer Gaede, and nurses Marjorie Macomber, and Mary Ann Burroughs; Arctic Missions missionaries Roy and Margie Gronning and Mel and Pat Jensen; Bureau of Indian Affairs school teacher and administers including Florence Feldkirchner; State Department of Education employees Robert Isaac, Harriet Amundson, and Herman Romer;

In regards to the Native people, it is my hope that by using actual names, their specific history will be documented by the State of Alaska, as well as within villages; and that this history, in story form, will be more easily remembered and transferred to future generations.

A portion of the royalties for this book will go to the Alaska Historical Society.

TABLE OF CONTENTS

Foreword 15
Part I   21
1923–1954 21
Growing into a Schoolteacher 23

Part II   35
1954 35
North to Alaska 37

Part III   49
1954 - 1957 49

1954 51
This Territory Called Alaska 51
Puzzle Pieces 63
If God Builds the Foundation 71

1955 77

The Unwelcome Visitor. .77

Romance Arrives 81

1956 89

Needed: Teachers in the Territory 89

All I Need is a Break 95

Chocolate Cake Flambé. .105

1957 109

Beware the Blows! 109

Easter Eggs—Boiled or Frozen? 113

Part IV   119

1957 - 1960 119

1957 121

A Stepping Stone North .121

Getting Acquainted 129

Making Myself at Home .139

School Bells 145

The Automatic Flu 153

No Doubt About it—Winter is Here! 163

Christmastime in Tanana. 169

1958 175

Potlatch Celebration. 175

Ordinary Village Life 181
An Uncertain Future 189
The Going Gets Tough 203
The Tough Get Tougher 219

1959 231
The 49th State 231
Further North? 239
Breakup 251
A Few More Alaska Experiences 255
Taking it Easy 261

1960 267
Changes, Chickens, and Conclusions 267
More Prescriptions for Adventure 275

Glossary 277

Suggestions for Further Reading 281

Reader's Guide 283

Songs and Music Sheets 285

Index 289

Endnotes 295

FOREWORD

Naomi and I had Miss Bortel for a second-grade school teacher in Tanana, Alaska. Naomi was a white girl and I was Athabascan Indian. Anna Bortel looked at both of us as children to be educated, without preference one for the other. We were different, but alike, and our school teacher set a foundation for how we viewed education and our future pursuits. We are examples of lives touched and shaped by Alaska education in the 1950s and 60s.

Naomi and I left Tanana, and our lives veered in different directions, yet we kept in touch sporadically over the years. In our adult lives we discovered, to our amazement, that our lives had paralleled each other's and we had gone into education ourselves. Naomi obtained a secondary English Education degree and then a master's degree in Counseling, which she used to teach post-graduate studies. I achieved a master's degree in Special Education, Pre-kindergarten through grade twelve.

More recently, we learned we share a passion to disseminate, learn from, use, and preserve Alaska history. Our perspective is not as academics researching the History of Education in Alaska or studying educators, or theorists experimenting with what works for Alaska students. My commitment was made evident in the thesis for my master's degree, "How Alaska Natives Learn and Changes to Alaska Education that Would Ensure Success." Naomi's dedication comes through the medium of her Alaska non-fiction writing.

Narratives of early school teachers, such as Anna Bortel in A is for Alaska: Teacher to the Territory, are living treasures, dug up from the past. These stories not only honor the educators themselves, but each of the students who are mentioned; and then, as the concentric circle widens, the accounts give insights into the communities in which the teachers served, therefore preserving distinctives of people groups and entire communities.

From the spirits of hunter-gatherers, pioneers, immigrants, explorers, clergy and missionaries, we are Alaskans: Alaska Natives, Native Hawaiians, Pacific Islanders, and others who came, who listened to the still small voice of our Creator who has given us a purpose to serve. We have taken our individual concentric circles and integrated them with others to make new beginnings from what was good in the past and good in the present to create good in our future. As educators we have the opportunity to mold lives, create positive memories, and build strong people who can meet the new world and change our fear, despair, or rebellion by working together.

—Sally Woods Kookesh, Koyukon Athabascan
M. Ed. Special Education-PreK-12 and teacher
at Eli Katanook Memorial High School
Member of Alaska Native Sisterhood Camp 7
Member of NEA Alaska, Chatham-NEA, and
National Indian Education Association
Proprietor of the Kootznahoo Inlet Lodge in Angoon, Alaska

THE STORY BEHIND THE STORY

Naomi:

In 1957 a sagging white Knights of Columbus building faced the legendary mile-wide Yukon River. Forty-eight Native and non-Native boys and girls attended school in two rooms. There on the dusty Front Street of Tanana, in an Athabascan Indian village with a population of around 300, I came to know Anna Bortel.

I was seven, and living with my family in Tanana, where my father served as the Public Health physician at the Tanana Hospital. Like the other first and second graders, I adored Miss Bortel. I remember her wide smile, twinkling blue-gray eyes, and quick chuckle. She transformed ordinary events into amusing stories, and her imagination made up for the scarcity of teaching materials. One day I packed up my blond, pig-tailed Betty doll and announced I planned to move in with her! Another time, I informed my mother, "When I grow up I wanted to be just like Miss Bortel."

Today, when I have the pleasure of visiting with Anna, I am struck by her keen memory and her indomitable attitude. What would have overwhelmed another person, served only to exhilarate her. Anna had a story inside her, which waited to be lived. She ranks with ordinary people who follow the stirrings of their hearts, and make an extraordinary difference in the world.

Anna:

I was a late-bloomer. I was not out to change society, nor did I intend to travel to the ends of the world. Instead, I was a mischievous little girl who liked to talk in class, beat up an annoying boy on the school bus, and made average grades. My schoolteachers and classmates never dreamed I would be a schoolteacher, much less venture to the unknown wilds of The Alaska Territory.

I was also very sociable. When we had guests for dinner, my more reserved older sister, Mildred, would gently kick me under the table to subdue my chattering. This social inclination probably prevented me from later becoming depressed in remote Native villages.

My parents were protective. My independence was not nurtured. Nevertheless, within this sheltered environment, my autonomous spirit emerged. Given this upbringing, it seems unlikely I would head north to Alaska, a trek that entailed driving up 2,000 miles of chuck-holed, dusty Alaska-Canada Highway, with no job at the end. My father admonished me, "Girls just don't do these kinds of things. I'd rather see you go on a ship to Africa." In the end, however, he was my chief admirer and cheerleader.

ABC

Naomi often asked me to write my Alaskan stories. I was reticent to do so, but she kept encouraging me. In 1991, I gathered up Alaska slides and flew from my home in Oregon to meet Naomi at her home in Denver. While I projected slides on to a blank wall and recounted fond village teaching memories, she jotted down notes and kept her transcriber tape recorder handy. I'd brought along a box of letters I'd mailed home weekly to my parents during my Alaska teaching. Over time, we poured over my worn diary, yellowed newspaper clippings, a file of correspondence with the State Educational Department, and boxes of photos. I spent days at an Oregon beach house reliving and writing my stories.

I am indebted to Naomi for editing, researching, adding more geographical/historical information, and organizing these stories into a book for publication.

PART I

1923–1954

GROWING INTO A
SCHOOL TEACHER

Snow swirled around our school campus of five army Quonset huts until it resembled an igloo encampment. In fact, by November, the snowfall equaled the previous year's total accumulations and visions of Valdez's record-setting depths danced in my head. Piles of snow provided excellent insulation around the huts, but plummeting temperatures meant an ongoing battle to keep our fickle oil stoves operating.

One evening, my two young co-teachers, Herman Romer and Harriet Amundson, and I welcomed the invitation to see nature films at the Public Health Hospital, which was one of the few diversions in this small Yukon River village of 300 people. Herman, a youthful looking Eskimo and Harriet, a hardy Minnesota girl, rowdily gathered their outdoor gear for the short walk in the minus 43 degrees dark night and begged me to hurry with my preparations. They'd completely forgotten our stove vigil, which was the outcome of inadequately designed narrow, three-quarter inch copper tubing which carried the oil from the outdoor tanks into the huts and to the stoves. With these polar temperatures, the oil would thicken and eventually slog to a stop. The stoves would shut down. We'd be doomed.

"We can't leave or the stoves will freeze up," I exclaimed in frustration.

My colleagues stared at me incredulously. They had already made the leap to the warm world of the hospital basement, where the movies would be shown, and where running water, consistent electricity, and most of all, dependable heat prevailed.

"We have to tap the lines to keep the oil flowing," I reminded them. I took a deep breath of courage, "Let's work on all five lines before we leave, and then one of us can run back in a few hours to go through the same procedure all over again."

We plunged into the frigid blackness. Powdery snow wrapped around our legs. The tapping rang loudly in the crisp air.

ABC

Thanksgiving came and went, as did Christmas. The New Year did not start with a celebration, but with body-shaking tears. Following a New Years Eve party, I'd worked endlessly on our oil lines. At 3:00 a.m., I collapsed in bed, chilled to the bone, and utterly worn out. I had reached the end of my rope and had no reserve to cope with one more minute of this pioneer life. Harriet struggled numbly with the lines at 4:00 a.m. Temperatures were freezing outdoors and now sunk lower inside our Quonset. She desperately fought to restore some heat. Herman quietly carried our potatoes and onions to his place to keep them from freezing. Our fortitude was nearing a numbing standstill in the winter battle.

On January 6, 1959 I wrote to Mr. Robert Isaac, at the Territorial Education Office in Juneau.

> Mr. Krazinzki, from the Anchorage office, told me to have larger tubing put in from the tanks to the stove, but I have to have someone who is willing to do it, and even then there is no assurance that the freezing problem would be solved. There is a large tube and heating cable on the one at the old school and it still freezes.
>
> Dr. Gaede suggested that I just not have school when it gets 40 degrees or more below, since it is wearing us teachers out

to fight to keep the fires going, and even then we can't get the temperatures up so the children can take off their coats.

One plunge of the thermometer to minus 50 caused us to send all the children home. Two days later, my chimney sooted up and would not produce heat. Again, I sent my class home. Doc and Ruby came over and together we cleaned it out. We were completely covered with the grimy residue.

Whatever had I been thinking when I'd started that long drive to the Territory of Alaska?

ABC

On May 10, 1923, a warm spring day with blooming white spirea bushes and fragrant purple lilacs, I was born to Clifford and Myrtle (Crosby) Bortel in Grand Rapids, Ohio, a small, quiet river town. My parents recounted the event, often on my birthday, and over the years I could visualize it in my mind. On that day, my father, who worked as an exterior and interior decorator, was wallpapering in a farmhouse across the Maumee River. He spent much of his day around people, and that suited him well with his outgoing personality. With my mother's imminent delivery due date, he made an unplanned trip home for lunch in his black Model T Ford. My tall and usually slender mother could not conceal beneath her long dress and bibbed apron that she was indeed heavy with child, but showed no symptoms of the grand event. Father rapidly downed a bologna sandwich, cranked up the Ford, and sped back to wallpapering.

The wallpaper paste was barely mixed when he received a phone call. "Come home right away!" urged my mother. "I'll call Dr. Drake and my mother."

My father hopped into his Model T and careened into the driveway in less than the anticipated 20 minutes of driving time. As was the custom, babies were born at home. Dr. Drake made a house call, and in spite of my screaming protest, around 3:00 p.m., ushered me into this wonderful world.

"Her name is Anna Marie," my mother unhesitatingly informed Dr. Drake. Grandma Anna Crosby proudly held me in her arms.

After assisting in this miracle of birth, Grandma took my three-year-old brother, David, and 16-month-old sister, Mildred, home with her to allow my mother to regain her strength and concentrate on my needs. Actually, Mildred, already pensive and shy, posed no problem, but David, an explosion of energy, would have depleted Mother's energy reserve.

I entered a world where bread sold for 9¢ a pound and milk for 56¢ a gallon. A new Ford cost $295. Gas to run it was 22¢ a gallon. Whooping cough and tetanus vaccines came into existence; however, they must not have been widely used since later, all three of us children contracted whooping cough.

President Harding held office and just that year he had pounded a ceremonial spike into the ground to complete the Alaskan Interior rail line. Nonetheless, our family had no reason to think about the Last Frontier. Weakened by the tour to Alaska, yet ill for only a week, the 57-year-old president shocked the nation when he died on August 2, 1923. Subsequently, Vice-President Calvin Coolidge was sworn in as president of the United States, a nation whose population had grown to 111,947,000.

ABC

When I was six months old, my father was offered a partnership by Mr. Long, an elderly man who owned a wallpaper and paint store in Bowling Green, a larger town about 16 miles east of Grand Rapids. We left our little town with its beautiful dam and old flour mill, and purchased a home on North Prospect Street, about a mile north of the store. Our Grand Rapids house was rented for $2.00 a month, but later when my father raised the rent to $2.50, the renters moved out.

When I was four, my parents built a house on an acre of ground on Napoleon Road, at the southeast edge of town. They felt this would be a better place to raise their three children. I cherished the two-story, yellow frame house with a broad screened porch across the front and shutterless windows. This house with four bedrooms, an attic, a basement, and a two-car garage was built for $5,000 in 1927. Delicate white-flowered spirea bushes clumped beside the house and all along the front and side yards.

Millie and I shared a bedroom upstairs. Daddy had used his decorating skills and painted a double oak bed with pink enamel. Going beyond the basics, he put decals on the headboard, with a fluffy, white rabbit over my side and a bushy-tailed squirrel over Millie's. In this bed, we little girls would talk about the day's events, laugh, and share our hopes.

ABC

Just like Daddy and Mother, I thrived on relationships. My best friend, Betty Smith, and I played house with our dolls underneath the back porch. Other days, we shaped mud into pies, decorating them with the ripe red seeds from Mother's asparagus bed. Muddy tar felt good between our toes, too. On very hot days, the tar softened on the asphalt road in front of our house, and we took off our shoes to squash the bubbles with our big toes. Sometimes, the steaming water inside the bubbles would catch us by surprise and spray our toes.

In late summer, my round-faced friend and I would scratch our legs and arms climbing the prickly thorn apple trees. Then we pushed aside the scarlet leaves and nibbled on the tiny fruits.

David did not allow girls in his bedroom, or on his bike. When he spent two summer weeks on Uncle Newman Crosby's farm with our cousins, Roger and Burton, I decided it would be my golden opportunity to learn how to ride a bike. He would never know I'd borrowed his bike. Up and down the hard-packed graveled driveway I practiced. I tumbled and picked myself up, and tried again. Eventually I ventured onto the paved road. I relished the feel of wind playing in my short bobbed hair.

One afternoon while helping Mother can cherries in the basement, I pleaded, "Why does David have a bike and Millie and I don't?"

Before she could answer, Daddy's voice boomed down the stairs, "Come quick! Look at this Blue Racer!"

We flew up the steps, thinking there must be a snake outside. There, before my wide eyes was a beautiful new blue bicycle! I jumped up and down, hugging Daddy and shouting "A bike! A bike!" I grabbed the handlebars, pushed off, and glided out to the road. No more riding David's boy's bike anymore. Millie and I had a wonderful girl's bike.

Mother tolerated all these childhood ventures, and the bumps and bruises didn't thwart my explorations.

ABC

David, Anna (age 7), and Millie Bortel (1931)

At age five, my parents enrolled me in kindergarten. The classroom, a mile north of our house, was located on the campus of Bowling Green Normal school, a teacher-training school, now known as

Bowling Green State University. Nap time on sundry colored pieces of carpet was an initial recollection of school. *"Why do we have to rest when we're not tired?"* I wondered. Lying still was inconvenient when a myriad of other possibilities existed.

I waited for the slow clock hands to make 20 minutes pass. Then I saw the silhouette. Jimmy, a rotund boy, lay flat on his back with his legs outstretched. Sunlight streaming in from the east windows accentuated his high, round stomach. For the longest time, the mound remained absolutely still. Then he coughed. His whale shape heaved up and down with each exertion, and his legs made sharp jumps. Time went by more quickly as he coughed intermittently and I anticipated his next move.

The next fall, I was old enough to wait with David and Millie at the bus stop to go to first grade at South Main Street Grade School. As I bounded out the door on that first school day, mother tried to straighten my out-of-control hair, which had turned from blond to light brown and was cut short with severe bangs. Impatiently, I waited in my new homemade, blue print dress with puffed sleeves, hopping on one foot, trying to catch sight of the school bus. Finally it arrived and my school life began.

I loved Miss Baker, who wore a black chiffon dress with a hemline that by design went up and down, making points around her legs. Instead of looking sour and making us think teachers delighted in scolding children, she praised us for doing good work. One day when my mother and I were walking down the street, I saw Miss Baker. Dashing from my Mother's side, I ran ahead, grabbed Miss Baker's arm, and impulsively exclaimed, "I wish you were my mother." As typical as it is for children to adore special schoolteachers, I wonder how my mother felt.

When I first rode the bus to school, I stood behind David and trusted him to protect me in annoying or scary situations. That didn't last. Soon I tackled life's provocations on my own. When we three Bortel children climbed on the bus, I'd find myself confronted by Harry, a plump red-haired boy who lived about half-a-mile from us. Wooden benches, worn smooth and shiny by years of transporting children, ran around the perimeter of the bus, and Harry deliberately seated himself at the opposite end of the bench seat where I always sat. Each school day, the scenario was the same. Harry smirked at me and gathered up all the force of his stout body. Planting his feet firmly on the floor, he pushed off from the bench's end, and blasted toward me. I braced myself, turned my back, and clung to the seat, hoping my fingers wouldn't get stuck in the gum, commonly disposed of beneath it. Chortling, he would slam into me, pushing me toward the front of the bus.

At breakfast one morning, I told myself that this would be the last day for such humiliation. When Harry climbed onto the bus, I glared at him. He sneered. I prepared myself as he launched himself toward me. The human cannon ball gained speed. My heart throbbed in my ears. After the impact, I jumped up, grabbed his stringy red hair with one hand and pounded on his head with the other. His freckled face contorted in surprise. I turned red and breathless. When I released my grip, he meekly retreated to his spot near the back of the bus. I never had trouble with him again. For years, I had trouble with a guilty conscience for giving him such a beating, even though my take-charge spirit came in handy when I beat on uncooperative oil stove fuel lines in Alaska.

All the same, if anyone had told me I would become a schoolteacher I wouldn't have believed it. A teacher role fit Millie, who was the studious one, but David and I were content to receive average grades. It was obvious to my teachers that I *did* enjoy my classmates!

ABC

At last summertime arrived. No sitting at school desks. Vacation time. Bare feet. We children went to Grandpa and Grandma Crosby's house in Grand Rapids. My Ichabod Crane-built Grandpa sometimes scared the younger grandchildren by clicking his false teeth when they neared him in his leather chair; but his love for his grandchildren showed through when he'd bring out his candy sack of peanut-marshmallow treats. Grandpa delivered the milk to several houses. Completing his route, he stashed the crate of returned empty milk bottles in the bushes and walked over to Huffman's Grocery Store. Behind the store counter and in a back room, men sat around black and red checkerboards. Cigar smoke and talk of politics filled the air.

Grandma looked his opposite, and the way a grandma should be—short, soft, round, and dusted with flour. Occasionally, she would go to the wall cupboard, get out a clear, cut-glass pitcher where she kept change, look at me out of the corner of her eye, and reach in for a nickel. After a quick, "Thank you, Grandma," I'd skip out the front door and breathlessly arrive at the gas station, where the clerk transformed the nickel into a quarter-pound chocolate candy bar. Slowly, I'd walk back to the house, unwrap my prize, and enjoy the thick sweetness of each bite.

Even though my grandparents lived in town, they had an ample lot with a barn, chicken coop, and a fenced-in chicken yard. As a city girl, this appealed to me. I tagged along after my grandma as she walked to the barn to milk Bossy, the milk cow. Grandma would hobble Bossy's back legs together so she wouldn't kick, and then stuff in the cow's switch-like tail, too. Adeptly she balanced herself on the three-legged milk stool, making the milk sing as it hit the bucket.

"Do you want a drink of milk?" she asked one evening.

"Oh, yes!" I answered.

"Stand still and open your mouth," she instructed me.

With anticipation I obeyed. Grandma aimed at my mouth and Bossy's warm milk zinged across the room and hit its mark. I gasped in astonishment and Grandma laughed until her eyes squinted and I thought she was crying.

When I wasn't watching Grandma hook rag rugs or piece quilts from remnants, I would go fishing with Grandpa. Before he would take Grandma and me down to the Maumee River, he and I would get a tin can, go out to the chicken yard, and move the long, weathered walking boards that ran across the yard. There beneath the damp boards we would dig for fishing worms. It seemed like a game of hide-and-seek as we would dig and they would squirm away. Eventually, we would have a can full of bait.

While we walked down to Grandpa's wooden rowboat, I would carry the can, stuffing in any contrary worms that were reluctant about their impending swim. It never occurred to me to be squeamish; this was just a part of life. Grandpa would situate his long-limbed body in the boat, dangle the worm on the hook, and then sit back while the red and white float bobbed on the water. My easy-going grandpa could sit for hours, whether the fish were biting or not. This style suited him, not me. Before long, I was whispering excitedly.

ABC

When I finished high school, I was not interested in attending Bowling Green State University (BGSU), only a mile from home. Instead, I set my mind on going to the Free Methodist College, Spring Arbor Junior College, 90 miles away. This choice had more to do with my desire for social life, than with education. My father, a frugal man, thought that, obviously, Bowling Green State University made more sense because it was less expensive and I could live at home. I resisted.

We presented our cases. I said, "I will work for one year, save money, and then I can pay to go to Spring Arbor." He conceded. Off I went, and promptly found part-time employment in a variety store and as a nanny. At the end of the year, my father willingly helped with my freshman tuition at Spring Arbor College.

After completing my freshman year, I returned home and enrolled for summer school at BGSU. Actually, I was surprised to find myself attending college—although back in the 1940s, what else could a young woman do who was not married? I was even more startled to find myself taking education classes.

After the war, teacher shortages were the result of low pay and poor conditions. Consequently, potential teachers could take specific classes and achieve temporary teaching certificates, if they agreed to complete their course work and obtain a degree. Therefore, while completing my college work, I applied for a teaching position at Crissey, Ohio, 22 miles from Toledo, and promptly signed a year's contract for $1,150. A real job, real money, and the bonus of my older sister, Millie, as the principal of the same school!

The following year, Millie and I accepted teaching positions in a larger school in Monclova, Ohio. After teaching for two years with the modified qualifications, I decided to complete my education at Greenville College in Greenville, Illinois. Once again, I looked forward to living in the dorm and making new acquaintances. As before, I was involved in a variety of musical groups.

Nearing the completion of my Bachelor of Arts in Education, I began to consider what I would do after graduation. A close friend, Dorothy Bronson, had come up with an idea, "Why don't you apply at Pekin, Illinois, where I have just accepted a teaching position?"

The interviewing process went smoothly. The school board was willing to hire anyone—that is, if they promised not to marry during the 1947–1948 school year. I signed the contract without hesitation.

My first grade students spilled over into every corner of the room, and sometimes I wondered why I continued to be a teacher. Rooms were crowded and children easily upset. One day, several little girls rushed into the classroom to solemnly report, "Mary is in the restroom crying." I hurried to see what had happened. It seemed Mary had never encountered a flushing toilet and the gushing water had frightened her.

Later in the fall, a pupil put a shiny red apple on my desk. That afternoon as I was clearing my desk, after my little students had gone home, I noticed with amusement the state of my gift. Just as Eve had been tempted in The Garden of Eden, some child had not been able to resist taking a large bite out of my apple!

The following year, the new Wilson School was completed and I transferred. It was the most modern school in Illinois, and every teacher's dream. In fact, teachers traveled from all over the state, including Chicago, to visit.

Anna teaching at Pekin School (1947 – 1954)

The newspaper carried non-stop reports and photos of the classroom activities and field trips of this model school. Daddy beamed when he pointed out my picture to people. "See how our Anna loves children, and how they love her, too." At age 28 I found myself in an enviable professional position.

Now, I had some money. Now I could buy a car and stop catching buses and rides with friends. In the summer of 1951, I withdrew $1,050 of my hard-earned savings, and purchased a shiny, new green 1951 Styleline Chevrolet with bulky outline and square cutouts around the wheels.

PART II

1954

NORTH TO ALASKA

· ·

At the age of 30, I knew I liked to travel and, a bit caught off-guard, that I liked teaching. And, I was single. Other women my age were married, with their lives and future decided as a wife and mother. Without that default, I was on my own to figure out what to I'd do and where I'd go. I don't know how exactly Alaska wedged its way into my heart and life, but I do remember starting to read books, such as *O Rugged Land of Gold* by Martha Martin, and articles about that distant and mysterious American territory. My heart and mind surged with excitement as I learned about frozen wilderness areas with access only by dogsled, remote Native villages, and the Northern Lights dancing across the Arctic sky. *My fascination is only a passing fancy–it will fade with time,* I told myself.

In May 1953, when the Free Methodist Mission Board offered me a teaching position at a Christian day school in Florida, I carefully considered the offer. Their letter outlined an opportunity to expand my career to teaching children of different ethnic groups. This appealed greatly to me; yet, to my surprise, the pull northward hadn't lessened, even with the knowledge and practicality that if I chose to head North, I would have to be on my own and without my denominational Mission Board support, since its affiliations did not extend into Alaska.

One winter night, in early 1954, I knelt beside my bed with my hands folded on the patchwork quilt. I felt God's presence and His very real summons to go to Alaska, despite the fact I didn't have a teaching position there. Some people would think this was a strange and illogical decision. Here I was, sought after by a Christian school. Furthermore, at Wilson School, I'd been offered a substantial increase, a $200 per year raise for the following year. That latter incentive did not tempt me in the least, thanks to the influence of my Grandmother Crosby, who had written in my autograph book when I was a child, "A good name is rather to be chosen than great riches."

I made the decision to go to Alaska. Colleagues at school raised their eyebrows.

"Will you live in an igloo?" one individual queried.

"The sun never shines in the winter," another declared.

"And, there's snow all the time," added another.

I packed up and returned to my parents' home in Bowling Green, Ohio.

That summer, Ernest Keasling, the Free Methodist General Conference Superintendent of the Young People's Missionary Society, wrote about my journey to Alaska in the *Young People's Missionary Society News*.

World Youth crusade theme of the YPMS for the past four years challenges young people in every walk of life. Just recently the call came to the central lay representative and Illinois conference YPMS president, Anna Bortel.

For years she has been promoting crusade but just this spring the Lord tapped Anna on the shoulder and said, "This time it is you." She leaves for Alaska this month.

When the Lord first called the youth leader, she wanted to be sure it was the right step so thought if a job opened up and everything worked out right, it was the leading of the Lord. But the Lord even knocked that prop out and her final commitment was she would go even if it meant scrubbing floors when she got there.

"The Lord has made things definite to me and I do praise Him," writes Anna. "I have always been interested in missions and had a great desire and a willingness to do mission work. Before I felt God wanted me right here, so I tarried as long as He led."

As of June 1, Anna resigns as lay representative and conference president. We are going to miss this sparkling girl on the council team but our loss is lessened when we consider the work she will be doing. Pray for Anna as she goes that the Lord bless her and reward her with souls.

—The Editor

On June 14, 1954, I awakened to sounds downstairs, letting me know that Mother was already in the kitchen. "It's important that you eat a good breakfast before taking a trip," she insisted.

I breathed deeply the aroma of Mother's pancakes, eggs, and coffee as I carried the last suitcase downstairs and out to the fully-loaded Chevy. I'd miss her loving care and delicious meals.

"Where is Daddy?" I asked, returning to the kitchen.

She was quiet a moment, "He got up early to go work on one of his rental houses ... Anna, he just can't say good-bye."

He feared he'd never see me again if I drove over the desolate chuck-holed highway to Alaska; his view into my future was dim. On this day of departure, Daddy would lose one of his girls. On this day, I grasped the edge of my dream.

Alone in the driveway, I hugged Mother. "We love you, Anna." Her voice caught. "Watch for bears!"

I closed the Chevy door and backed out the drive-way. Mother stood weeping and waving. I checked my watch: 9:30 a.m. I was finally on my way to the great Territory of Alaska.

ABC

Before I'd left Ohio, my finger had found Valdez (Val-DEEZ) on a map; a tiny dot of a seaport in southern Alaska that lay tucked into one of the bays within the large Prince William Sound. Between Ohio and Valdez stretched 4,408 miles.

I'd learned about this small town through church officials who connected me with Wilson and Jay Stein, a young couple who was starting a Free Methodist church in Valdez. When I wrote them in February, 1954, Jay eagerly responded, "We have been earnestly praying that God would send workers this way."

My correspondence with Jay painted reality into my mental picture of Valdez and heightened the allurement of Alaska: *Do you know that snow piles up to 300 inches? Then you'll need rain gear, too, for the wet spring and fall. We really can't buy much here, in the way of clothes, but we order from Sears & Roebuck out of Seattle...*

I couldn't wait to experience this intriguing new life. If only I could close my eyes and be there. Jay suggested that the easiest method to bridge the gap between here and there was to drive to Seattle and put my car on the ferry, in order to avoid the Alcan Highway. This would cost $150 to $175 and only take about five days. If, however, I chose to drive, she advised that it would be prudent to have a traveling companion: *Be prepared for only 2,000 miles of pavement and then the gravel roads, deteriorating to dirt and mud... gas will be very expensive 57¢ to 85¢ per gallon; however, once here it is 34¢.*

Dorothy Fisher, a young woman who had stayed with me in Pekin, was compelled to join me, and she figured she could find some kind of summer work there. I knew she wouldn't whine no matter what we faced on this unknown journey, and I'd taught her to drive, which would be an enormous help with over 4,000 miles to cover.

Jay offered several job possibilities. She and Wilson had worked at the salmon cannery, which ran in July and August. Wilson earned over $400. (Men usually made more than women, since men worked longer hours.) Room and board would be provided.

Another prospect was to work with the youth and children of their fledgling church group. I could volunteer for a while, but in the long run I needed money to exist. Jay also advised me to send my transcripts to the Department of Education in Juneau, with a description of my prior teaching experiences. In addition, she suggested that I send applications to the school boards in Valdez, Ninilchik, Homer, Anchorage, Fairbanks, Seward, Chitina, and Glennallen. I felt confident I'd find a job soon after I arrived.

ABC

I headed to Sterling, Illinois, for Dorothy, or Dot as she like to be called. She was ready to go with her blue jeans cuffed around her ankles, showing off white bobby socks, and navy Ked sneakers. We were off!

Our first day was idyllic, driving about the Mississippi River in northeastern Iowa through German settlements. At noon, we picnicked in a park and in the evening cooked alongside the road. We were prepared for cooking with my aluminum camp set and a gasoline Coleman burner Daddy had sent along. Fried pork chops were our first gourmet dinner. Eventually, with 451 miles behind us, we made it to St. Cloud, Minnesota.

Dorothy cooking on a Coleman burner beside Anna's 1951
Styleline Chevrolet.

I carefully recorded daily details in my diary:

June 16, Mandan, North Dakota, 391 miles

We bought day-old rolls and donuts, but couldn't find any oleo—it's just "butter country" here. [1] We stayed in Mandan, where we found a cheap hotel ($3). There was no bath soap, so we took Dreft (a laundry soap) showers.

June 17, Harlem, Montana, 482 miles

We prepared a delicious supper of liver and onions. After I played my accordion and Dot wrote her boyfriend, Bob, we strolled around town.

June 18, Calgary, Alberta, 403 miles

We exchanged our traveler's checks for Canadian money and on $40.00, I lost $0.85. Considering how expensive things will be in Alaska, we splurged and bought banana splits. We walked around town and saw our first totem pole.

The hotel is loud with raucous laughter, people stumbling into the non-sound-proof walls, and drunken expletives.

June 19, Slave Lake, Alberta, 333 miles

We fled Calgary at 5:40 a.m and drove to Edmonton. Since we were heading into rougher terrain with more primitive roads, we purchased a shovel and a log chain, in case we needed to be pulled out of a ditch, or had to clear something out of our way.

At 1:10 p.m. at Westlock, Alberta, we bade farewell to paved roads and started through the dense north woods on dirt roads, or should I say muddy roads? For the first time, I wondered, Am I doing the right thing? Can we make it? In one place, a tree had fallen across our pathway. Feeling like real pioneer women, we got out and hefted it off the road. We prepared our supper—chili, bran muffins, and jelly. I relish outdoor cooking!

June 20, Valleyview, Alberta, 130 miles

The excitement for the day was seeing our first wildlife—a black bear! In the distance, we sighted him ambling along the road, but by the time we caught up to him, the roly-poly black shape had disappeared into the tall underbrush.

June 21, Fort St. John, British Columbia, 210 miles

The treacherous road between St. John and Dawson Creek in British Columbia

This is the longest day of the year and certainly what seemed to be the longest day of driving. Today's rains turned the roads into muddy, slippery ruts. We crept along at 20 to 25 mph. Just this side of Smokey River, we were cautiously descending a hill and as we came around a curve, there sat a semi-truck jack-knifed across the road with barely a car's width between it and the embankment edge.

I descended the hill. I could see a mud-splattered black car approaching from the opposite direction. Between us lay a one-lane bridge. I looked over the road shoulder into the canyon. What a drop-off.

"I don't think this is going to work," I said, gripping the steering wheel. We edged toward the bridge and slowly started up the hill. His car hadn't left us enough room to pass. We stopped and reversed down the incline to let him go by. When I returned to first gear, the car wouldn't budge. Dot opened her door. She could not get a foot-hold to stand up. The slick, gumbo mud was so wet that it was like stepping on a film of soap on glass. We turned and frowned at each other.

Within moments, we heard the lumbering construction caterpillar coming toward us. The driver gave us a big toothless grin. He had dried mud to the top of his knee-high boots, as well as splats on his canvas coat. The bulldozer cleared the dirt behind us so we could back up. Without a second thought, the driver swung down, sank deep into the mud, and hooked a cable to our car. His lack of teeth didn't matter in this situation. We were grateful he pulled us up the hill.

As we pulled out of Dawson Creek, we recognized the Mile 0.0 milepost, which signifies the official start of the Alaska-Canada Highway. After driving 47 more miles, we arrived at Fort St. John. To reward ourselves for our hardy spirits we bought steaks.

Tonight, we are staying in a hotel—at least that is what the sign says in front. It doesn't have running water unless we run after it, but there is a bed.

June 22, Fort Nelson, British Columbia, 251 miles

We really broke the speed limit as we kicked up dust at 30 to 40 mph.

June 23 Watson Lake, Yukon Territory, 334 miles

Last night, we had one narrow bed and the mosquitoes attacked me all night. About 1 a.m. I got up in the dusky light, lit a match (since there was no electricity), and tried to locate the source. The elusive critters stopped buzzing and went into hiding. I smeared myself with 6–12 mosquito repellent, slid back under the blankets.

June 24 Krack-R-Kreek, 369 miles

Nothing is broadcast over the radio, without a human voice there is just the bumping of the tires on the washboard road as we swerve around potholes. It would be lonely to travel alone, not being able to share in the beauty of the scenery or the humor of various trials. Few cars travel this highway. We toured Whitehorse and ate a wonderful roast beef dinner in a restaurant for $1.25. Before heading back to the main road we visited Sam McGee's log cabin, the legendary character in one of Robert Service's ballad poems.

Here in Krack-R-Kreek, we're staying in an old army barrack. We were given a pan of hot water and a bottle of drinking water.

June 25 Log Cabin Lodge, 369 miles
We're almost there! Only 227 miles to Valdez. After going through customs, we stopped at Tok Junction to give information about the car, and at 2:40 p.m. we entered Alaska! We exchanged our Canadian money for U.S. money and lost 3¢ on the dollar. Our last night before reaching our destination!

The Territory of Alaska!

On June 26, 1954, we bumped toward our destination. The past 12 days, we'd skimmed over dusty, rough roads with hairpin turns that burned up brakes and unraveled nerves. These stretches had been interspersed with rewarding views of flowing ribbons of murmuring water, which momentarily crept toward the highway, then abruptly turned away and disappeared into alders and spruce. Now the Chugach Range loomed before us.

"No wonder they call these the 'Alaskan Swiss Alps,'" I remarked to Dot.

Even at the end of June, snow filled in the distant valleys and striped the hills. Nearby, pink wildflowers clung together with wet, green, spongy moss on the slick gray-black shale edges. At the treeless summit of Thompson Pass, trickles of gray water ran alongside the road, and in and out of dirty snow caverns. We rounded a curve. Never had we seen mountains whose peaks looked like shark's teeth. Ahead of us, Worthington Glacier, gritty with age and carved with deep turquoise ruts, gave the illusion of pouring onto the adjacent road.

Thundering waterfalls pounded on rocks and welcomed us to Keystone Canyon. We pulled off the road to experience the spectacular, deafening effects of Bridal Veil Falls, which cascaded down with frothy fringes. The moist air clouded my glasses. We drove off, marveling at the creamy devil's heads, luxuriant green ferns, and mountain ash, which crowded into narrow canyons along the road. At a second scenic stop, Horsetail Falls divided and produced two luminous white showers against black outcropped rocks.

When we left Keystone Canyon, Lowe River became our companion. Sandbars with bleached-white driftwood mottled the flat, silty-gray, glacier river.

We had to be close to our destination, but I couldn't see a body of water anywhere. *If we are nearing Valdez, which is on a bay, why can't we see an opening?* At that moment, seagulls overhead signaled that the bay was close by. A once obscure dot on the map was about to take on three-dimensional life. "We made it!" "We made it!" I shouted as we caught sight of cabins poking out of the woods and the large blue-green bay unfolding before us. The theme song for our trip came to my lips with more meaning than ever:

> He holds my hand, Jesus holds my hand...
> ...The road may be long, but my Savior is strong
> And He holds my hand.

ABC

The epic construction of the 1,520 mile Alaska-Canada Highway (Alcan) began on December 7, 1941, with the Japanese attack on Pearl Harbor, and later on Dutch Harbor in the Aleutian Islands of Alaska. The danger of invasion brought a startling reminder that there was no direct land route from the lower United States to the

Alaska Territory, which had become a strategic military outpost, and that travel to and from Alaska was restricted to water.

In the spring of 1942, the combined forces of the U.S. Army Corps of Engineers, the Public Roads Administration, and civil engineers began hacking into the vast wilderness with D-8 "swamp Cats." Natives, trappers, and prospectors joined the rigorous pioneer efforts. At one time, 11,500 troops, 7,500 civilians, and 11,000 pieces of equipment worked on the road. Dawson Creek, Watson Lake and Whitehorse awoke one morning to thousands of construction workers demanding food, shelter, and entertainment. Alongside the cabins, grocery stores, and post offices, popped up rows of prefabricated barracks and warehouses. A town's population could be 350 one day and 1,000 the next or vice versa.

Within eight months, with approximately eight-miles-per day, the goal of making a road was achieved; albeit with 90° turns, 25 percent grades, and timber truss bridges.

On November 20, 1942, the Alaska-Canada Highway officially opened with 133 bridges and 8,000 culverts (six per mile.) This progress was achieved in spite of plunging winter temperatures that snapped steel and solidified oil in crankcases; and heavy rainfall and spring-thawed bogs that swallowed trucks and bulldozers. In the sharp blizzardy air, "God Save the King" and "The Star Spangled Banner" rang out from the 18th Engineers Band.

Stout-hearted travelers met the challenge of the Alcan, coming prepared with extra spare tires and reserve gas cans. In the 1940s, mileposts were put up at communities along the highway (beginning with Mile 0 at Dawson Creek) as reference points to guide travelers through the wilderness and serve as mailing addresses for local inhabitants. In 1949, *The Mile Post*, a thick travel guide, identified milepost numbers with gas stations, food, and lodging accommodations, and points of history and interest.

ABC

Alaska: 586,412 square miles. Alaska boasts the tallest mountain in North America–Mt. McKinley, towering 20,300 feet. Some

55 peaks are over 10,000 feet high. The early native Aleuts called it, *Aleyeska*, "the Great Land." Early Russian settlers heard the word as *A-la-a-ska*. In 1867, Secretary of State, William H. Seward purchased Alaska from Russia for about 2¢ per square acre. Many Americans believed it to be a wasteland of ice and snow; subsequently, it acquired the nick-name of *Seward's Folly* and *Seward's Icebox*.

PART III

······································

1954–1957

1954
THIS TERRITORY
CALLED ALASKA

Valdez town and seaport on Prince William Sound (1954 – 1957), before the Good Friday Earthquake in 1964.

"We look a little worn from our journey." Dot grimaced.

We stopped at a swiftly rushing stream, washed our faces and hands in the ice-cold water, and combed our hair. The rippling stream repeatedly washed the flat gray river rock and invited us to toss a stone or two before facing our new world.

"Now we're ready for our debut," I said in high spirits. "Valdez, here we come!"

At 4:00 p.m. on June 26, 1954, we drove into Valdez. Even with uncertainties, the future looked as bright as the afternoon sun that hung high in the huge Alaska sky. Dot pulled out the directions and the precisely drawn map to Andrew and Louela Taylor's trailer. Although Wilson and Jay Stein had been my initial contacts with Valdez, they had returned to Missouri for two months and had temporarily passed the hospitality baton to the Taylors, whose arrival from Cincinnati, in a dilapidated truck with all their belongings, barely preceded mine. Louela hoped to obtain a teaching position, and Andrew expected to use his carpentry skills to build the church and to serve as pastor as well.

With Dot's navigation we found the travel-sized trailer house on Alaska Avenue, parked behind the Steins' house, which we were to sublet in their absence.

Jay had written to me earlier, *Valdez has really boomed. A modern house rents for between $80 and $100 per month; however, you may rent ours for $50.*

The Taylors opened the door and Andrew's handshake matched his slow, comfortable Louisiana drawl. Louela looked like she'd been expecting company; although, she had no idea we'd be arriving just then. Her fitted bodice dress with full-skirt flattered her figure, and her dark hair was secured neatly at the nape of her neck with a wide ribbon. Their two pre-kindergarten sons, James and Roy, stood back and studied us. At that moment, I had no idea that Roy would be one of my students, and that this little boy, who seldom spoke but worked diligently at his desk, was a vascular surgeon in the making. Louela urged us to stay for supper, which we did, even though I wasn't sure how we'd all fit in the tiny trailer. The delicious meal of sockeye red salmon, baked whole, with sliced onions was only the first of such entrees in this northern country. Already we felt more like friends than strangers.

"Well, the sun's still up. Let's see the town," drawled Andrew.

"The sun is always up, there's no hurry," laughed Louela. They both radiated excitement like kids at a new playground.

We drove down to the docks where water lapped against the piers, which held the dock high above the water, allowing for the ebb and flow of the tides. Even though I knew the bay flowed into the ocean, I saw no sign of an exit. It was as though the mountains held the bay in a giant bowl.

Back from the docks lay a neatly designed town. The straight gravel streets appeared to be carefully engineered. Assorted wooden structures lined up along McKinley Street, while several churches were scattered across the checkerboard town.

Alaska Ave. in Valdez, (1954-1957)

Both Keystone and Alaska Avenues dead-ended into the docks with nearby salmon fisheries. Seagulls shrieked and searched for dead delights on the shore or floating in the water. In this town and tucked into outlying forested areas, 600 people lived in winter and 1,400 in summer.

Even with its precise layout, the town still presented a decidedly disheveled appearance. Later, when I commented to a neighbor about the unkempt yards, with weeds flourishing, woodpiles unpiling themselves, and clotheslines standing askew, she reprimanded me, "We like our town this way. We don't need criticism from outsiders."

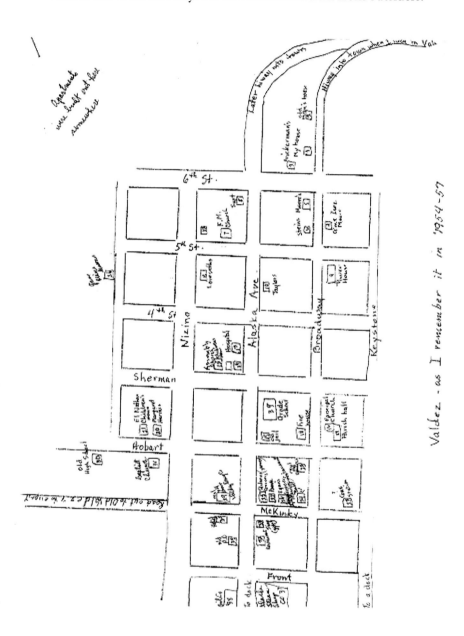

Town of Valdez (1954- 1957)

This rough-and-ready attitude extended into the business section, where the boardwalk would never have passed a safety inspection. Gingerly we walked around sagging sections, and then as
Dot stepped off the end of one board, it flew up behind her like a
teeter-totter.

"Walking in the dusty street might be safer," joked Andrew.

We explored the town and found only the bare necessities at Bill
Egan's Valdez Supply and Gilson's Mercantile. These two grocery
stores carried a variety of canned goods and produce at varying prices.
We meandered around making observations and comparisons:

> boat eggs–$0.79 a dozen, and carried by boat from Seattle.
> fresh eggs from across the Bay—$1.00 a dozen
> hot dogs—$0.67 per pound
> a sack of flour—$3.65
> bread—$0.40 a loaf
> hamburger—$0.80 a pound

A bank, a gift shop, two restaurants, the Pinzon Bar, a drugstore, a
dry cleaner, a post office, a gas station, and a hospital rounded out
the community's minimal services.

"I will be roughing it without a five-and-dime store," I quipped.
"And a shoe store that carries size 10AAA!"

All the same, I floated euphorically above these minor inconveniences, which at this point seemed amusing.

ABC

Aunt "Pedo" Esther Peterson and Aunt Louise Segerquist at a garden in the Matanuska Valley,
near Palmer, Alaska, while on the way to a conference at Lazy Mountain Children's Home.

Before we could even launder our traveling clothes and hang them on the clothesline, the Taylors had introduced us to their recently-acquired friends. Aunt Louise (Segerquist) and Aunt Pedo (Esther Peterson), as the children called them, immediately invited us to help in the El Nathan Children's Home. These women cared for eight children, ages six to 19. Aunt Louise was middle-aged and widowed. Aunt Pedo was close in age. Her red hair flew around her jolly face and her sense of humor offered a balance to Aunt Louise's earnest reticence. After years of service, these dedicated and over-worked women were grateful for any assistance, and at once, I was elbow-deep in flour baking caramel cinnamon rolls. The tall sun had slipped behind a cloud for the day, and it felt good to be in the kitchen with the oven's heat permeating my body. Following our initial sunny greeting, the bashful sun made only rare appearances. The consistently rainy, cool days which kept the weeds and luxurious underbrush thriving, drew us towards the oil space heater as our bodies adjusted to the climate.

Between baking projects at the Home, I changed aprons and switched to cutting the children's hair, I even gave Toni hair permanents to several of the girls—which were a bit tricky since most had very thick, straight hair.

Like many other people, I thought most Alaskans were Eskimos. Seeing the children with similar skin color but eyes with various slants, I was confused.

"We have Aleut (AL-lee-OOT), Indian, and part Polish children, but no Eskimos," Aunt Pedo explained to me. "In the early years, El Nathan had about 100 children," she continued. "In many cases, their parents were in the hospital with tuberculosis, or had died from that disease."

I wondered what *was* farther north, and how the Eskimos were different from the Aleuts, and what happened to the children if their parents were not at home. Perhaps there were orphanages like here, or at least some kindly souls who cared for and loved those children, too.

Later, I met Margaret Keenan Harrais. The outspoken 82-year-old woman was the town commissioner, and her presence and voice commanded attention, I paid attention when she described the initial efforts by Banche Nason to start the home in 1935.

"We started the hospital by lifting on our own bootstraps," she said, looking me squarely in the eye. "The Home, however, did *not have* bootstraps. It did *not* have *one dollar!* But they did have faith in God–'El Nathan' means 'God-given.' They now have the main building and four cottages, also 17 lots, 12 of which were donated."

I could tell she was proud how this little community had stepped up to the challenge; and, in no uncertain terms, she recognized the source behind its achievement.

This wonderful wilderness woman, born in Ohio like me, had arrived in Skagway to teach in 1914. By 1916, she was school superintendent in Fairbanks, where she met her husband, who was a miner in the 1880s. Margaret fanned the flames of my frontier spirit and I deeply admired her impressive example.

The Free Methodist Church group had met in the Steins' home, where Dot and I were house-sitting temporarily. We agreed to continue with this arrangement. Fifteen to 18 faith-seeking adults and children crowded into our borrowed house. After discussing our interests and experiences, Dot volunteered to teach the beginners and Louela the intermediates. Since Andrew would preach, I took the adults. Friendships developed naturally as we worked together and shared a common focus.

ABC

Dot was hired on quickly at *Dorothy's Restaurant.* Unfortunately, the $12 a day job with $2 in tips only lasted two days. Apparently the work was slower than they'd expected. I took in some ironing which added to the grocery fund. Before the Fourth of July weekend, a neighbor lady came over.

"The clerk at the hotel says they are out of rooms. It is quite common for local people to house the tourists at this time of year. Would you be interested?"

I thought for a moment, "Our davenport does turn into a bed, so I imagine we could keep someone."

We concurred that $5 would be sufficient.

"Looks as though we'll be able to eat for another week," said Dot, half-jokingly.

The Fourth of July in Valdez drew people from all over Alaska, and we soon received a call from potential roomers, a couple who had driven from Elmendorf Air Force Base in Anchorage.

"Valdez is the most beautiful place," said the captain.

"Yes," chimed his congenial Southern belle wife, "This is our fourth year to visit here."

All the races and contests for young and old took place on Main Street. We stood on the sidelines for the pie-eating, egg-throwing, bicycling, and three-legged races, but when it came to the nail-pounding race, Louela and I competed against each other, putting our novice skills to the test. Louela took first place and received $2.50. I didn't fare as well but still received 25¢. In lieu of shooting off fireworks, the city officials paid every person who entered the contests. This resulted in greater participation. Besides, with the long daylight hours, fireworks in the sky would have been unimpressive.

To supplement our pantry stock, we picked salmon berries and high-bush cranberries outside of town. Besides "living off the land," the El Nathan Home shared moose meat from the road kill donated to them. This introduction to Alaskan wild game with its strong taste didn't appeal to me.

"Not all moose tastes this gamey," Aunt Louise assured us.

ABC

Salmon, a staple of life in the area, was as abundant as the wild berries. My first salmon fishing occurred within days of our arrival. The Taylors loaded up a bunch of us into their truck with sideboards and jolted up the Richardson Highway to the Chitina cut-off. After quite some time, we entered a notch, where the railroad had previously traveled. It resembled a tunnel with an open top. After closing the mine, the rails had been removed and now vehicles traveled on the skinny road. Following more lurching, the truck shifted to a halt, and we all tumbled out.

Apprehensively, I studied the steep rocky decline. We climbed up, rather than down, and walked along a rocky ridge. After traversing a distance, we started our descent at about a 45 degree-angle to the treacherous, swirling Copper River. I found myself on hands and knees creeping down the sheer rock and gravel face, trying to find hand-holds and secure ledges for my feet. One wrong move and the precipice would offer no pity, letting me slide straight down onto the rough boulders or into the agitated glacial waters. Once at the bottom, I caught my breath and balanced on a large rock, rooted firmly into the hillside, but jutting out over the water far enough to extend a five-foot-diameter dip net, which was attached to the end of a long pole. The object was to entrap unsuspecting fish, while at the same time, not get dragged into the current.

Without delay, Dot scooped up her first salmon and squealed in delight.

By 9:00 p.m. I'd caught two salmon. One measured 29 inches and weighed six pounds. Other people had caught many more. Altogether, we tallied up around 65 slippery, tail-flipping fish. The El Nathan family would be well-fed this winter. Even though plenty of daylight remained, we were wet, mosquito bitten, and chilled to the bone.

We crept up the rocky trail with numb fingers reaching out to pull us to safety. Andrew dragged back most of our hefty mass of fish. The rest of us could barely balance ourselves and our unwieldy dip nets. Too tired for words, we forced ourselves into the truck and sat close together to borrow body heat.

Back at the El Nathan Home we completed our "fishy" business, and proceeded to can our commodities. I'd never worked with, let alone seen, a machine that sealed tin cans. The process kept me spellbound.

"Look! They are round," I said in disbelief. Now the salmon resembled those I'd seen back home.

ABC

When I asked about a daily newspaper, Louela replied, "There is no daily newspaper. You will find information and news taped on the store windows and at the post office there will be public notices."

Sure enough, once a week, the *Valdez News,* which was a news-sheet, was printed and posted.

One particularly gloomy day, when gusts of wind splattered big drops of rain against the windows, the lack of a daily paper, along with other nonexistent services and conveniences, hit me. Alaska was not only romantically rustic, but remotely removed. The reality of isolation was sinking in.

I huddled near the stove wrapped in a thick-yarned afghan. Steam from my hot cocoa rose against my face and I closed my eyes, before taking a sip. When I opened my eyes, the vapor had blurred my glasses. My vision had been blurred when I'd imagined Alaska, but how could I have imagined reality for something for which I had no comparison? Jay *had* written that it was a nine-hour milk-run flight from Seattle to Anchorage, with numerous stops before the plane actually reached its final destination. Dot and I had felt every bump of our 4,408 mile, 12-day expedition. The truth was, that to reconnect with the United States was a journey, not just a quick jaunt.

There were few radio connections to the United States, or even to Anchorage. In most cases, all we could get was sporadic static in the evening, which some desperate soul had dubbed, the "Static Quartet."

Glancing out the window, I watched heavy clouds rolling down the encompassing mountains, obscuring the sky, and once again replacing the soaring sun that had welcomed us to this much anticipated destination. Pressed in by mountains around me, a flat sky above, and a large body of water before me, I experienced an uneasy confinement. My usual buoyant personality felt flattened, too, which was an uncomfortable awareness. I drained my cup of cocoa, pulled a coat over my sweater, and drove to El Nathan Home.

Aunt Louise noticed my pensive mood. "The weather is down on the deck. Some people feel trapped here." She looked at me intently. "Days can turn into weeks of drizzle, and endless white snow merges the sky and ground."

It dawned on me why the local people referred to traveling to the lower United States as going "Outside." When I'd first heard that term, I thought it meant "going outdoors." I was learning that it referred to returning to fully-stocked grocery shelves, sprawling green lawns, cheaper gasoline, paved streets, and sources of entertainment and refinement. I suspected that it might also mean a respite from rows of days without energizing sunshine. This was only mid-summer. This was not even winter.

The unquestionable call to Alaska went round and round in my head. I took a deep breath and squinted through a rain-drizzled window toward the rugged mountains that pierced holes in the clouds, "I know I'm where God wants me! But, can I survive here?"

Aunt Louise hugged me, "Everyone needs people, but especially up here–but getting Outside every so often sure doesn't hurt either."

ABC

On May 4, 1790, a Spanish expedition sailed north from the newly-established Spanish base at Nootka on Vancouver Island. The commander, Lieutenant Salvador Fidalgo, was directed to explore the coast for possible passageways to Hudson Bay. He eventually entered Prince William Sound and carefully examined the bays, naming one of them Valdes, (which later became "Valdez") but failed to find a waterway leading to Hudson Bay.

Prince William Sound continued to draw interest because it was the most northerly ice-free port on the west coast of North America. Between 1887 and 1889, Valdez was established as a port of entry for thousands of gold seekers who stormed through Valdez on their way to the Klondike gold fields. The Valdez trail, which passed over Valdez Glacier, threatened many of the early hopeful miners with life-taking crevasses, snow-blindness, and exhaustion.

In 1901, the War Department spent nearly $100,000 to open a pack trail which led over Thompson Pass from Valdez to the gold fields of the upper Yukon basin. General W.P. Richardson, president of the Alaska Road Commission, directed the improvement of the trail in 1907, and consequently left his name on the Richardson Trail. *Improvement* meant that it was passable for horse-drawn stages and wagons, and a regular stage service between Valdez and Fairbanks. The no-frills trip usually took a week by stage or fast horse-drawn sled, and the $150 ticket did not include lodging. Consequently, roadhouses popped up along the way to accommodate travelers.

Between 1920 and 1927, the Richardson Trail was widened and graded, making it minimally passable for automobiles and buses, and forming an unbroken stretch of gravel road between Valdez and Circle, a distance of about 535 miles.

On Good Friday, in 1964, the strongest earthquake ever recorded in North America shook the town. The epicenter of the 9.2 Richter Scale earthquake was in northern Prince William Sound. The dock and part of the town collapsed into the bay and the town was relocated.

Valdez, which originally served as a port for gold seekers, later became a port for oil. In 1974, construction began on the trans-Alaska pipeline. The 45 inch-diameter, 800-mile pipeline extended from Prudhoe Bay on the Arctic Ocean, down through the Brooks Mountain Range, near Fairbanks, up Thompson Pass, down Keystone Canyon, and into Valdez. On August 1, 1977, the first tanker transported oil out of Valdez. In March, 1989, the oil tanker, Exxon Valdez, ran aground, spilling 11,000,000 gallons of oil, again attracting national attention to Valdez.

PUZZLE PIECES

Life in Valdez was fun–but I still had no permanent, income-producing work. During the day, I went fishing, peeled logs for the church building, baked sweet rolls, biscuits, and cookies at the El Nathan Home, picked berries and made berry pies. People, popcorn, picnics, prayer meetings, Bible school programs, and playing table games filled my evenings.

Once I gained a sense of the community, I contacted three school board members, besides Mr. Butcher, president of the school board.

At one meeting Mr. Butcher asked abruptly, "Have you come to Valdez for any other reason than to teach school?"

Unflinchingly, I said, "Yes, I am interested in helping with the work at the Free Methodist Church."

His expressionless face sagged into a scowl.

A school board member protested vehemently, "We don't want any more Bible-toting teachers."

In resignation that perhaps my teaching experience would not be the means to a job, I pounded the dusty streets for other jobs. At the end of July, I was offered a position as clerk at Hotel Valdez for $150 a month. I was thankful for permanent work, yet felt uneasy. The night before I was to confirm my acceptance, I couldn't sleep. I needed the income, but was this the right source of income? What about my experience as a teacher? On the other hand, I remembered how I'd told God I'd do anything–even scrub floors.

ABC

Dot had been a great companion for me, but now she was ready to fly back to her boyfriend. At the same time, Aunt Pedo and Aunt Louise were planning to attend the Child Welfare Conference in Anchorage. On August 1, the four of us started out for Anchorage in my Chevy.

After some false starts, due to torrential rain, a cracked transmission, and reorganizing in Aunt Pedo's blue van, we arrived later than expected in Anchorage. We hugged Dot good-bye at the airport. She'd been a major part of my trek to Alaska. Even though I'd made new friends, Dot was a tie to my life in Ohio; now I was on my own.

Attending the Child Welfare Conference was an unexpected opportunity to learn more about Alaska's children, as well as about other teaching opportunities. When I heard about villages in Interior Alaska, I thought, *Wouldn't it be an experience teaching in a Native village along the Yukon River?* I sought out individuals who had been farther north and plied them with questions about the living situations, stores and conveniences, the weather, and missionaries. Contacts with educators were fruitful. When Dr. Dorothy Novatney, Deputy Commissioner of Education in Alaska, heard of my experience and availability, she instructed me to find A.A. Ryan who was in charge of military schools. Before the day concluded, I'd been offered a teaching position on the military base at Adak, on one of the Aleutian Islands that stretched off the southwest corner of Alaska.

I felt the tug of war. *Hey, now I can teach!* pulled one way. *I think God wants me in Valdez,* yanked me away. I returned to Valdez without signing the contract.

On August 18, a drippy Friday evening, I had just snuggled into a warm blanket and was reading a book in the living room near the oil heater when a knock on the door interrupted my concentration. There stood Mr. Butcher.

We stared at each other. Without any social greeting, he stated his mission, "I think they could use you in school." He paused, shifting his tall, thin frame in the doorway, "Are you still interested?"

"Oh, yes!" I burst out.

Mr. Butcher responded, "I received a letter from the new superintendent and he thinks I should hire you." As he turned to leave, he muttered over his shoulder, "I guess we should be glad to get you."

The next day, Mr. Butcher tracked me down with a phone call at El Nathan Home. "Anna, consider yourself employed. I'll get a contract to you."

He still acted as if he didn't want to see me, much less talk to me. In rapid-fire he outlined my job. Rather than simply teaching one or two elementary classes, it sounded as though I'd have a composite of groups, ranging from kindergartners in the morning, to working with the general music program, to possibly doing clerical work in the office! This diverse list of responsibilities surprised me, as did the stunningly high salary of $5,180 per year with future raises implied.

It wasn't as though he had a change of heart. Mr. Butcher reminded me that he and others still opposed my *religion*. "You must be okay with the years of teaching experience you've accumulated, and without any negative repercussions in regards to your religion," he said coolly.

As it turned out, my first year was a hodgepodge of teaching:

Kindergarten

9:00–11:00 a.m.

(In a small room adjacent the superintendent's office)

Secretarial work	11:30 - 12:00 p.m.
8th grade reading	11:15–1:45 p.m. (In the former jail building)
7th grade reading	1:45–2:15 p.m.
High school typing	2:15–3:15 p.m.
Choir/Chorus	3:15–4:00 p.m.

I hadn't expected to sprint between classes. I heard rumors that when the new hospital opened, I might find my students in an old hospital ward. I wondered, *Could these unusual environments be educationally stimulating?*

After signing the teaching contract, and in celebration of my greatly improved financial situation, I marched out to buy a hamburger at *Dorothy's Café* too bad Dot couldn't share the moment with me.

ABC

I adored my kindergartners. I hoped to nurture these children as little human beings, rather than treat them as mere receptacles of primary colors and the numbers one to ten. I awoke each day in anticipation of spending the morning with them. Before the ground froze and snow covered the road, I dodged gray puddles in the sandy-gravel streets, thinking about fun learning activities, and inventing inside games in case the soggy skies leaked during recess.

Ironically, my kindergarten students met in an 18-foot square room filled with tubas, French horns, trombones, and other musical instruments. Why they were stored there was beyond me, or, why the kindergartners were placed in this room made no common sense. The kindergartners were delegated to this room of temptations, yet, the inquisitive little people never overstepped their boundaries.

Each day began with sharing time. We sat in a semi-circle on short, small chairs. The children always surprised and charmed me with their intimate revelations. One day, it was Penny's turn to share. Her chair was next to mine, and before she started speaking, she leaned against me, with her blond curls tumbling upon her cherub face. "Go ahead," I whispered.

Taking a deep breath, she asked her classmates, "Should three-year-olds still be wetting their pants?"

I stifled a laugh. Not a single child thought this was amusing and for some time Penny and the other five-year-olds wrestled soberly with this issue; all the while she unconsciously reached over and played with the back of my hair.

Then she turned to me and said, seriously, "Miss Bortel, what do *you* think?" I felt the gentle spray of moisture on my face as she exhaled with each lisped word.

Another time, a boy explained that he awoke to find a longshoreman in bed with his mother. I listened intently as these small folks grappled with big concerns, and unreservedly offered their opinions.

On some occasions, literal language and abstract concepts created confusion. One fall day, a child carried a leaf to class and asked why the once green leaf was now yellow. This teachable moment resulted in a mini-lecture on frost.

One boy piped up, "I hope Jack Frost doesn't land on me and change my color."

I started to grin, then recognized the solemn faces around me, pondering that same thought.

And so my mornings would end. Usually, it took ten to 15 minutes to get the kindergartners dressed to go home. In the winter, we'd search for misplaced mittens, untangle wool mufflers, and cope with wet socks. One day, I was struggling over little Jimmy, trying to get his boots on. Worn out from trying to stuff his feet into too small boots, I let out a sigh. At that moment, the small almond-eyed Native boy leaned over and kissed me. With my morale boosted, I hugged him, successfully yanked on his boots, and sent him smiling out the door. There were many rewards for teaching the ABCs.

At the teacher's reception I read an essay by an unknown writer, which described so well my precious group of children. Later my adaptation was printed in the October 6, 1956, Valdez newspaper.

What is a Kindergarten class?

A kindergarten class is a group of five-year-olds, none of whom look, act, think, behave, or grow in exactly the same way.

A kindergarten class comes to its teacher with assorted needs, ranging from Kleenex to affection. It has stars in its eyes and loose teeth in its mouth, questions on its mind, and Band-

Aids on its knees, forgiveness in its heart, and peanut butter cookies in its lunch box.

A kindergarten class can put a variety of things on its teacher's desk: bouquets of flowers, wilted leaves, a turtle, a rock collection, a cookie with one bite out of it, or an "I like Ike" button for the teacher to wear.

A kindergarten class loves to share with the teacher all the happenings at home whether speakable, or unspeakable. The teacher must look at every new dress or shirt, and share the joy of a new toy that arrived after sending 25¢ in with a Wheaties box top.

A kindergarten class teacher's lesson plans are interrupted by skinned knees, broken zippers, a measles outbreak, untied shoes, and the need for a hug.

A kindergarten class teacher realizes that she must strive "to possess the green thumb essential to the culture of the human plant."

ABC

The *Life-in-Valdez* puzzle was coming together. I had friends and a permanent job. Next, with the Steins scheduled to return in another month, I needed to find a permanent residence. The day after Mr. Butcher came to my door with the job offer, the Alaskan Steamship representative and his wife, invited me over for lunch. I had no idea why Mr. and Mrs. Burnham had sought me out.

We ate at a chrome dinette set with bright yellow padded chairs. A couch, along one wall, was more like a daybed with over-sized cushions. The light-colored linoleum was chilly beneath my feet, even though the oil space heater was nearby. Sheer tie-back curtains framed the living room window, in front of which stood a rectangular wooden stand covered with lace doilies and a collection of plants. A blond chest of drawers was placed across the room from the couch. Large pictures covered the walls.

I figured this was a nice social gesture and we engaged in agreeable conversation, comparing my first impressions of Valdez with their more seasoned perceptions. John Burnham talked easily and often. Ilene Burnham kept smiling, but was more contemplative. She was a pleasant hostess, but her eyes looked unhappy.

At a lull in the table talk, John Burnham turned to me, "Anna, we are moving out of Valdez and wonder if you would like to purchase our home."

I looked around the modest home. I'd taken in the living room and had caught a glimpse of the kitchen and bathroom when Ilene had swung through it with lunch fixings.

"It has a bottled gas stove with a good oven, a refrigerator, a new electric water heater, its own well water, and a washing machine," he quickly informed me. "We added a bathroom with a shower and I'm now connecting a drain pipe to the city sewer system."

I'd checked around town and was aware of prices. Rentals were going for between $75 and $125 a month, which didn't include utilities. A trailer house with a lean-to sold for $5,000 to $6,000.

John added, "You can pay $1,500 down and the remaining $1,000 later—without interest."

Such a miracle! How could I refuse?

The all-business man didn't give me conversational space to respond. "You know that it is extremely expensive to move household items in and out of Alaska. Consequently, most people sell their belongings at reasonable prices or even take them to the city dump—"

Ilene apologetically interrupted him, "Which is why some people go *shopping* at the dump."

"Yes," I interjected, "recently someone found a wonderful supply of Franciscan dinnerware there."

John continued his sales pitch, "In our case, we'd like to leave all the furnishings with you."

I was flabbergasted and nearly choked on my swallow of water. I'd only brought along necessities and didn't have enough to fill out a house. "You mean the plants and knick-knacks, too?" I asked.

I accepted their generous offer. Without delay, I wrote to my parents about my new home at the end of Broadway. I trusted that along with my announcement of a job, that this would assure Daddy that his daughter was well taken-care and would not freeze to death or go hungry in this far-away place. I added that Wilson lived nearby, and would be handy and available if the need arose. At this moment, I didn't know how urgently I'd need his help later.

Margaret Keenan Harrais typed up the deed and mortgage and recorded the transaction. "I'm glad you're buying a house and putting down roots," she told me, "I have no use for people who shift around."

I figured I'd stay rooted until God planted me somewhere else.

IF GOD BUILDS
THE FOUNDATION

I'd anticipated meeting Wilson and Jay Stein, who had been so insightful in preparing me for my first Alaska experience. Finally they returned to Valdez. As young as Wilson was, his hair had retreated to the point that he had more landing space for mosquitoes than the rest of us. He was a soft-spoken person, somewhat behind-the-scenes, and a dutiful husband, finding ways to serve his wife.

Jay was a neat young woman with red wavy hair. Her studious-looking glasses suggested reserve, but in everyday events she was outgoing; when given the occasion, she was a good speaker. Clovis, their toddler, did not warm up to people easily, and at first, clung shyly to one of his parents' legs. I'd never met a child who remained wary of me for very long. Soon we were friends.

Over dinner, Jay Stein filled in the history of the church. On August 31, 1950, they'd arrived here by steamer, the *S.S. Aleutian*, to start a Free Methodist church. Then, on December 7, 1952, Rev. Auburn and Bessie Witt accepted the challenge from the Free Methodist conference to come organize the first Free Methodist Sunday school in Alaska. There were nine people present for the first session: Rev. Auburn and Mrs. Bessie Witt, Mr. Wilson and Mrs. Jay

Stein, Mrs. Hannah Thompson, Donna Look, Ronald Look, Jan Look, and George Davis.

A lot was purchased from Armis Jarvi for $1,000. On October 12, 1953, logs and lumber for a building were purchased from George Johansen in Glenallen, for a total of $553.06, which included transportation. Later in that month, excavation was begun using the town's caterpillar—and without a charge. However, winter set in solidly a few days later and the ground froze for the long winter. Now I was part of this living history.

ABC

I wanted to assist in this mission, but I was somewhat in a bind since my savings had been depleted by the purchase of my house. I watched the Taylors and Steins spend unselfish hours and dollars on the church, making personal sacrifices. After much deliberation, I shared with the group one Sunday, "I want to buy the windows and the doors for the church."

During prayer time, I said, "Lord, I don't know what I'm going to live on for the next several months, but this is your work. I'm trusting you to provide."

Soon after, a schoolteacher inquired about room and board at my home, until she could find a place of her own. Consequently, Joyce Nicolai came to stay with me. Her generous payments prompted me to say with the psalmist, "My cup runneth over." Her rent adequately provided for my groceries and house payments.

ABC

"Snowshoes included," Mr. Burnham had told me when he handed me the keys to my new home. After only a few head-first plunges, I learned to walk heel-toe, always lifting the waffle-like grids.

During a typical autumn, the locals anticipated snow in Valdez within six weeks of a dusting on Sugarloaf Mountain. This year, however, snow descended upon us within 16 hours of the dusting;

which should have been a clue as to what to expect the rest of the year. Valdez boasts more snow than anywhere else in Alaska. Three hundred inches is normal. In 1954 into 1955, we would be exceeding that statistic. The Indians and Eskimos refused to live in Valdez—they declared it to be too windy and too snowy. They were right. After I left Valdez, I would watch for news about the snowfall there. In 1989, the National Weather Service recorded 560.7 inches (46.7 feet) of snow.

On into the frigid fall the men laid out the foundation and peeled logs, a task that became more difficult as the logs dried out and the bark hardened. I asked the hardware man, who had built a log house, how the logs would be finished. He directed me to boiled linseed oil. "This first, and then varnish," he instructed. Since I'd grown up with a father who was knowledgeable about paint, stain, and finishing, I just wanted to know.

The brisk days and fresh snow on the mountain tops signaled the rapidly approaching winter. With the ongoing tasks of daily living, teaching, hunting, and caring for children, we wondered how we would complete this building.

I maneuvered fairly well with chains on my tires and ban-ice in the car's gas tank. I also kept the snow brushed off my car when it was parked, lest I lose it and never find it until spring. Already, several cars had been damaged when snowplows attempted to remove what looked like a snow pile! Around town, the snow, pushed high on either side of the streets, resulting in driving tunnels. Cars could not be seen in advance, and drivers approached corners cautiously. If we did slide along the streets, the tall snow piles would cushion us when we skidded off course. Fortunately, claustrophobia was not my problem; otherwise, I would have panicked with the high snow and frequent, low skies. I was always grateful that the snow-grader swerved off the street to clear a spot for my car; aside from this courtesy, I was totally responsible for the snow on and around my house.

One task was to dig out the oil barrel before calling the fuel oil man. This required snowshoeing around the house and trying to guess where the barrel stood on its four-foot framework. In the summer, the barrel was a convenient height. But in the winter, I actually had to dig *down* to find it. *There must be a way to shorten this reoccurring hit-or-miss investigation,* I said to myself.

Finally locating the buried barrel, I looked up. Near the house roof remained a narrow strip that the snow had not entirely covered. Counting from the edge of the house, I pinpointed the shingle directly above the oil barrel, and made a mental note of this for the next digging expedition.

I never got used to snowshoeing *over* my clothes line in the winter. In summer, when I hung out clothes, I couldn't believe that snow had reached such an incredible depth. With the extreme physical changes in the environment between summer and winter, it seemed as though I lived in two entirely different worlds.

The heavy powder created extra house maintenance. The composition roof on my kitchen and bathroom had neither a steep pitch nor a metal surface, as did the main part of the house. Consequently, the snow did not slide off. When two or three feet accumulated, I'd have to snowshoe up with my shovel. To break the monotony, on one occasion, I made a chubby snowman on my roof. Laughing, I thought, *If only my family could see me now!*

ABC

On December 23rd, at 7:00 p.m., one hour before the Sunday School Christmas program, we saw the last nail pounded into the flooring. We were filled with amazement, gratitude, and joy.

After the first of the year, Rev. Burton Root, the conference superintendent, from Washington State, came to speak. Near the middle of his sermon, a tremendous rumble shook the building. Before we realized what was happening, the deep snowpack on the roof slid down, crashed through a window, and avalanched halfway across the front of the sanctuary.

The stunned speaker looked all around, and observed the snow pile below his pulpit and at the feet of his audience. After a moment of disorientation, his eyes turned to his notes. "I think I've lost my train of thought," he solemnly concluded.

Following that sensational service, we jokingly told our guest speakers to keep their snowshoes handy behind the pulpit!

Anna (middle of back row) with her Sunday school class in front of the Valdez Free Methodist Church. The young people are from El Nathan Children's Home. (1955)

1955
THE UNWELCOME
VISITOR

March 23, 1955
Dear Friends,
   Keep your letters coming! We get our boat mail on Monday and plane mail every day except Sunday. Sunday was the day before spring, but you would have thought it was mid-winter, for we had 50 mph gusts of wind. Even though the sun has been shining, I've had to burn lights due to the snow packed against the storm windows. We've had 319 inches of snowfall this winter ... I had an uninvited guest ...

I thought I'd been living alone, but sometimes, late at night, I'd hear little footsteps scurrying around. I discounted this as my imagination, during the twilight stage between wakefulness and sleep. Then one day, my vague dream-world visitor left startling, identifiable clues.

On March 13, 1955, I invited Reverend Carl and Dorothy Anderson to my house for dinner. Carl, an official in the Free Methodist Church, had flown to Valdez from Seattle to conduct a special service. At the service, six adults and 11 young people became charter members of the Valdez church. The older gentleman made up for his short stature with his booming voice, and we were inspired by his passionate words of challenge and inspiration; as well as excited about this history-making event.

That noon, over roast beef, mashed potatoes and gravy, and homemade rolls, our talk shifted from the church to life in Valdez.

"Don't you ever get lonely up here?" asked Dorothy, admittedly a city girl.

I responded quickly to the sweet, little white-haired lady. Oh, no," I laughed. "There are always people to be with and things to do. I sincerely appreciated her concern, but honestly had not felt lonely since I'd arrived over a year ago.

Carl pushed the issue, "What about living all alone?"

Alone? My mind turned to the sounds of scurrying footsteps. I'd like to be alone, but perhaps I really wasn't. I replied, "Jay and Wilson are a short distance away."

Following dinner, the Andersons wanted to visit El Nathan Home. I cleared the dishes, but left the remaining roast on the counter to cool before storing it in the refrigerator. Several hours later, I returned. Intending to clean up the dishes, I walked into the kitchen and nearly stumbled over the roast on the floor.

What is this doing on the floor? I crossed off the list of possibilities. An earthquake? No. Strong winds? I stood speechless. *Perhaps I am not alone. Perhaps something was living with me.* If this *something* was large enough to pull a roast off the kitchen counter and rudely invite itself to Sunday dinner, what would prevent it from taking a bite out of me for dessert?

I turned around, and walked back out the door toward the Steins. Interrupting their Sunday afternoon naps, I told them my tale.

Wilson volunteered, "I'll go hunt for the critter."

"You go," I said, "I'll stay right here with Jay."

It wasn't long before Wilson returned. "I didn't discover anything besides chunks bitten out of your roast—he must like your cooking! I'll set a trap and we'll see if your visitor will introduce himself."

I didn't care to be alone with my guest. I walked back to my house with Wilson, packed an overnight bag, and returned to the Steins for the night. Wilson set a steel trap in my kitchen, and without the nocturnal sounds of scampering feet, I slept soundly on their hide-a-bed.

The next morning, Wilson left to check his trap, and within short order, returned with his catch.

"He's still alive!" I exclaimed.

"Yes," said Wilson, "They have thick necks, and the trap spring must have been weak."

"He's beautiful," I responded. "Look at that pure white coat and the black tip on his tail!"

"Only so in the winter," replied Wilson. "Just wait, in summer, he'll turn brown and blend into that environment."

Wilson explained that the foot-long creature was an ermine, much like a weasel.

"Its small size can fool you about its aggressiveness," he cautioned.

Since it was Monday morning and nearly time for school, I decided to carry my houseguest to school in a very large glass jar. The children crowded around "Herman the Ermine" and chattered excitedly. They wanted to stroke his soft fur, but if I'd remove the lid, he'd bite their hands and try to escape. Still, I didn't want to miss a teaching opportunity. I informed them that in times past, the robes of royalty had been trimmed with winter-white ermine fur. They wanted to declare him a classroom pet and couldn't understand that such a lovely animal could be a pest.

Even though Herman was a nuisance, I didn't have the heart to kill him. Carl Anderson painlessly disposed of him. After that, I *did* live alone, without mysterious nighttime noise, and with my food intact, and with a tiny ermine fur to remind me of my unwelcome visitor.

Herman the Ermine entertaining the school children

ROMANCE ARRIVES

June 1, 1955
Dearest folks,

My garden is up. I could really plant a lot of stuff here but my difficulty is getting it plowed up. I've spaded everything and it is hard work....I turned carpenter and last weekend sawed and pounded, fixing the upstairs...Now for a bedtime story. Right after school was out—three school girls in the fourth and fifth grades–came by...

"Miss Bortel, he wants to meet you. Don't you want to meet him?" queried the girls who jumped off their bikes and surrounded me with this exciting news. "He's a police officer for the Alaska Territory and works at the weigh station, just outside of town," they added.

How could it be that I'd been teaching in Valdez for a year and was not aware of this individual? "So, what does he look like?" I quizzed the girls.

They giggled and looked at each other; then one said, "He's taller than you, with very dark eyes, brownish-blond hair ..."

"Okay," I agreed. "I'll meet him."

The girls shrieked, bounded onto their bikes, and with braids flying, left me in a small tornado of dust.

Several days later, I was vacuuming my Chevy when I heard a vehicle approach and stop. Looking up, I saw a jeep, and recognized a man who fit their description. When he came closer, I stopped cleaning, and stood beside my car. He walked self-assuredly toward me with a big grin and reached out to shake my hand. "Hi, I'm Al McGregory."

"Your students really like you," he teased. "You should have heard what all they told me."

I laughed. "Okay. Now tell me about you. What do you do at the weigh station?"

While I sized him up and gave silent approval to his clean-shaven face and extra-long blue jeans, he proceeded to tell me about the trucks that carried freight from docked ships to the interior of Alaska. There were limits on the truck's weight, and he and another officer enforced the restrictions. *He could add some fun to my life,* I thought watching him.

"Tomorrow is my day off. How would you like to go on a picnic?" He was quick to make plans.

Picnicking up the Alcan had not diminished my fondness of picnics. "That would be great! Where will we go?"

His brown eyes twinkled. "Up the road. I'll be by at ten. And don't worry, I'll bring the lunch."

I knew that with only one road in Valdez, that *up the road* meant heading out of town. I didn't know what a bachelor would make for lunch.

Boy! Was I a schoolmarm all aflutter that night. Sleep eluded me as I thought of various endings to this fun, real-life story.

I woke to overcast skies and a soft off-and-on drizzle. It would take more than gray moisture to tread on my spirits. Besides, a little rain would sharpen the colors of the cottonwoods, spruce, and wildflowers.

I looked in the mirror again and again, checking every perspective, and changing my sweater twice. I was still primping when at 10:00 a.m. a knock on the door ended my deliberations.

Al greeted me, "A great lady and a great day! Let's get going."

My heart was pitter-pattering when I climbed in to the Jeep.

"It's a bit soggy, but we'll just drive until we're out of it," he said confidently.

One of the first questions I asked was how he found out about me.

"I saw you in the post office and wanted to meet you." He smiled.

That temporarily satisfied my curiosity, but then I had more questions. As we drove through Keystone Canyon, away from Valdez, only the deafening waterfalls interfered with our nonstop conversation. His folks had come from Rogue River, Oregon, where his father was a logger and his mother taught school. Following in his father's footsteps, Al had logged before driving up the Alcan to Anchorage. He changed to police work at the Anchorage airport.

"But, city living isn't for me," he said, "I like Valdez and the solitude. Here I can breathe and stretch out."

By noon, we'd driven 59 miles, and, as Al had predicted, we were out of the drizzle. We found a scenic spot overlooking a lush green valley. The abundant wildflowers and thick grassy carpet were beautiful but damp, so the jeep tailgate became our lunch table. The heavy clouds turned off their sprinklers, and a small patch of sunshine brightened the day. Al spread out the food— thick vegetable stew cooked on his Coleman stove, chunks of bread, bananas, and chocolate chip cookies. Not bad. We devoured the food, talked, and laughed.

I was soaking in the breath-taking views and when Al suggested we tidy up our outdoor cafe and start the trip back. After driving only a short distance, however, he declared we must stop.

"It's time you had a lesson shooting a revolver," he announced in a silly, emphatic way.

I burst out laughing. "You expect me to compete with an officer of the law?"

My protest was of no use. After shooting a number of rounds, I stopped and smiled, satisfied by my marksmanship.

"Okay," Al conceded. "You're a good sport. Let's go."

The miles back to Valdez flew, and I regretted that the day had disappeared.

The jeep rumbled up to my house, and Al thanked me for accompanying him. "Perhaps we can go for another jaunt up the road sometime," he suggested.

I thanked him for a wonderful day and walked into my house, reflecting on the satisfying day.

A few Saturdays later as I graded papers, I heard a knock on my door. There, leaning against the door frame, stood Al. "Anna, tomorrow is my day off. How would you like to ride up to the Tiekel Roadhouse[2] and have lunch?"

"What fun!" I responded.

Tomorrow finally came, and the morning sun brought with it a spectacular day. With much laughter we drove up the Richardson Highway about forty miles to where George and Rosie managed the roadhouse.

"In years past the highway in this area was not kept open in the winter," Al informed me.

"That sounds pretty isolated," I said, "Just the two of them. No neighbors nearby. Fathomless winter snows."

We parked in front of a patch of arctic blue lupines. Al came around and opened my door. I jumped out and we started walking toward the cabin.

"Do we knock or do we just go in?" I asked. Before Al could answer, a short, stocky man, with suspendered blue jeans, who we assumed was George, opened the worn-smooth timbered door and greeted us with a vigorous, "Hello!" George shook our hands firmly and we stepped into a small entry way filled with an assortment of coats hung on pegs. Al ducked through the thick-beam doorway. Our host seated us with the flair of someone who is accustomed to providing fine dining experiences for the best of folks.

A woman appeared from nowhere. Her dark, gray-streaked hair was pinned back from her face and a clean white apron covered her long skirt. In an old country accent, Rosie presented the menu: "haumburger" and "peekles" or "aw-plesauce" or roast "bereref" sand-wich with either "peekles" or "aw-plesauce." She patiently stood with hands folded in front of her as we deliberated a moment. We conferred and decided to order one hamburger, one roast beef sandwich, pickles, and applesauce. This way, we could split our orders and try everything. Selecting a soda pop completed our decision-making.

In broken English, Rosie relayed our order to George, who walked into the next room. Through the doorway we saw him lift a trap door, and disappear beneath the cabin. Al and I looked at each other and simultaneously mouthed, "What?"

Within minutes, George reappeared from the cabin depths with the delicious makings of our lunch, which he presented to us with a flourish. Both orders were delicious, including the "aw-plesauce" and "peekles." Time stood still as I savored the meal, absorbed the old-time charm of the setting, and sat across from the most engaging and attractive man.

Before climbing back into the jeep, I requested a visit to the privy. George pointed me down a well-worn trail toward the river, a short distance away. I'd seen outhouses, but this one had its own character. For one thing, it perched over the river. Furthermore, on the upstream side of the privy, a box filled with bottles of soda pop was half-submerged. The cold clear water rushed over the bottles was refrigeration.

Gingerly, I opened the creaky door of the sagging, weathered privy. I wasn't prepared for what met my eyes. Staring down through the two-holer, I watched the water tumble over the rocks, hurrying down the hillside. Truly this was a water closet, and a self-flushing one at that!

ABC

Our excursions continued, but my feelings of exuberance diminished as our conversations turned to personal values. Al did not share my spiritual values. He stressed that he was a good person and that he wouldn't hurt or take advantage of anyone.

"Don't worry, the good life I live will get me to heaven," he assured me.

This troubled me. My desire for a husband and children was great, and I cared deeply about Al, but my faith came first. I couldn't be married to someone who did not share this commitment. As a result, the friendship cooled and weeks went by without conversation or Saturday outings.

One evening, I answered the door and was taken aback to find Al. After several awkward pauses and small talk, he blurted out, "Anna, I've missed you so much. Please marry me right away."

My voice caught and I said, "Al…I just don't know how.…"

"Anna, I've got to have a girl I can trust," he interrupted. Fervently, he grasped my hand. "I know I can trust you."

I fought back tears, and admitted, "I've so enjoyed spending time with you.…Yes, I've wanted to be loved and be a wife and mother, but I can't be married to a man who does not share my faith."

"Anna, I don't mind if you go to church," Al pleaded.

I shook my head and my response came out as a moan, "That's not the same…I don't think you understand how significant this is to me."

His head dropped to his chin and he stared at the floor.

I tried to explain, "Al, I really care about you, and I know you care about me, too, but unless we're of one accord spiritually, marriage will not work."

The room got silent. We stood together, but apart with our deep emotions. Neither of us moved for a long time. Finally, with a dejected look and slumped shoulders, he left the house. On his way out, he paused in the doorway, glanced at me one more time, and said in a broken voice, "Anna, you have a standing proposal."

I didn't hear from him for quite some time, but after awhile, Al returned with another plea, "Will you marry me Anna? I trust you and love you."

"Al," I questioned, "What is your aim in life? What is your desire?"

He quickly answered, "To have a home and family."

I agreed with him, "I want that too, Al, but only if God is the center of our home will it be a happy one."

He sat silently, then straightened his shoulders, and said in his deep bass voice, "I know what kind of life I want to live and I'm going to live it."

His heavy footsteps across the floor and out the door gave emphasis to his decision. My heart ached. Even if it meant being an old maid, I knew that I'd made the right decision. We had shared fun times and friendship; however, my first Alaskan romance had come to an end.

That experience left me on guard. As was the case in most of Alaska, there was a dearth of marriageable women, and I soon became the object of another man's fancy. One Sunday evening, as I'd just started walking home from church, another town bachelor asked to drive me home. Half a block turned into a drive up the road and we shared small talk. It didn't take long before I sensed that he, like Al, was in pursuit of a wife. Following additional conversations, I realized that although we found each other interesting, we had some religious differences. After what I had experienced with Al, I did not want to trifle with another man's affection. Breaking up was difficult so I wanted to end any thought of romance right away. I explained to him how I felt. He was disappointed, yet understanding, and we parted on a friendly basis.

That summer, I returned home to Ohio. One afternoon, my sister, Millie, came in the front door and exclaimed, "Anna, you have a letter from Al."

I read the letter and realized that Al was giving me a final chance. If I didn't respond, he wrote, he would marry Ruth, one of my co-teachers, who he'd started dating after I'd left for the summer. I did not answer the letter.

Al married Ruth.[3]

1956
NEEDED: TEACHERS IN
THE TERRITORY

Few teachers were applying for positions in Alaska. In fact, the previous year, the Territory was forced to resort to newspaper and magazine advertisements. Don Richards, put these facts in the *School News:*

> At the first regular meeting of the newly formed Valdez chapter of the National Congress of Parents and Teachers, commonly known as PTA ... went on record as favoring a resolution drawn up on behalf of Alaska Education Assn for a salary raise in teachers pay, salary raises for Superintendents and other school personnel, allowing outside teachers equal consideration of time spent in teaching as Alaskan teachers, and a few other provisions all designed to help alleviate the serious teacher shortage problem.
>   ... It is no secret that there is a shortage of trained teaching personnel in the nation's schools ... The National Education Assn. states in an annual report that, "with 1,197,000 students last year, the U.S. now has a shortage of 130,000 teachers and 120,000 classrooms. There are 840,000 students getting only part-time schooling and 80,000 teachers without standard certificates, partly because of low salaries, 97,000 teachers will drop out of teaching this year.

As the Valdez newspaper pointed out in a January 5, 1956, article, *Of all the applicants that do apply, a very small percentage actually show up, and some of these quit before school starts.*

Teaching was not without its complications in Valdez. In the winter, snow piled up until only one-third of the windows allowed the pallid winter light into the classrooms. Unlike the school-yard rules in Pekin, Illinois, where I restricted the children to the school ground during recess, here I admonished them not to play *on* the school roof. The children were easily entertained building snow forts, tunnels, and towers; and what could be more fun than sledding down mountains of snow piled high around the school lot?

Even inside we had to contend with the elements. During my third year, Superintendent Don Richards, shared both the hurdle and the humor in the *School News* section of the local paper:

> The faculty is seriously considering a radical change in its curriculum. For the balance of the year, instead of "Industrial Arts" or "Shop," we may offer "Aqua Sports" or "Swimming," or perhaps, "Applied Essentials of Marine Management." These changes would be the result of the approximately six inches of water in the Shop.
>
> To attempt to teach at this time would undoubtedly lead to a short course in electrocution; or, should we say, a short circuit. We do not feel that our students should die with their boots on.
>
> All fall, we have been anxiously awaiting the moment when the water would subside back into Sewer Creek, so that the floor would dry out. The long-awaited moment arrived last week. We took the plug out of the drain to allow the water to run out; instead, it ran in. Mr. Kulstad promptly replaced the plug.
>
> Due to the excellent facilities of Sewer Creek in our shop, we might get a subsidy from the Territory to establish a fish hatchery. If anyone has a better use for this room, please contact the superintendent at once.

One day, when I left school at 4:00 p.m., I reflected on that quote and my compelling desire to come to Alaska. My boots crunched on the hard-packed snow in the below zero temperatures, and I looked up at the high moon and star-speckled afternoon sky. No matter the short, dark winter days, and yard-deep snow. Leaving the Territory had never entered my mind.

ABC

In college, I thrived on singing in trios, quartets, octets, and musicals such as *The Messiah*. In addition, I played piano, organ, and accordion. I hoped I could instill this love of music into my students. The superintendent, Mr. Barney, recognized my musical interest, and my first year of teaching he asked me to assist him with the High School Chorus.

I wrote Millie my frustration:

> Mr. Barney wants me to take kindergarten a half day and be free to help him with music, and what-have-you in the afternoon. I am tired of that teaching schedule…I had girl's chorus by myself today. We're trying to get ready for the music festival in Anchorage and we don't have but one sheet of music. Mr. Barney was directing the other day and right in the middle of things he stops and says, 'Miss Bortel, you come up and direct, I'm tired.' Yesterday he tried to get me to take the boys but…it's hard for a woman to sing male parts and after I impressed that upon his mind, he took it…

My annoyance was not at the students, but directed at his assumptions and unpredictability. The children were a pleasure to work with, even though they had not done much singing before and loved the songs, rhythms, and sheer fun of music. The time together was personally rewarding.

Before long, requests for my music teaching and directing extended outside the classroom and into the community. For Thanksgiving 1954, the churches had combined services and I'd been asked to facilitate the musical numbers.

The third year, my responsibilities included teaching both kindergarten and music classes. The music instruction spanned the entire grade school, including full-blown musical performances.

ABC

On November 21, 1956, the school held its second assembly program of the school year. The elementary grade music group, junior high group, and the high school girls' ensemble sang under my direction. The Thanksgiving keynote address was then given by State Senator Bill Egan, and appropriately so; this was his birth place and hometown, and he'd graduated as valedictorian from Valdez High School in 1932.

In addition to Margaret Harrais, he was another interesting person I crossed paths with in this end-of-the-road indentation of the Alaska territory. Like many other Alaskans, he was a pull-up-by-the-boot-straps kind of man and had been raised in a mining family, where at a young age he had to help support his struggling family. He did this by working in a local fish cannery. By age 14, he was driving dump trucks for the Alaska Road Commission. People listened when he spoke. He was authentic and understood their concerns—and I was told that he remembered everyone's name. I listened because he, like Margaret, provided snapshots of Alaska's past, all the while modeling true Alaska character and spirit, and stimulating my curiosity about what lay farther north.

Senator Egan and Tommy Harris, who was also from Valdez, both served as representatives to the Constitutional Convention in Fairbanks, in 1955 and 1956. Even though Alaska was approved for statehood in 1955, it would not be admitted to the union until January 3, 1959. Bill Egan would be the first governor for the 49th state—and re-elected again in 1970.

ABC

I moved from classroom to classroom, releasing the regular teacher for a coffee break. In kindergarten and the lower grades, I played music games with the children, acquainting them with musical concepts and the fun of learning music. Twenty lively kindergartners exuberantly took to the rhythm band instruments and by Christmas knew every beat to "Jingle Bells."

Because the children didn't come to me in a music room equipped with piano and risers, I taught music without accompaniment. Before a program, we would go into the auditorium to do final practices with the piano, unless an a cappella number had been chosen. This was the process for preparing the *Little Blue Angel* operetta for the annual Christmas program. The lack of time spent practicing on stage left me nervous for the actual event.

The night was clear and cold, with no wind. Snow crystals filtered through the air and reflected in front of car lights and flashlights. Vehicle tires squeaked on hard-packed below-zero snow, and children's excited chatter filled the silent night.

Although the program didn't begin until 8:00 p.m., a number of us teachers, along with parents, had come earlier to set up and decorate. A basketball hoop hovered above the stage, but we hoped to draw attention away from the un-holiday piece of hardware with greenery and red bows in front of the stage. Ed Nickerman, a fellow teacher, who volunteered to be the stagehand and help wherever needed, climbed on a ladder and hung large, foil-covered cardboard stars from the ceiling above the platform. Center stage, back, was a tall spruce tree with decorative balls and colorful lights.

The program started nearly on time with musical selections and a medley of Christmas carols. The first act of the *Little Blue Angels* followed. The girls looked splendid in their short, sheer dresses of light blue, cream, and white. Satin belts and attached silver stars sparkled in the floodlights. Just as we'd practiced, they stood poised with their hands folded at their waistlines. I didn't know how they stayed warm enough with bare legs and short sleeves.

Between acts, other music groups performed. At the close of the program, Santa Claus come ho-ho-ing out with candy treats for every child in the audience.

In my opinion, it went off quite well; and the comment all over town was "The best in years."

ABC

Of all my myriad musical responsibilities, the Junior High a cappella choir became my pride and joy. One day we were in the auditorium practicing for an upcoming performance. In close, three-part harmony, the students sang the touching Negro Spiritual, "Steal Away." Unknown to us, an inebriated man had wandered in. When he heard the singing, he pulled himself out of the corner, stood up shakily, lifted his lined face and palms upward, said, just loud enough for us to hear, "Ahhh, *that* is beautiful," then sat down weeping.

As is the case in many pioneering settlements, school, church, and general community life was intertwined. More and more, someone knocked on my door, caught me in the grocery store, or waved me down on the street to ask if I'd put together a musical number or two for a public occasion. When a student died of cancer, his mother asked me to arrange music for the funeral, using an adult choir. Since the churches in Valdez all had small congregations, we sometimes combined services. I chose singers from various churches and we blended our voices, and our care, for the grieving family. Music was a part of this shared spirit and connected our community in times of celebration, worship, and sadness.

ALL I NEED IS A BREAK

I stomped the snow off my boots before pushing open the door to the post office. "Say, Fran, did the mail make it in today?"

"Yes, first time in three days," the postal clerk responded. "The plane managed to sneak in before the snow started again ... everyone will be glad to get their Christmas cards."

Winter was such an unpredictable time for air traffic and mail delivery. Besides the hazards of inclement weather, the Valdez airport lay close to the base of the mountains. Without visual contact, pilots dared not take chances.

To my pleasure, Box 14 yielded a letter from Rev. Howard and Jessie Lower in Anchorage. I pulled off my mittens, crammed them in my pockets, and read the Lowers' invitation: *Why don't you come to the city and spend Christmas with us?* The Lowers were starting a Free Methodist church in Anchorage, and I'd met them at a conference. The Washington Conference news had recorded the historical event.

Alaska Sends First Alaskan Delegate

The Valdez Free Methodist Church, first of our denomination to be organized in Alaska, was well represented ... by Miss Anna Bortel, charter member of the church and school teacher in Valdez. Thus to Miss Bortel goes the distinction of being the first Free Methodist delegate in history from Alaska. She gave a good report concerning the progress of the Valdez church, and showed colored slides of Alaska.

I stuffed my hair back into my parka hood, and turned to Fran, "I can't believe it. I've been invited to the city for Christmas." I'd taught for over a year in Valdez, and the disorganized school system was taking a toll. "I love music, and the kids are putting so much concentration into the Christmas operetta. But, even with these rewards, I'm feeling a bit worn out."

"Sounds like you need a break," Fran responded. "I'd say if you've got the chance, go."

In my first Alaska Christmas letter, I'd described the winter setting.

Christmas 1954

If you'd like a little northern hospitality, stop in and I'll have some coffee and sugar Christmas cookies...since before Thanksgiving...we've had snow and cold weather for so long.

I wish you could step outside my front door tonight and look at the full moon, snow-covered mountains, and the star-studded sky. I'm still amazed that I'm in Alaska—that I actually got here. I realize that God gave me the courage and strength to undertake such a trip.

This is my first experience living in a small community and I'm finding that friendships mean everything. We have one road out of the village and in the winter time we are practically village-bound, or should I say, isolated. There is a high mountain pass about 27 miles from here. They keep the road open all winter but not too many venture out. I haven't been ten miles away from here for quite a long time.

The days are short now. The eastern horizon is getting pink about 8 a.m. When I came out of school after four today the moon was shining.

Two weeks later, on an atypically sunny day, I rubbed the fog off the inside of a plane window and watched Valdez disappear below me.

Landing in Anchorage, I felt revitalized by the bustle of people and the festive holiday decorations. The three grade school and high-school-aged Lower children reached for my suitcase and in near unison said, "Hey, will you make us pizza pie?" Their mother shushed them for their forwardness. I assured them that I'd love to. This Italian specialty had just been introduced to the United States.

Oh, what a wonderful Christmas in the city! I enjoyed to the fullest the candlelight church services, children's Christmas programs, meeting interesting people, and shopping at a dime store. Besides gifts for the Lower family, I bought items I couldn't buy or mail order out of Valdez: rick-rack trim, fabric, a record, and colorful kitchen towels. Every minute refreshed my soul and spirit. I read the newspaper and listened to the radio. In the evenings, we ate popcorn and fudge, and then stayed up until the wee hours talking and laughing. After a week of that kind of nourishment, I was ready to return to Valdez and wholeheartedly plunge into the remainder of the school year.

ABC

Anna returning from Ohio on Cordova Airlines DC-3.

On the day of my return flight, the sun refused to shine, and Cordova Airlines refused to promise my arrival in Valdez. "If the weather clears enroute, we'll get you back," the unflappable ticket agent told me. "If not, we can get you as close as Cordova."

I'd only be a half-hour flight from Valdez, yet, still stranded. I remembered my initial apprehension. I'd been so airsick flying to Anchorage that I didn't just want to "fly around" and return to Anchorage. Walking toward the silver DC-3 airplane and tossing good-bye kisses to the Lower family, my optimism waned.

Instead of flying directly to Cordova, the air carrier changed course and flew to Middleton Island. The air was rough, and there was water beneath us. The overly cheerful stewardess gave us her memorized monologue of "In case of an emergency landing in the water..." In these hostile temperatures we all knew her words were meaningless. Even when the pilot notified us that we were landing, dry ground failed to appear, and the murky waves only rose up closer. I held my breath and prayed.

At long last, the plane wheels grated on the run-way. Men got on and off the plane. Only men lived on the island, men who worked on the national defense warning system there.

In Cordova, I transferred to a small plane. I was the only passenger and my seat was next to the pilot's. He raced the engines and proceeded down the runway, even though the land and sky touched each other. I held on to my seat and prayed, again.

Just before lift-off, the pilot abruptly chopped the power and aborted takeoff. He turned to me, "The pressure isn't right. I'm not sure I want to go winding around the mountains with this poor visibility."

Back at the one-room airfield office, an airline official informed us, "I hear it's snowing by the foot in Valdez." Then she readily added, "But, it's only a skip and a jump once Valdez opens up."

"I guess I'll boost this town's economy by staying in one of its hotels," I responded gloomily.

"Since our sole revenue is fishing, that would be much appreciated," said an old-timer sitting on a worn vinyl chair. He scratched his chin with a hand-carved walking stick and then used it to point me in the direction of the Windsor Hotel. Outside, the snow kept falling in heavy flakes and the sky hugged the ground.

In spite of my dejection, I made myself explore the town; which, with its many-layered history, turned out to be more interesting than I'd expected. The area around Cordova was originally home to the Chugach Eskimos. When the Gold Rush in the late 1800s brought in hopefuls from outside Alaska, Cordova added other dimensions. In 1902, the first oil fields in Alaska were discovered 47 miles east of the coastal village. Then in 1911, Cordova became the railroad terminus and port for copper ore from the mines at Kennicott, up the Copper River. Times, needs, and explorations had changed over the years. Since the 1940s, fishing had served as the economic base, including a title of "Razor Clam Capital of the World."

At this moment, Cordova was a winterized fishing village, with any exciting work or activities in hibernation.

I ate my meals at a restaurant where fishermen and local towns-people socialized. At lunch one day, the room was crowded and I couldn't sit in my usual corner. Several men eyed me as they walked past my table and I quickly averted my eyes to my book. A few minutes later, something plopped into my vegetable soup. Jerking back in surprise, I realized one of the men's beer bottle caps had flown over and landed in my soup. I couldn't hear all they said, but I felt uncomfortable with their boisterous laughter.

At another meal, an enormous black dog pushed his way through the restaurant door. He stood for a moment, turning his massive head from side to side. Then he lumbered slowly in my direction. The men around me hooted and hollered. The bear-like creature sat down in front of me and settled his massive head on my lap, his brown soulful eyes searching mine. Realizing I had nothing to fear, I slipped him a cracker and whispered, "I know just how you feel."

A few days later, the telephone rang, awakening me in my hotel room. "We will pick you up and take you to the airport in 30 minutes," a voice announced.

Quickly, I dressed, repacked my suitcase, and gulped down my Dramamine to prevent air sickness. There was no time to spare; yet, I reminded myself not to fly on an empty stomach. Tucked into my suitcase was an orange I'd brought from Anchorage. Fresh fruit was such a treat in the northland, that I quickly devoured each juicy section.

The gray morning sky didn't hold promise, but we buckled our seat belts and took off. The pilot's voice over the sound system interrupted any further conversation, "We can't make it into Valdez, so we're going to try Gulkana. We've called ahead for transportation to take you to Valdez." Gulkana was 118 miles from Valdez by the Richardson Highway.

Before long, I felt so drowsy that I could barely enjoy the fresh coffee and donuts the smiling stewardess brought us. I blinked my eyes. In a daze, I heard someone ask, "Are you okay?" I recognized the stewardess, and struggled to speak.

Out of the blue, obnoxious fumes filled my nostrils and my head jerked up. I saw her hand with a broken capsule beneath my nose. For a second, I was awake, but just as quickly, my head plopped back to my chest. The plane lurched through the sky and soon my meager breakfast lurched out of me. The miserable flight was never-ending.

Eventually the plane found its way out of the rough air onto solid ground. I staggered down the steps. Wet flakes slapped me in the face. I took stock of my other flying companions, four men. A short distance away, I saw another man in an army parka beckoning to us. Through the white dimness, I recognized Bernard Whalen, a longshoreman from Valdez.

"I'm your guide for the rest of the journey," he said, as he ushered us to his Oldsmobile station wagon. "We'd better get going," he urged. "The highway department is fighting a losing battle to keep Thompson Pass open."

Doors slammed, and the car wallowed away through the deep snow. Bernard hunched forward at the wheel. Few words were exchanged as all eyes strained to discern the tall poles planted beside the highway to mark the edge of the road. We all knew that nothing protected us from the valley below.

"At least we'll have good traction with all of us in here," someone said.

For a while, I felt hopeful about ending my horrific ordeal; but, as we neared the pass, wind joined the snow, together conspiring against our efforts to master the mountain. "The conditions haven't improved since I came through before," said Bernard, momentarily straightening out his arms and stretching his shoulders.

At that exact moment, the car slammed into a drift. Bernard shifted into reverse in an attempt to back out, but to no avail. "There's a shovel in the back…" his words were lost in the gusty wind as all four doors seemed to open automatically. The men zipped up their coats, jumped out, and moved into action, shoveling, pushing, and rocking the car between first gear and reverse. No luck. The car sank deeper into the snowy quicksand. Although it was only early afternoon, the January sun had retired for the day, leaving us in darkness.

"Hey! Someone's coming!" Bernard shouted. At first, it looked like just another vehicle, but then when we saw it was a snowplow, we all cheered. The snowplow backed over to us, and the equally powerful-looking driver climbed out.

"It's you again," he said affably to Bernard. "You mean you're going back over the mountain?"

Bernard tried to explain, but wind whipped the words out of his mouth.

The driver yelled out, "I'll escort you over Thompson Pass."

With little effort, the snowplow freed the car from the drift, and we resumed our extraordinary trek to Valdez.

"It won't be long now," Bernard informed us, his eyes glued to the snowplow taillights.

We arrived in Valdez around 4:00 p.m. It was obvious I'd been out of town. My Chevy was buried. "Here, follow me and I'll forge a path," offered Bernard, hoisting my suitcase out of the station wagon.

He cut a good trail through the waist-high snow, and I pushed my way after him. After we dug the snow away from my front door, I stumbled into my house. My home, sweet home.

Later, I learned that the pass had closed behind us and some travelers were stuck in snow drifts for three days and three nights.

They had food with them, but I wondered how they had kept from freezing to death. While I'd been gone, winds had reached 60 mph. Siding had blown off the Stein's house.

ABC

Home to me also meant friends, and after my Cordova *break* I was eager to see familiar faces. I turned up the stove to re-warm the place, and plunged back into the wintry night, over to my new pastoral friends, the Eckmans. Leonard and Wilda were a few years older than me, with a school-aged boy and girl. He had come to pastor our church and replace Andrew Taylor. Wilda answered the door and the smell of something delicious baking rushed out. After quick embraces, she said, "Welcome back! You really took a break from school didn't you?"

"I don't think I'll need another break for a while," I responded.

"Well, tell us about it," Leonard said.

I thought of the bear-like dog, the flying beer cap, the juicy Christmas orange, the spirits of ammonia. "If you don't mind, I think I'll just sit here, and enjoy your company first." I sighed.

I needed a break from my break.

Anna's Alaskan Pizza Pie

Make a bread dough with shortening, flour, water and yeast. Add enough flour to make a stiff dough. Let rise once. Roll out on a cookie sheet with edges. Layer the following ingredients:
- tomato paste
- fried moose burger, seasoned with garlic salt, oregano, pepper, and diced onions
- globs of cream of mushroom soup
- grated Velveeta cheese or whatever cheese is available
Bake at 400° for 20 minutes

My pizza- pie-making fame began after I ate in a pizzeria in Melrose Park, Illinois with my Italian friend, Josephine Casurella. We were youth officers in the Free Methodist Church attending their New Year's Eve conference rally in Chicago. I tried to copy the ingredients, and experimented on my relatives. No one in Bowling Green had ever heard of pizza. By the same token, none of my Alaskan friends had ever made pizza. In Alaska, I had to adapt different ingredients, due to availability.

CHOCOLATE CAKE
FLAMBÉ

The springtime weather teased us. Following an intense winter of snow and wind, thawing and freezing now took turns. We'd turn our heads toward the sky, feel sunshine on our faces, and have hopes that winter had relinquished its grip. But then when we opened our eyes, piles of snow remained around us. I faced waist-high snowbanks outdoors and ankle-deep snow remained on top of my kitchen and bathroom roof. The snow, crusty on top, but melting underneath, formed long, drippy icicles on the roof edges. Above my north kitchen window, the drips fell onto the regulator of the propane tank.

One lazy Saturday morning, I was inspired to bake Mrs. Halbert's Cocoa Cake for my dinner guests. In slippered feet, I padded into my kitchen and across the chilly linoleum floor. Pulling open the short curtains, which enclosed my cupboards, I reached for flour and sugar. Methodically I stirred together the ingredients, poured the batter into a glass pan, and licked traces of sweet-stuff from the wooden spoon. I moved toward my stove with the cake, thinking warm thoughts about my wonderful little home in Alaska.

I loved my house. I thought the bathroom, added on to the kitchen, and the steep stairs to the upper bedroom tucked under the roof, made it quaint. Nonetheless when my sister, Millie, who was a Home Economics major, had come came to visit, she thought the place lacked a color scheme and focus. All the same, she persuaded me to study the Sears catalog and select wallpaper. I'd purchased a sewing machine and we'd turned out green-gold-beige striped slip-covers and matching curtains. I had to admit that the pretty floral kitchen wallpaper pulled together the haphazard colors elsewhere.

At this point in my musings, I turned on the propane-fed oven and opened the door to put in my cake pan. To my astonishment yellow flames shot out. I jumped back in horror! Greedily, the flames licked out toward the cupboard. No languid daydreams now.

"My house will burn down!" I screamed.

Frantically, I grabbed the oven knob and turned off the oven. The flames continued untamed. The fire was out of control. I slammed the door and jumped back.

Without grabbing a coat, I raced through the living room and out the door, slipping and sliding toward the Steins in my floppy slippers.

"Oh, Lord, don't let my little house burn down," I puffed and prayed as I ran.

Pounding on their door, I screamed, "Help! Help! My house will burn down!"

Jay jerked open the door and I stumbled in. There sat Wilson hastily yanking on his shoes. Before I could say another word, he bolted out the door, and rushed pell-mell toward my house, careening between the banks of snow on either side of the road, his shirt tails flying.

I stood motionless in shock. Didn't he know he'd forgotten something? I looked at Jay, her eyes wide in disbelief.

"He, he ..." I couldn't blurt it out.

He was clad only in a flannel shirt and undershorts.

"We slept in late today," Jay said, reading my mind.

As the cold seeped into my slippers, my thoughts returned to the fire in my house. I chased after Wilson. Ahead of me, he stood hip deep in snow, beating the ice off the propane regulator with his shoe. Then, he dashed inside.

By the time I reached my front door, the "steeplechase" firefighter hurried past me on his way out.

"Everything's okay now," he panted, pushing his glasses back on his nose.

His blue flannel shirt, cold red legs, and unlaced shoes made a comical sight. I wasn't sure if I should laugh, or if I should cry in relief.

Hesitantly, I entered the house, put the cake into the oven, pulled up a chair, and sat guard until I was confident there would be no more outbreaks.

That evening, I served the notorious cake to my dinner guests. "The regulator was frozen and the gas pressure came at full throttle," I explained to them.

On later occasions, Jay, Wilson, and I told and retold the story. Laughter, good friends, and a little excitement would help us all make it through the deep-snow months—and the spring that struggled to come.

Mrs. Halbert's Cocoa Cake

- 1 C. brown sugar
- ½ C. cocoa
- 1 C. granulated sugar
- ½ C. (or more) boiling water
- ½ C. oleo
- 1 heaping teaspoon soda
- 2 eggs
- salt
- 1 C. sour milk
- 1 t. vanilla
- 2 ½ C. flour

Combine cocoa and boiling water. Add more water if consistency is too thick. Let cool. Mix together sugar, oleo, and eggs. Add soda to sour milk. Mix cooled cocoa mixture into sugar mixture. Alternate flour with sour milk mixture. Add vanilla. Mix well.

Pour into 9" x 13" cake pan. Bake at 350° for 30 minutes or until toothpick comes out clean.

P.S. Check gas regulator before turning on oven.

1957
BEWARE "THE BLOWS"!

The winter wind whipped up frightening problems. So was the case in January. I thought the Friday afternoon would never end. My body ached. My throat scratched. At long last, the remaining student stopped by my desk with "Bye, Miss Bortel." I opened the school door to drag myself home. A blast blew me back into the building. I pulled my wool muffler (scarf) around my neck and tried again, this time succeeding in getting out the door and into my car. I felt as though I'd tangled with a monster. Once home, I fought my way out of my car and through the howling wind. My front door slammed behind me, emitting a cloud of snow. I crept up to the bedroom within the pitched roof, crawled into bed, and pulled the flannel sheets and pile of blankets over my head.

Drifting in and out of a fitful sleep, I attempted to find a comfortable position, and tried to stay warm. In my feverish state, I could hardly distinguish between my dreams and reality. At one point, I thought I heard the water pump running, a common problem with my inadequate foundation. When this happened, I had to boil water to pour around the pipes. I rolled over and swung my feet over the bed. But when I stepped out on the icy floor, all I could hear was the blowing wind.

The house shook as each gusty blast pummeled it beneath the heavy blanket of snow. As Ed, the sixth grade teacher, commented during my first winter in Valdez, "Come January, we live in a constant hurricane."

The eerie mental and physical battle against the wind resulted in general irritation among students and teachers. Yet, neither the snow depths, nor the freezing water pipes, nor the wind itself was the worst villain during these times. The most dreaded of all was "the blows."

"The blows"! I shot up in bed.

The wind would blow down the chimney stack of the oil heater and snuff out the flames. Then when the oil ran in, contact with the hot stove would ignite the oil and an explosion would result. As often as this occurred in Valdez, it was still a dramatic newspaper story—and a nightmare.

Valdez Newspaper, Dec. 1956

"High Winds Irritate Furnaces"

About 2 a.m. last Saturday morning, the fire siren sounded off. Gusty winds were prevailing. Trouble had developed at the home of Howard Woodford where the furnace "blew up." The Volunteer Fire Department, which arrived promptly, found everything under control.

Looks like Howard and Tiny will be spending some time digging out from under the thick layer of greasy soot resulting from the accident. Sounds like a complete redecorating job will be necessary. Some consolation, tho, they shouldn't have to do any spring-cleaning!

I'd experienced "the blows" once before and never wanted to go through it again. Now, sitting up in bed, the house shuddered and I shook. The cold air seemed to penetrate the mattress, reaching into my tired and feverish bones. Then pulling my blankets around me, I grabbed my pillow and stumbled down the stairs to the living room davenport.

Outside, the wind shrieked. Inside, the oil heater danced on the protective metal sheet beneath it. I argued with myself, *You must get some rest ... You must be vigilant.* Many people refused to sleep during these times, since they feared fires, but as the night wore on, I wore out. In the morning, I awoke with the gales continuing outside, but the stove intact inside. I'd made it through the night.

All that day and throughout another night the fury refused to be tamed. I wondered what was going on outside. I tried to look out, but could find only a crack of light coming through the top of a living room window, and a small open circle toward the upper corner of my front door. My front door was snowed shut. *What if "the blows" would come? I'd have a fire and I wouldn't be able to get out.*

Curiously, and slowly, I turned the door knob and pulled the door toward me. There against the hard snowbank was the imprint of my front door. I stared in despair. I closed the door and returned to guarding my stove.

About noon, I heard shouting outside my door and recognized Wilson's voice, "Hey, Anna, are you okay?"

He'd shoveled the snow away from my door. I opened the door a crack. My voice cracked as I hoarsely thanked him; after which I shut the door and returned to my den. The wind gave no indication of subsiding.

Sometime during the night, I awoke, startled by the silence. No roaring wind. The house felt warmer. I'd survived. I snuggled down in my covers and slept soundly. The next morning, I awoke without aches and pains, back to my usual self.

Well, I wonder what I've missed out on? First I had to get out of my house. I dug colossal chunks of snow out of my doorway and carried them into my shower to melt. Once I broke out of my imprisonment, I searched for my garbage can. I discovered it lodged in a snow bank, a block away. The town was buried in snow, and in many cases, only roof tops showed above the tremendous drifts. When I returned to my house, I climbed on top it, and I stood on a ridge by my second-story bedroom window. Now I felt better. Now I was having fun.

Anna on top a roof ridgeline by her second-story bedroom window.

After surviving the weekend's illnesses and adventures, I carried my blankets back upstairs. What a surprise met me when I reached the top. The determined white stuff had shoved through the cracks around the window and now behind the twin beds was a drift of snow. I carried lumps downstairs and tossed them out the door. The next fall, I put heavy plastic over the windows to prevent this frosty intrusion.

As much as the Valdezians were used to snow and wind, on Monday school was out for a snow day. Even the locals could only stand so much.

"The Valdez Wind"

(Music and lyrics by Anna Bortel)
The wind blows in the morn-ing,
It blows all through the day.
And when the day is o-ver,
I can hear it say, Oo-oo-oo-oo-oo-oo.

EASTER EGGS–
BOILED OR FROZEN?

"Ladies, I know we are engulfed in over 250 inches of white winter stuff, but it is not too early to start making plans for an Easter egg hunt for the children of Valdez." I brought up this idea when we were discussing new items of business at the Dorcas Club.

The Dorcas Club, a non-denominational group of Christian women, tried to emulate the Biblical Dorcas, who was described as "full of good works and deeds." Our deeds ranged from donating a record player to the school to making afghan blankets. Rummage sales and bake sales produced our revenue. At one meeting, Margaret Keenan Harrais reported that within the past two years, 22 afghans had been delivered–four to the local hospital, and 16 to the Veteran's Administration Hospital in Washington D.C. Although the Club was given credit for these good deeds, truthfully, Margaret had crocheted most of the blankets herself.

One year, all the chambers of commerce in Alaska sent gifts to President Eisenhower. The Valdez Chamber of Commerce requested the Dorcas Club's help in furnishing an afghan. What an honor for our obscure group! Senator Bill Egan delivered our gift to the president, and later we saw ourselves recognized in the Anchorage newspaper.

Now I could just see us embarking on more history-making. My exuberance was not shared. Instead, my announcement was met with cries of protest.

"Whoever heard of an Easter egg hunt in Valdez?" said Katherine.

"Where in the world would we hide the eggs with knee-deep snow?" queried Ruth.

"We've never had an Easter egg hunt before, and it would be ridiculous to try one now," chimed in Dorothy.

The more the members deemed the event impossible, the more determined I, their president, became. After all, children in Washington D.C. attended an annual hunt on the lawn of the White House, and children in cities throughout our entire country looked forward to this event. Why should the boys and girls of Valdez miss out on the excitement? True, there were obstacles, but we could do it!

After much discussion, the noise subsided, and the women resigned themselves to what they considered to be an inevitable disaster. A committee was formed to work on publicity and another to organize the event. The egg-decorating group decided to use dark, rather than pastel colors so the eggs would stand out against the snow; and even to wrap some eggs in gold paper. The finders of the latter would receive a prize.

"We'd better be sure there are enough eggs in Valdez to dye," I reminded the egg-dyers. "Who will notify the grocery store?"

On the weekend of April 21, a small crowd gathered at a large open field on the outskirts of town. Excitement filled the frosty air as 10:30 a.m. approached. Children threw snowballs, parents pulled their younger children on sleds, and dogs barked and cavorted. Below the crusty springtime surface the snow was heavy and sticky. One of the Dorcas women explained to the eager troupe how the event was to take place. I hadn't imagined that children had to be told what an Easter Egg Hunt was about. I'd assumed every child would just know.

Instructions were given, children looked around expectantly, Dorcas Club members shook their heads in skepticism. I blew the whistle. The hunt was on. Children scrambled in the deep snow, trying to pick up eggs with slippery mittens. Emotions ran high.

"Miss Bortel, Larry's dog ate my egg," sobbed one kindergartner. I grabbed the happy-go-lucky dog and tried to comfort the child. "Go look for other eggs."

Another voice called, "Miss Bortel, come quick! George's boot came off. It's way down in the snow and his foot is freezing." George leaned on his friend, Michael. I let go of the dog and dug into the snow. Indeed, the boot was stuck and no amount of tugging would release the obstinate object.

"Wait here, and someone rub George's foot, I'll be right back," I said, then rushed as fast as I could through the bottomless snow, to the road, and down to my house for a shovel. After some pulling and panting, we reunited George's foot with his boot. Instead of complaining about the cold boot, George thanked me profusely, which caused him to lose his balance, and plunge head-first into a snow bank. I shook my head. The happy little clown pulled himself out and laughingly reentered the hunt. Within minutes, he returned with one of the prized gold-wrapped eggs.

"Hey! Look what I found!" he waved his trophy above his head. At that moment I knew it was worth the effort to bring this extra-special experience to the children of Valdez.

First Easter Egg Hunt in Valdez (1957)

ABC

Easter eggs rolled on the snow and the school year rolled toward an end. My teaching responsibilities were scattered about with uncertainty. The superintendent and school board had decided that I should take over the high school vocal music in addition to the grade school music. This required taking the high school choral group to state competition. I felt uncomfortable and unqualified. My background was elementary education, not secondary music. Furthermore, the superintendent had informed me that since only six kindergartners had enrolled, and 12 were necessary for a class, *and* the first grade teacher was not returning, therefore, I would be teaching first grade, rather than kindergarten which I'd anticipated. I felt shoved beyond my competencies and as if everything was spinning out of my control. Once again, thoughts of teaching farther north crept into my mind.

Even though I was content during most of my three years in Valdez, as early as one month after my arrival, my curiosity had been aroused about what lay farther north. Granted, I'd become accustomed to Valdez's hundreds inches of snow, which at first made me feel as if I'd drown in the powder and not be found until springtime; and the mountains, which initially left me feeling constricted, now felt cozy and secure. The bay, which changed with the tides and seasons was still alluring, but I'd listened to the El Nathan Children's Home women pray for missionaries in the Interior villages. At the Teacher's Convention in Anchorage I heard several teachers tell about their adventures in remote villages. I imagined yapping sled dogs, dark-eyed Indian children, and dancing Northern Lights. Sometimes I'd lie awake at night and imagine what that would be like. It wasn't that I was bored with Alaska, but I was restless and wanted to see more of the territory. I wondered what else Alaska had to offer.

My desire to experience untried northern experiences pulled me north; and now, the unappealing teaching situation gave me the push I needed. I'd heard that *Sometimes obstacles are messages from*

God to redirect our ways. I didn't want to be hasty, or a quitter, but I wanted to be listening for God's direction.

ABC

"What's that nasty rumor about you leaving?" asked George Gilson. I was standing in front of a shelf of baking powder, vanilla, and spices, when the tall owner of Gilson's Mercantile sidled up behind me and peered over my. I jumped with a nervous laugh. George was the president of the school board. The town might not have had a daily newspaper, or TV news, or even complete telephone service, but that didn't slow down communication—or gossip.

I was taken aback by his question *and* how emphatically he'd said it. How did he know anything about this? I'd divulged to Superintendent Don Richards that I felt compelled to venture farther north, and that I had a three-part strategy. I didn't expect my words in private would become public news. I'd outlined to Don that I would establish myself in Fairbanks and find a job. Teachers in Alaska came and went unexpectedly, so I anticipated hearing about openings. This would hopefully be a toe-hold in the right place for the right time. Next, I would start graduate work at the University of Alaska. Finally, I would remain available for a teaching position in a village. Don hadn't understood my reasons, and apparently, he had not kept them confidential. As is often the case in such situations, he and other people added their explanation. Everywhere I went I felt like a microphone had been shoved beneath my nose.

Tangled into my decision to leave, the wild rumors, and children asking, "Who will teach us music next year?" the school board threw me another curve, that of an astonishing pay raise. Somehow this classified information also got out and blew like a blizzard around town. Ironically, rumor had it that the school board was favoring me. I shook my head. It hadn't been that long since the school board had opposed "another Bible-toting teacher" in Valdez.

If that wasn't enough evidence of favoritism, Don Richards put on a surprise birthday party—for me. He'd learned of my May 10 birthday through the school secretary, and even though he'd never done anything like that for other teachers, he planned a Friday after-school celebration. I enjoyed the party even though the snowballing news labeled the party as a bribe to get me to stay in Valdez.

Try as I could, my logic made no sense to anyone and it was like explaining why salmon swim upstream. The suspicious questions saddened me, but I felt at peace about following the urge to go north.

PART IV

1957–1960

1957
A STEPPING STONE
NORTH

Now if only I can squeeze in this last box, I mumbled as I packed my dependable Chevy. Although it was the end of May, the morning air was chilly. Summer finally showed signs of returning to Valdez, and I could see blades of grass pushing through the sandy gravel around my house. My friend Myrtle, a retired Oregon teacher, who had decided to teach in Alaska, stood beside the car, and handed me a lunch. The smell of fresh bread escaped from the sack.

"Please tell all my friends good-bye for me," I requested. Exhausted from packing, I dared not trust my emotions for additional farewells. Myrtle's tearful brown eyes met mine and it was a damp good-bye.

With each step, my decision had been confirmed. Due to the population decline in Valdez, houses were not selling. I thought I had my house sold to two incoming teachers, but when that fell through, I rented to Al and Ruth McGregory. Eventually they purchased. Finding a place to live in Fairbanks came together, too. One of my student's parents sold me their 30-foot, two bedroom Rollo-home trailer near Fairbanks.

Now, I started to my next destination—365 miles north to Fairbanks. Agnes Rodli wanted a ride to Fairbanks to visit friends so I had companionship. She was leaning towards becoming a certified school teacher and this gave us plenty to talk about. The drive out of Valdez through Keystone Canyon with its Bridal Veil and Horsetail Falls reminded me of my first impressions of Alaska.

ABC

Just as promised, my newly-purchased trailer had been moved to Northaven Cabins Court in College, about five miles outside of Fairbanks. The $30 a month fee allowed me the use of toilet, shower, and laundry privileges, and electricity hook-up. I didn't mind carrying water for my drinking, cooking, and washing dishes from the public wash-house. I would enjoy this temporary camping environment.

I unloaded my car and crammed all my earthly possessions of kitchen utensils, bedding, books, clothes, and sewing machine into the back bedroom of my latest home.

The university was a mile away and I explored as I walked along. Even though summer green touched the rolling hillsides and purple lupines had started to bloom in clumps, I missed the towering mountains of Valdez with their hoary crowns and the constant rise and fall of the bay. Fairbanks seemed flat and drab in comparison.

I selected three classes: Creative Activities for Exceptional Children, School Music Activities, and the Elementary Science Workshop. I paid the $55 enrollment fee and purchased books. Unlike when I was a child, I was eager to enter a classroom and be a student!

In the Music Class I introduced the song, "Valdez Wind," which I had written in the minor key to capture the feel of a harsh, bone-chilling wind that Valdezans experienced.

"You need to have your song copyrighted," the teacher exhorted.

I appreciated her affirmation, but didn't think I was ready for publication.

I kept busy with my graduate projects. I took in my little Coleman camp stove I'd used for cooking on the Alcan, and we heated up water to record the boiling temperature. When a rolling boil would appear, the water would vaporize into steam. Then we held marshmallows over the flame to observe the change in property matter; for another project we used different colors and shapes of plastic balls to create a planet system. As extraverted as I was, I very much enjoyed interacting with professors and students. Some instructors were from Alaska and their lessons were tailored to the rural villages, but then there were the ones who were new to the Territory who seemed more interested in learning from their Alaskan students than teaching. A visiting professor from Texas spoke of "those who teach out in the brushes," referring to remote villages and areas which are not connected by roads or rail system. This comment brought hearty laughter from several members in our class.

"It isn't 'brushes,' but 'bush,'" replied a young female student.

The professor asked, "Why can't one call it 'brush,' just as well as 'out in the bush'?"

"That just isn't Alaskan terminology," she countered.

Knowledge about teaching in the *Bush* extended outside the classroom. One evening, a study group met at my trailer. Cramped together around my small table, over blueberry pie and hot drinks, we momentarily forgot our project while a teacher from Nome entertained us with her explanation of the sanitation system in her village.

"I don't have a flush toilet," she began. "We use chemical toilets because of the permafrost. Just behind the toilet can is a trap door to the outside of the house."

The twinkle in her eye indicated something comical was to come. We leaned forward in our seats. "You know, one has to be careful because when the "honey wagon" driver comes. He pulls the trap door open to empty the can.

We convulsed with laughter.

She continued, "One time, I locked myself out of the house. I decided that the only way to get in was to squeeze through the trap door. It was a tight fit, but I made it!"

Our noses wrinkled, and we looked at each other in disgust.

Eventually, we did get to our project, but listening to these episodes was an education in itself.

ABC

Between classes, I checked the bulletin board in the hallway at the university. One day, I saw a notice that stopped me in my tracks. My heart skipped a beat.

Wanted: Elementary School Teacher for the Tanana Day School on the Yukon River

I'd heard about that village perched on the edge of the tremendous Yukon River, and the bits and pieces of facts and observations had sounded appealing. I scribbled down the information and I ran to my car with thoughts bouncing around in my mind. *I've always wanted to teach in a village. Here is an opening. If I am ever going to teach in a village, I'd better do it before I get any older and have aches and pains of arthritis.*

As much as it seemed the perfect answer, I went home to think and pray, before making a decision. Within the day, I felt at peace about teaching at Tanana (TAN-na-nah), and wrote a letter of application.

A week later, a call summoned me to Dean Cashen's office. Both Mr. Robert Isaac from the Territorial Education Office in Juneau, and Mr. Windsor, from the Bureau of Indian Affairs (BIA), wanted to talk with me. Mr. Isaac quickly made me feel at ease. As soon as we'd exchanged handshakes, he announced with a smile, "Your teaching contract is on its way from Juneau." I gripped the edge of my seat to refrain from ricocheting around the room in excitement.

Following this introduction, the two men proceeded to discuss what teaching would be like in Tanana.

"The Tanana Day School is under the Bureau of Indian Affairs, or the federal government; therefore, they hire the head teacher," said Mr. Windsor.

"The second teacher is hired by the Territory of Alaska," Mr. Isaac clarified. "This is the only dual teaching system throughout the Territory."

In all other situations, the Alaska educational system had separate systems for Native and non-Native children, with the Territory supplying teachers for the non-Natives, and the Bureau of

Indian Affairs providing teachers for the Natives. There were no high schools for the Native children, except for vocational school at Mt. Edgecumbe in Sitka. The Tanana school enrolled 40 students, of which 12 to 15 were non-Native. Although I would teach all first and second graders, I would meet the requirement for a teacher for non-Native children.

The year before, this overlap had created tension and there had been problems at Tanana between the BIA head teacher and the Territorial-hired second teacher. Leaning forward, Mr. Isaac detailed the upcoming arrangement, "Miss Feldkirchner, the new BIA head teacher, will teach the third through eighth grades." After a momentary pause, his eyes not leaving mine, he said, "And, I hope there won't be friction."

I got along with most people, so doubted there would be hostility; all the same, his tone of voice made me apprehensive.

The conversation moved away from teaching to life in Tanana. "Most of the children will be Athabascan (ATH-uh-BAS-kuhn),[4] that is Indian, not Eskimo," Mr. Windsor told me.

"You do know that Tanana is one of the coldest spots in Alaska," Mr. Isaac said, returning to a more nonchalant tone. "Anywhere from 40 to 70 degrees below zero."

At this moment, I could welcome cooler weather. I'd noticed the climatic change from Valdez's moderate coastal climate to the more extreme temperatures of interior Alaska. Fairbanks' current 70 to 80 degrees made me feel lethargic and I realized I'd adapted to colder temperatures. In outlining how to prepare for my move, the men urged me to bring plenty of warm clothing, but otherwise all I'd need would be personal items and linens everything else would be provided.

"There is a nice hospital complex about 400 yards from the school, a Civil Aeronautical Authority (CAA) station[5] toward the downriver end of the village, and a White Alice site[6] eight miles up from the village," Mr. Windsor continued with the briefing. "Air service is regular, about every day or so, and it's only an hour's flight from here."

"And, there is a Northern Commercial Store," interjected Mr. Isaac. I knew this was a general store.

Within a few days, the contract arrived.

Now, I had more decisions. I wanted to keep my trailer home and ship it by river barge to Tanana. However, the first of August, a letter arrived from the State Department in Juneau stating that a nice two-bedroom trailer home, located on the hospital grounds, awaited me. Quickly, I put a *For Sale* sign in my window, and within a day, I had a buyer.

In the midst of last minute preparations, I met Miss Florence Feldkirchner, who had been Outside visiting her siblings, and now returning to Tanana. I judged her to be 20 years my senior. Her solid build and dark dyed hair were pulled up in a bun, befitting her name. While we visited in my crowded trailer, she sat with her back straight against the kitchen chair and no-nonsense shoes planted firmly on the floor. With little emotion, she told me she'd been teaching at Fort Yukon, and described basic facts of teaching there. As we talked, I visualized the year ahead. *She'll "wear well,"* I convinced myself. *She's my opposite.* It wouldn't be long before we could try out our team efforts.

In the interim, I placed all my worldly possessions, on a Yukon River barge. The deck of the heavily loaded barge rose a mere foot above the water line. Only a scant sheet of plastic protected my boxes of cookware, photo albums, quilts, knickknacks, and winter clothes. I hoped and prayed that the Person who had walked on the water could keep my treasures out of the water!

One last item remained. I wasn't sure if it was a simple possession or a friend: the light green Chevy with familiar curves and many miles on its odometer. If it could talk, it would recount miles of fond memories and sharp curves of adventures. I'd been told that I wouldn't need a car in Tanana, but I'd miss my loyal companion.

As it turned out, new friends purchased the Chevy, and they subsequently sold it to a family who used it to pick up children for Sunday school. I was grateful that my car had entered God's service as well.

ABC

Summer classes ended in late August. Exams were taken, tourists pulled up stakes from my campground, and traces of morning frost subtly transformed green leaves to golden. The day came to fly to Tanana. In the 1950s, women schoolteachers did not wear slacks, so even though I was flying in a small plane—in Alaska—and going to the Bush, I dressed carefully in a two-piece, black-and-white checked suit with a modest length straight skirt. When I walked out to the single-engine Norseman, I stared at the plane uneasily. *How in the world will I get in?*

No rungs or steps. All the other planes I'd flown in had some sort of steps. I glanced down at my tight skirt and shifted my carry-on bag and handbag to a more comfortable position. Then, I stood in front of the plane. Impossible.

The pilot, an unpretentious man with wisps of brown hair poking out of his plaid cap, stood beside the plane chewing on a toothpick. I could feel his eyes trace my skirt and then he seemed captivated by the hills in the distance.

My throat tightened and I coughed.

"Uh ... try this lady," he said quietly, pointing toward a tread spot on the low wing.

I edged up my skirt to allow more agility—and blushed. He looked away in embarrassment.

I wasn't the helpless type, but, I thought, *I could use a hand or a shove*. He just shifted his weight. Red-faced, I bent forward, hiked up my skirt above my knees, and with every seam straining, lifted my weight, and boarded the plane.

Having accomplished that feat, I sat wordlessly. The plane rattled down the runway, and noisily invaded the quiet sky.

Twenty minutes later, I recognized that unlike the route to Valdez, we did not follow mountain passes or fly at high elevations to miss mountains. Instead, the Tanana River guided us, as it wound back and forth cutting between the old spruce forests. Steep riverbanks, undermined or sheared off by river erosion, and hills on either side provided the only variation in this wide wilderness. In late summer, the river flowed low, with driftwood littered sandbars often surfacing. I actually enjoyed this relatively flatland flying, with only overgrown hills to fly over. Surprises of yellow aspen splashed black-green forests. Blueberry leaves already touched by fall blanketed the ground with deep red tones. Orange swamps added to this autumn palette.

Suddenly, the pilot shouted over the engine's racket, "Look! See the bear over there in the clearing?"

The bear had plopped himself in the middle of a blueberry patch, taking a last chance to dine before hibernating. The pilot's tongue seemed loosened, and he pointed out geographical interests, as well as animals that his trained eye had spotted. In less than an hour, the Tanana River[7] approached the legendary 2,298-mile-long Yukon River. The powerful bodies of water met in a mile-wide junction and, after interruptions of islands, sandbars, and detours, emerged as one enormous entity.

"There's your village," the pilot exclaimed, motioning toward the buildings strung along the riverbanks.

We flew closer and started to descend. There were no long-distance roads in and out of the village. No wonder I didn't need the Chevy.

I'd thought Valdez was isolated with access by only one road, which was occasionally closed during the winter, but here, there were *no* roads to another town.

Aloud, yet more to myself than to the pilot, I said, "So this is life in the Bush."

"Yep," he said, "the next village is seventy miles downriver."

Taking a deep breath, I acknowledged that I was about to begin a new chapter in my life in Alaska. I'd stepped farther north.

GETTING ACQUAINTED

Village of Tanana on the Yukon River. L to R: CAA complex, Public Health Hospital
complex, Tanana Day School. (1957)

The pilot banked the plane over the river. I stretched my neck trying to see my new community. At the downriver end, a group of
boxy green-roofed, white-sided houses were arranged in a square.
Nearby, a compound of red-roofed rectangular buildings was positioned at right angles beside the road. Following these buildings
other structures rambled some with tall, flat store-fronts and others
with glinting tin roofs. Before I could see more, the plane made a
final descent. The wheels touched down on the gravel strip and the
propeller rotated to a stop.

Climbing out of the plane proved slightly easier than the climb in. This time gravity was in my favor.

A short man, clad in a green army jacket greeted us, "Hey! Are you the new school teacher? I'm Warren Thompson."

"Yes, I'm Anna Bortel," I said. We shook hands.

His gray whiskers parted and he shot a spit of tobacco juice out the side of his mouth. He repositioned his cap. "Hop into the pickup while I load this freight and the mail."

Identifying his pick-up was easy. It was the only vehicle at the tiny airport office-shed.

After dropping mail bags, crates, and my two suitcases into the back of the rusted pickup, Warren pulled himself inside and slammed the door, twice, to get it to stay shut. The road curved toward the riverbank and then paralleled at a distance of about 25 to 30 feet.

Warren chuckled, "There's not much to point out, but right here is the CAA camp." He gestured toward two-story, steep-peaked houses in neat rows. They looked like a neighborhood in the States.

He kept up a steady flow of conversation as we drove on a one-lane dirt road, more like a walking path, which took us past the red-roofed complex, he identified as the "hospital and stuff." We lurched to a stop beside a swing set in front of an aging white building with olive trim. Dust swirled up around my ankles as I scooted out of the pickup. A sign hung on a post. *Tanana Day School* was hand painted in narrow black letters. Above it was a black, cast-iron bell. I wondered who would ring that bell in just nine days.

Anna Bortel and Florence Feldkirchner by Tanana Day School (1957)

"Miss, the door to your living quarters is here on the side."

I walked around the corner and there stood Florence Feldkirchner in a crisp, navy print housedress.

"Anna, welcome to Tanana. How was your trip?" She shook my hand. "Please come in."

Before I could answer her questions, I realized she had guests. "Anna, I'd like you to meet..."

My mind failed to register the first three men's names, but they were dressed a bit formally for this back-country place, and even wore narrow dark ties. All I heard was that they were with the BIA and had just flown in an hour before my arrival. I wondered if they had come to observe our meeting and to assess if Florence and I would be compatible for a year together in the Bush.

"And, this is the Rev. Coleman Inge, the Episcopal priest," Florence completed the introductions and offered me a cup of coffee. I settled into a worn over-stuffed chair. The aroma of cinnamon streusel coffee cake and easy small talk made for a pleasant introduction to Tanana, Alaska.

ABC

The BIA team left for another village down river and the white-collared Rev. Inge excused himself as well. He was a friendly man, and I appreciated meeting him. Florence asked, "Would you like a tour of our facility?" She had arrived before me and had obviously settled in and become acquainted with the living quarters and classrooms.

"Oh, yes!" I followed her.

The living room, eating area, and kitchen were actually one large room. She took me to a door off the kitchen.

"This is an important room," she said straight-faced.

She opened the door. I gasped and then chuckled. I was glad to see that beneath her precise veneer she had a sense of humor. A few steps up and several feet across was a toilet set on a platform. I named it "The Throne Room." She elaborated, "It is oddly designed due to the obstacles for plumbing, but most of the village does not have running water or indoor plumbing, so we are fortunate. The school children use the outhouse behind this building."

When I wrote home, I tried to describe my unusual living quarters.

The old Knights of Columbus building that houses the classrooms and teacherage is a romantic place that walked out of the last century. The ceilings must be 12 feet high, and the floor slopes down on one side. BIA has the teacherage furnished with modern furniture—some new and some quite worn, which stands in contrast to the ancient building. An oil furnace heats the entire building, and in the teacherage we have electricity, a refrigerator, and hot and cold running water.

The classroom section consisted of two rooms with double doors between. The doors were wide enough so when opened, created a space adequate for combined class events. The floor sagged towards the doors and it was obvious where a pencil would roll if dropped. From above, light bulbs hung on cords and glared from the tall ceilings.

"This back room will be your classroom," said Florence.

Except for the factory-type bottled water on a stand, the rest of the room was a standard classroom with bulletin boards, a pencil sharpener, bookshelves, school desks, and a chalkboard with printed alphabet marching across the top.

"Now, do you want to unpack, or would you like to walk around the village?" asked Florence.

"Unpacking can wait," I replied. "I want to see the village."

Looking at my suit, she suggested, "You might want to change your clothes and take along a sweater."

A few minutes later, we walked outside and started upriver. There was no need for caution when walking in the middle of the lane since no cars or trucks appeared. The river seized my attention and I detoured to the ten to 15 foot bank that broke off abruptly to a gravel shore along the muddy water. The vast river consumed much of this new environment and I stood gazing at the heavily treed island, a half-mile across the water.

Back on the road, the first house we passed was a two-story frame building suggesting years gone past. At first glance, it seemed typical of any small town, but as I looked carefully, I saw metal bars stretched over some of the windows. I questioned Florence. She replied, "Someone told me it used to be the village jail. Now, Lewis and Lucy Kalloch live here. See their wonderful vegetable garden?" She hadn't been in Tanana for any length of time, but she'd been quick to assess her new environment.

Straight lines of bushy potato plants, onions, beets, Swiss chard, enormous cabbage, and fringed carrot tops ran within the garden which was mixed with a jumble of bright flowers. Multi-colored sweet pea vines climbed the wire fence. We moved on. A non-Native man and Athabascan woman ambled across the road and sat down on a backless, board bench facing the river.

"Oh see, there they are at their usual afternoon spot," Florence said.

In the near future, the Kallochs would invite me in for tea. I'd learn that Lewis had come to Alaska with other gold rush hopefuls, and when his gold finds were what he thought was adequate to provide for a wife, he'd married Lucy. I'd experience the marvelous home they had, with a water pump standing right in the middle of the kitchen, beautiful antique dishes, and vintage pictures. I'd wonder who, over the years, had eaten off those china pieces. I'd watch the way Lucy would smile with her eyes at him, and the way he treated her like a new bride, hovering a bit to see if she needed help.

This generous pair would share with us their 15-pound cabbages and other jumbo produce, grown in the sandy loam under the midnight sun.

Florence continued her commentary, "This is the Episcopal parish house, where the Rev. Inge stays. And up there a ways ... see the building with a belfry? That is St. James Episcopal church." The dark-green church stood out in an assortment of otherwise white buildings and log cabins.

In 1884, when Congress passed legislation to set up a civil government in Alaska, Alaska was divided geographically among the religious groups. Since the Church of England already had missions along the Yukon, this area was assigned to the Episcopal Church. That, however, didn't prevent other denominations from coming in later.[8]

Before we reached St. James Church, we walked in front of the Northern Commercial Company Store. The door stood ajar and we went inside. Curiously, I inspected the array of kerosene lamps, wool gloves, laundry detergent, bananas for 30¢ a piece, cans of green beans at two for 75¢, eggs $1.25 a dozen, and a loaf of white bread for 70¢ nearly twice the cost as that in Valdez.

I'm glad I shipped my groceries out.

Florence read my expression. "That's why it's better to order food for a year and stock up when you happen to get into Fairbanks."

St. James Church, a clean-looking building with a steeply sloped roof, sat among irregularly spaced spruce trees, short willows, and tall wild grass.

Next in line was a short white building.

"Look at that white picket fence!" I exclaim. I expected to find a tidy lawn inside this boundary, but instead, unruly wild grass grew against the pickets and a potato patch sprawled about in one corner. In the middle of this disorder, a small wading pool with a half submerged sailboat bobbing about indicated that a child must be nearby. The fence continued around a small white building, with long, low windows and a wood slat walkway. Beside the door, a sign read *Tanana Chapel*.

My tour guide swatted mosquitoes around her neck and kept walking. A rough-sided post office with a faded sign and a glass front, followed by several more houses and cabins, marked the end of Front Street, as Florence referred to this narrow road.

"Now, we can return on Back Street," she said.

We took an immediate left, and sure enough, about a block later we came to a street that ran parallel to what she had referred to as Front Street. There were no signs with these nomenclatures, just common knowledge.

"If you were to go right and follow this upriver, you would come to gravel pits, the old Indian burial ground, and another road splits off and goes eight miles up the hill to the White Alice project. Morrison-Knudson is the contractor, and they have over 100 men who work there."

White Alice antennas that reflected radio signals. (1957)

The previous December, a ceremony at Elmendorf Air Force Base in Anchorage had marked the beginning operations of this modern national defense system, which would serve both as a sentinel for North America and as a communication system for the most remote sections of Alaska. Right now, communication outside of Tanana was possible by two-way radios only.

"Have you seen the White Alice?" I asked. Florence shook her head and said, "The project is to be completed in November and then the construction workers will all leave—perhaps then we could go up ... Now, look over here."

She motioned toward a nearby log building with a tin roof, a corrugated tin-siding entrance, and tall magenta fireweed growing three and four feet high around its sides. "This is the Community

Hall where dances, movies, celebrations, potlatches, and community business meetings take place."

Across the street, a cabin with wild bluebells pressing against the window and growing out of a coffee can caught my attention.

Gregory and Margaret Kokrine live there," said Florence. "I understand that they are old-timers here. He's Apache Indian."

More time-tested cabins nestled in the willows where occasional wild rose bushes pushed against the undergrowth. The pale pink, cup-like blooms added a delicate sweet scent to the fresh, woodsy air. Huskies stood on their dog houses wagging their curled tails and barking greetings. Washing machines squatted on the front porches with drying laundry hanging overhead. A hint of spruce smoke drifted from several cabin stovepipes. It all seemed so quaint and idyllic.

Some villagers stared at us and several adults waved. A few children followed us. "See you in school," I called out. They giggled and hid behind one another. Wild grass swayed in the gentle breeze and occasional bursts of stalky blue flowers shot up unexpectedly in the overgrown clutter of dog sleds, wood chopping blocks, and piles of tin cans.

Our jaunt brought us back behind the school building—with our shoes well dusted.

"Here is the Catholic Church and tiny quarters where the itinerant priest stays," said Florence. "Actually, the Catholic Church owns the land the school is on."

The late August sun perched high in the sky, but the afternoon air had become crisp, and I pulled my sweater about me as we strolled behind the school outhouse and across the playground.

"I believe it's almost time for soup," announced Florence. "Mr. Thomas will be waiting."

Mr. Thomas, a BIA worker from Anchorage, was to paint and do repair work before the opening of school. He'd found a room in the village, but ate meals with us. Florence pushed on the unlocked teacherage door and went inside. I walked back over to the riverbank. The churning river commanded attention in much the same way as the majestic Chugach Mountains asserted their presence in Valdez. This flat, water-splotched country felt strange and I missed the mountains that had securely swaddled me close. Here, the mountains didn't crowd in, but stood farther back. I stared across the water that at this hour reflected the gathering gray clouds.

ABC

Mr. Thomas sat at the table, his narrow shoulders slumped forward.

"I thought you'd stand out there all day," the small man greeted me. His pale face barely showed a smile.

Before I could respond, Florence set before us steaming bowls of thick soup with chunks of meat, canned corn, and small bits of garden carrots. The hearty aroma didn't conceal the evidence that Mr. Thomas was a chain-smoker. This was my introduction to Florence's culinary skills which she had acquired as a cook in World War II. One swallow and I knew she'd brought a touch of class to the bush country.

I named this re-occurring specialty "Feldkirchner Soup." It required leftover vegetables, any kind of meat, and broth or leftover gravy. A heavy rim of black pepper lined the bowl when one finished eating.

When I learned that the trailer house by the hospital was unavailable, and that I'd at least temporarily live with Florence, I knew that eating her meals would be no hardship.

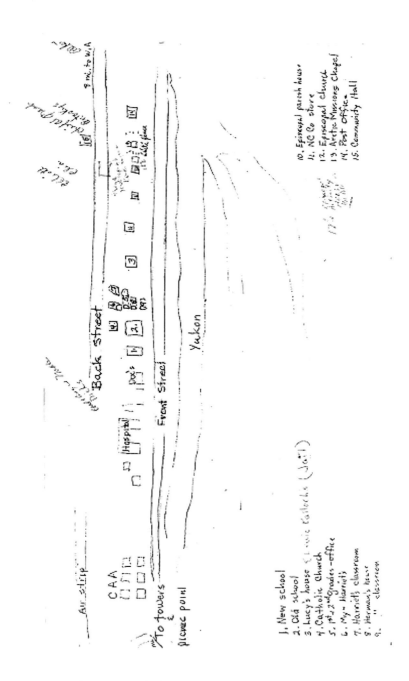

Quonset Hut School Camp in Tanana, Alaska (Winter 1958)

MAKING MYSELF
AT HOME

"Girlie, if you want your classroom painted before you start teaching, you'd better get busy," Mr. Thomas informed me. School would commence in three days. I reasoned that I did like to paint, and while my father never let me do any interior painting at home, I had enjoyed his permission to paint the Adirondack lawn settee one summer.

"Will you pay me if I paint my room?" I bargained.

Mr. Thomas eyed me for a moment and paused to press out a cigarette in the ash tray. "Okay, but we'll have to fill out a work order to submit for the work you render." He let that thought hang in the air, and then as though he was doing me a favor added, "The amount will be $2.80 an hour."

He had been authorized to hire Native help, but Harper, the man he had selected, had nonchalantly walked in the door this Saturday of Labor Day weekend with an explanation of his inability to do so, "You know, this is a holiday weekend."

Mr. Thomas, stroked his straggly goatee and didn't say a word.

"I can't work when it's holiday time," the man tried to enlighten us. He took off his army-green wool jacket and settled into a nearby chair with elbows on his knees and his head in his hands, indicating he was in no hurry to leave either. Now it was up to me.

I donned my oldest clothes. Mr. Thomas assigned me the upper half of the walls, which meant I was the person to climb up the ladder to the 12-foot ceilings. He stayed on the floor, reaching as far as he could stretch. After ten hours of painting, I looked at the beautiful bright classroom and reveled in my accomplishment.

ABC

The next morning, Sunday, I slept in and nursed the aches and pains from the previous day's work. But, by afternoon, I found myself sitting in the sunshine on the wooden backless bench overlooking the Yukon River. On my left sat a vivacious Athabascan woman, Mary. Her dark eyes shone, and her first words were about my coming to teach her children. It always made my job easier when parents supported my efforts, and I squeezed her arm. On my right was a bundle of energy: Margie Gronning. She and her husband were Arctic Mission's Missionaries. Margie's fairness contrasted with the other woman's golden brown skin.

It seemed Margie had been waiting for someone to show up who would share her love for this village. Both women were quite the talkers and a delightful conversation ensued; when it turned to the origins of this riverbank village I found myself enthralled. A variety of events had overlapped in this area near the confluence of the Tanana and Yukon River.

"It is called Nuchalawoya (New-cha-la WOY-uh) or 'Where two great rivers meet'," she said proudly. "For many years it is a meeting place for our people. We come together to trade furs, talk about problems, settle hunting boundaries, and celebrate, and go on our ways."

In approximately 1891, Rev. Jules Prevost, an Episcopal bishop, had decided to move the Mission of our Savior from the mouth of the Tozitna River. The selected site was 11 miles upriver, past the current village of Tanana, to a bluff that overlooked the Yukon River, by the Nuchalawoya junction. The Mission development consisted of a church, sawmill, school, dormitory for children when their parents left for fur trapping, hospital, and graveyard. Subsequently, an Athabascan village grew up around the Mission.

This central location with easy river access evolved into a strategic juncture for the Native people and early traders. In addition, the army had assessed its worth as an ideal site for an army post. In 1898, the military established Fort Gibbon, about three miles downriver of the Mission establishment. Then Tanana, a settlement of non-Natives, sprung up between it and the Mission. This area included stores, saloons, a four-story hotel, warehouses, a post office, boardwalks, and potato fields. The entire vicinity had over 1,000 people, and some historians even claim records of 3,000.

Although Fort Gibbon and Tanana were adjacent to one another, military authorities refused to call their post "Fort Tanana" and Tanana post office personnel stubbornly retained "Tanana," rather than adopting "Fort Gibbon." Obviously, this resulted in confusion. Further tension developed when the Tanana post office refused to deliver letters addressed to Fort Gibbon, and Fort Gibbon telegraph office denied knowledge of telegrams sent to Tanana.

Mary enjoyed talking about the village and interjected stories about her people. "We Natives mostly live upriver and the Whites live downriver," she said.

I thought of the layout with the CAA houses and hospital complex at one end and then cabins at the other.

"I remember when a fence made a dividing place where the school is now," the woman elaborated.

During the 1940s, the demographics changed. First, White man's diseases, such as measles, hit the Mission and a large number of people died. Then, the government assessed the redundancy of having two schools, one at the Mission and one in Tanana, and decided that the Mission school would be closed. When the Mission hospital burned it was replaced by a hospital in Tanana. All this resulted in the majority of Natives moving into Tanana. The Natives, however, still used the burial grounds up by the Mission.

"You would find it very interesting to talk to Gregory and Margaret Kokrine," interjected Margie. "They can tell you stories of times back in those olden days when so many people lived in Tanana."

I turned to Margie, "What brought *you* to this village?"

Margie explained how she and her husband, Roy, had worked at two children's homes, first at This-Side-of-Heaven Children's Home in Kasilof (Ka-SEE-loft) on the Kenai (KEEN-eye) Peninsula, and then at Lazy Mountain Children's Home at Palmer. Although the 65 children were Aleut, Indian, and Eskimo, they'd felt drawn to work more directly with the Native people in the village. This sounded a lot like El Nathan's home.

"We arrived in Tanana in January 1955—with a bitterly cold introduction to village life of 50 degrees below," her body trembled as she recalled that day. "It was hard to have a two-month-old son and no indoor plumbing!"

I stared at her with admiration. Inside this petite four-foot ten-inch woman was a tough, rugged Alaskan woman.

Deep rumbling interrupted our conversation.

"What's that?" I asked.

"Oh, a barge is coming from upriver," Margie said offhandedly.

River barge on the Yukon River. Island in the background (1957)

Sure enough, not one, but three barges vibrated into view and were pulled sideways against the beach to unload. I could see the name *Tanana* on one and *Yukon* on another. There wasn't a dock structure, so the boxes, barrels of fuel, lumber, and miscellaneous items were piled upon the narrow beach. Amidst the heaps I found my personal items, Boston fern, and my $200 worth of canned and packaged groceries. I wondered if I'd ordered the right amount of cornflakes, rice, pears, lemon Jell-O, canned peaches, flour, green beans, sugar, shortening, and other groceries to last the year.

ABC

By the time I'd recruited help to haul my belongings and supplies to the school house, it was time for the evening service at the Arctic Missions Chapel, to which Margie had invited me. I walked through the picket gate. I wasn't sure if I should knock on the door or walk right in. Before I had a chance to do either, the door opened.

"Welcome," a voice said above me. "I'm Roy Gronning. Margie told me about you."

I gawked a moment and then found my manners with a, "Pleased to meet you." Diminutive Margie was married to this Paul Bunyan. All the same, the large man was laid-back and unassuming. We talked, and then he introduced me to the others. Alice Peters, the Public Health Service Hospital secretary, gave me a warm smile and greeting. She was an attractive woman with a cloud of white hair.

"This is Grandpa Sam Joseph," said Roy. He stood with his arm around an older Athabascan man. "He is a special friend of ours and babysits our children."

I reached to shake Grandpa's gnarly hand and then sat down on a chilly folding chair. The room was the size of a one-and-a-half car garage. Roy lit two gasoline lanterns and hung them from the low, sloping ceiling, where they flickered and temporarily smoked. In the middle of the room squatted a fat barrel stove, constructed from a 55 gallon gasoline drum turned on its side with metal legs welded beneath for support. A wood box with a hinged lid wide enough to make a seat, rested against one wall. An upright piano completed the furnishings in the linoleum-floored room.

The group was meager, about 15 adults and some children, but the kinship was enormous. We prayed together, and then sang "Amazing Grace" in simple harmony.

Arctic Missions Chapel attached on right, to the mission house. (1957)

SCHOOL BELLS

"In ten minutes I'll ring the school bell," Florence warned me.

I'd awakened early for this first day of school, although Florence was already up and dressed by the time I'd reached for a cup of coffee. I wore a narrow skirt with a loose long-sleeved sweater. Florence's dress with full skirt and large-buttoned bodice softened her stiff posture. We both wore nylon hose and pumps with a slight heel.

Impatiently I paced around my classroom, then opened the door and watched the children appear around the building. Some children were laughing and chasing each other. The younger children clung to their mothers. Suddenly the bell clanged. Children scrambled to the door from all directions.

Florence organized 25 students into a noisy group of grades three through eight, and they marched into her room. In my room, 24 first and second graders wriggled into their desks. Several of the youngest children, who were initially reluctant to leave their mothers, forgot their anxiety and became absorbed by the fall leaves pinned onto the bulletin board. I looked over my class. The boys and girls were predominantly Indian with dark skin and raven hair. One boy apparently had both a Native and non-Native parent. Along with his dark eyes, he had sprinkles of freckles and red curly hair. I learned that two girls, Naomi and Ruth Gaede (GAY-dee), were the new doctor's daughters. The younger girl, Ruth, kept to herself shyly, with her shoulders pulled up slightly and her eyes downward. The second grader, Naomi, ran her fingers over her new Big Chief tablet and played with a freshly sharpened pencil. Her eyes darted around the room, taking in the September calendar with rural farm scenes, and watching a small group of children poking at one another. I suspected the girl with tight blond curls wearing a frilly blue dress came from a CAA family.

I introduced myself, then proceeded with first things first, as previously instructed by Florence; that is, I distributed vitamin pills to be washed down with cups of orange juice. Along with tablets, pencils, and crayons, the class materials list included a cup for this daily ritual. The procedure seemed strange to me, but it was a part of the health program required by the BIA school practice. Rather than leave out the non-Native children, I dispersed portions to all the students. Florence informed me that the government would also send tomato juice and hard cheddar cheese at other intervals.

The boys and girls, accustomed to summer outdoor activities, could barely restrain themselves in the classroom. I tried to maintain order with physical activities and a serious countenance.

"Miss Hotel…" a young Indian boy raised his hand and opened his mouth all at once.

The corners of my mouth turned up on my otherwise my controlled face. I wondered if he even knew what a *hotel* was. I thought of our assigned textbooks. How foreign they would seem to these children. For example, after lunch, I read a story and pointed to the picture of a red building with a silo. I asked, "Does anyone know what this is?"

The children sat for a moment, and then one Native girl volunteered, "A look-out tower?"

"Anyone else want to guess?" I asked.

"It's a barn and silo, just like my grandpa has in Kansas," responded Naomi.

I could see the limited general knowledge some students would have. Later, they opened their books to a story about children going by train to see their grandparents. My students were fascinated with the train and asked questions, such as, "Could it go on the river?" To help them visualize a train, at recess we played *train*, coupling and uncoupling cars, being a caboose, and so on. Unlike me, the mournful whistle in the middle of the night was not a known element of their lives.

I noticed Alfred Grant, the village chief and school janitor, behind the door. He was watching me teach. This became a common practice for the eager-to-learn chief, and occasionally he'd even fit his bony frame into an empty desk for the lessons.

At day's end, I managed to herd the children into line, and then they shot out of the room. I dragged myself down the hall to our living quarters, and fell into the same overstuffed chair I'd snuggled into the first moment I'd walked into the teacherage. Whew! Had I learned a lot this first day. I closed my eyes and heard my father's words to me early in my teaching career, *Anna, you can help a child decide whether he is going to like school and go on to college by the atmosphere you create for him in his first year of schooling.*

What atmosphere have I created today?

Day two came and went, and in the evening I walked to the Wednesday night prayer meeting at the Arctic Missions Chapel. When I entered the room, I spotted a man in his thirties with a wiry build and crop of black wavy hair. He spoke energetically with Roy. Near him, trying to talk to Margie, sat a pretty dark-haired woman. A squirming two-year-old, with the cutest double-chinned face and a mischievous grin, grabbed most of her attention by snatching at her glasses. She tried to restrain his chubby arms, but he was quick and determined. Ruth did her best to distract the toddler and patiently waved a stuffed toy in his face. Naomi sat next to Ruth, and talked to her blond-haired classmate from CAA.

"Anna, I'd like you to meet Elmer and Ruby Gaede," introduced Roy. "These are their children, Naomi, Ruth, and Mark. Doc has been here a week, and Ruby and the children flew in on Monday."

The Gaedes had come from Anchorage, where Elmer Gaede had served at the Anchorage Alaska Native Service Hospital for two years. Before I could find out much more, Roy waved a long arm, indicating it was time for the service to begin. Margie led us in choruses and songs, and accompanied with her autoharp. We were new to each other, but "What a Friend we have in Jesus" and "Tell me the Story of Jesus" were old favorites for us.

ABC

I absolutely fell in love with my first and second graders, and although the children's liveliness did not wane, I did manage to harness it by the end of the first week. In fact, several weeks after school had commenced, I had the nerve to ask, "How would you like to have a pet show on Friday afternoon?"

They weren't sure what I meant. After I explained, their eyes got big, and I could see their imagination working.

"Oh that would be so fun," shrieked Pee Wee, my hyperactive student who frequently gnawed on my desk. At this moment, she tucked her feet beneath her and balanced precariously on the edge of her desk seat.

"Let's do it! I'll bring my puppy," pitched in freckle-faced Chris, the boy with soft brown eyes and red curly hair.

Friday arrived. The pet show would be in the afternoon. The students worked hard all morning and at noon lined up obediently to leave for lunch in their home and to get their pets. Like a dog team waiting for a race, they bolted when released. I didn't see how they had time to swallow their food before they returned to school. Furthermore, I had no idea how or where they had acquired some of the pets.

Jimmy proudly paraded in with a beautiful blue parakeet in a cage. *Oh, oh,* I thought. *I'll be up on the ladder trying to retrieve that bird from the ceiling.* Next came Rudy, trying to hurry and at the same time carefully balancing a fish bowl with eight gray guppies swimming in the sloshing water. Two roly-poly husky pups yipped at one another and the children. The bird put on a splendid show, obeying his young master, sitting on Jimmy's finger and shoulder, and *not* soaring up among the dangling light bulbs. A black and white puppy with a tiny curled-up tail whimpered when I picked him up. I cuddled him, stroked his soft fur, and whispered in his ear, "Would you like to sing us a song?" He opened his mouth wide, stretched his pink tongue, and let out a tiny yowl. I repeated the request and again he yowled. The children whooped in delight.

Before I knew it, the afternoon was over, and Florence's students rushed through the double doors, wanting to see what they had overheard. The rest of the children exploited the bedlam, until I shooed them out as well. I surveyed the room. Desks were pushed against the wall and bits of animal fluff skittered from the draft of the just-closed door. A blue feather rose and resettled beneath a chair. I let out a small yawn and headed toward the hallway. I was tired, but it was a good tired. Next week, just maybe, the children would be motivated to write stories about The Pet Show. Now, it was Friday, and I had weekend plans for fun with new friends.

ABC

I stretched lazily and unwillingly exited my snug hibernation. Slowly I plodded into the kitchen. Fortunately, Florence had put the coffee pot on. With a full mug in hand, I lined up ingredients to make waffles: powdered milk and powdered eggs. The eggs smelled like soy meal. Florence had warned me they made baked goods heavier. Marjorie Macomber, a nurse from the medical complex, and I had planned to hike downriver from the village. I'd been told not to go off alone outside the village, because of bears, so I welcomed her companionship.

When I'd approached her about a Saturday exploration, she'd responded without hesitation. In the same way my daily conversations revolved around unusual bush teaching incidences, hers were filled with situations unique to a remote hospital. "This beats any post-graduate review course!" would become a statement I'd hear often. We shared the same wide-eyed amazement of where we found ourselves in life.

A timid tap on the door announced her arrival. Her black coarse hair was pushed off her face as if she'd already been biking–downhill. A camel-colored camera strap was around her neck with a 35 mm slide camera case near her waist. She was ready to go to exploring. I suspected this same attitude was what made her the perfect nurse for the Bush: ready for anything and more astonished than anxious at what might show up in her path—or examining table or hospital bed.

By the time we left, the morning air was already warm and the blue sky was empty of clouds. We climbed on old, clunker bikes and laboriously pedaled down the road toward the CAA complex, our fat tires leaving wide imprints in the damp dirt. Once past the complex, and beyond the end of the airstrip, the road ascended. We pedaled past thick timbered woods with willows, large silver birch groves, and fireweed that sought to overtake the road. The vegetation was so dense we couldn't see far into the forest. After several miles of steadily pumping uphill, we ran out of steam and decided to hide our bikes in the undergrowth, and continue by foot.

Walking made it easier to focus on our surroundings. Golden aspen showed off their fall apparel and shimmered against a back drop of pearly birch bark and dark spruce. At one point, we meandered off the road and followed a moss-edged game trail to examine some gone-to-seed fireweed that were changing from narrow green leaves with pink flowers into dried-up curly leaves with whitish cotton-like puffs. The spruce trees weren't unusually tall and grew up like match-sticks, rather than full-bodied Christmas trees. The pungent smell of wet and decaying leaves hung in the air. In the shaded areas, partially frozen, three to four inch deep moss squished beneath our feet as we walked back to the road.

"Oh!" I gasped, finding massive paw prints in the moist soil. Obviously a bear had recently shared our route. Marjorie and I stared at each other with our mouths gaping. After stunned silence, I blurted out, "Bears have terrible eyesight and if we make noise they will be afraid and never come close." I hoped this feeble attempt at courage would calm us both.

"It's the middle of the day. May, may, maybe he's heading toward the dump that we passed," stuttered Marjorie.

"I guess it's a good time to turn around anyway," I said, "I hope we make it around the dump without finding him scrounging for supper."

I cleared my throat and broke out with "Home on the Range." When I ran out of words, I created my own verses.

"Anna, you don't sound very scary," Marjorie blurted out. Nearing the dump site, we tried to act brave, and laughed loudly and hollered threats to any potential bear; all the while, I wished we'd taken a gun. I scanned the dump. My heart raced. Fueled by fright, we skirted the dump quickly without seeing any wildlife, besides the greedy black and white camp robbers (Canadian jays) that screamed at each other and at us. They didn't budge from their reeking smorgasbord.

We found our bikes. The road descended, but the bicycle chains needed to be coaxed and it was still a hard push down to the village.

"I can't believe it's nearly five o'clock," I said when we walked through the doorway of the teacherage. I am starved." Before we'd left, Florence had pulled out a package of frozen moose meat. It was thawed and waiting for me to turn it into supper for the three of us. Real potatoes from our neighbor's garden added to our fare of strips of moose dipped in flour and fried in oil. Marjorie kept trying to help with the preparations, but once Florence walked in, she became involved in exuberantly replaying our adventures to Florence.

We'd made the most of a late summer day along the Yukon River, survived the mystery bear, and polished off a delectable Alaska dinner. What more could we want?"

THE AUTOMATIC FLU

Girls in Anna's JOY Club (1958)

"Br-r-r, but it's cold out there." I shuddered as I closed the chapel door and wiped my boots on the rug.

Temperatures dipped below zero the first of October, and it was evident that we could not win the race against winter. I removed my glasses and rubbed the condensation off the lenses while I stood by the wood barrel stove rotating my body to absorb heat on all sides. Eventually, the dry heat from the stove warmed me.

"Are you ready for JOY Club?" asked Margie, smoothing out a flannel background on the flannel board.

JOY represented the concept of Jesus first, Others next, Yourself last. Margie taught the first and second graders in this after-school club, and I instructed the third and fourth graders. This way, I didn't have my usual school students and could get acquainted with other youngsters. I heard laughter and the tramping of feet and then the children pushed through the door, bringing a wintry blast with them. Even though I'd taught school all day, I loved to teach Bible stories and make them come alive to my children; and, the children loved to sing "Jesus and Others and You," and "Into my Heart." They were ready helpers to position flannel characters on the board.

On this particular day, one of the youngsters had just placed a picture of a blind man on the flannel-graph as I taught how Jesus could heal sickness.

"Miss Bortel, the Automatic Flu is going around, and we need Jesus," said Arvid, tugging at my sleeve. The personal application wasn't what I had expected. Arvid was small for his age, but his mind wasn't behind on any accounts.

"You mean the Asiatic Flu." I squeezed him close. He shook his mop of black hair in silliness. "Yes Arvid, we do need Jesus."

The next day at school, I noticed empty seats; this was unusual since the children enjoyed school and seldom missed a day. Whenever I questioned the whereabouts of the absentees, the students attributed it to the Automatic Flu—a name that had stuck. I gave up correcting them and let Arvid, who had not only named the flu, but could also describe the symptoms in detail, be the spokesperson on the matter.

"Miss Bortel, Dorothy has the Automatic Flu and won't be here today," said Sally. "She's wondering if you can wait to finish *The Story* until she comes back."

The Story was something I'd started during story time. Every day after recess, I'd read from a book. Last week, however, I'd been in an imaginative mood, so I'd made up a story about taking the class on a winter hike across the frozen Yukon to the island. It seemed the perfect setting for a mystery. We all knew that no one lived on the island, but the story raised the intrigue of possibilities. Although the river defiantly flowed at this time, I speculated about its frozen state to come, and what it would be like to venture across to the distant winter wonderland. The children sat spellbound as they experienced the story I construed.

On the island, we tramped about the knee-deep snow in the woods until suddenly we spied smoke lazily curling from a smoke stack that poked up behind a ridge. Where could the entrance to this region beneath us be?

Chris and Walter, who had plowed off in a westerly direction, called out, "Come! We found it!"

Hurrying over to them, we saw snow-packed steps leading down to a rough, short wooden door with dulled metal hinges.

"Who wants to knock on the door?" I asked. No one said a word.

The girls giggled and trembled with fright. The boys stared in awe at the hatch which would tip back into the wall of snow when opened. They looked at my face for reassurance that everything would be okay.

"I'll do it, Miss Bortel," Freddie finally spoke up. Chris and Walter hesitantly followed Freddie down the steps. Freddie pounded with his mittened fist. No one breathed. Snow slid off around the door as we waited. No one answered. We all let out our breath.

Chris looked up from staring at the door and said in a shaky voice, "Shall we try to open it?"

Freddie backed into Chris, who backed into Walter. "Teacher, you go first," he finally said in a frightened voice.

They made space for me to come through. I pulled open the door, which fell back out of our way. I had to duck through the entrance and wait for my eyes to adjust to the darkness. We put our arms out to touch the sides as we made our way in the tunnel. This lasted only for a short distance because the sides disappeared and we were left to wander in the spooky darkness. All of a sudden, our solid footing gave way to mushy matter.

We took off our mittens, squatted down, and proceeded in a duck-walk. Some strange force pulled our hands downward, and we touched a liquid on either side that made our fingers tingle. "Ohhh," we murmured softly as we waddled along.

"Look!" gasped Naomi, startling all of us. In front of us was a pinpoint of light. We inched our way toward it, and as we drew closer, we could tell that it came from a keyhole in a door.

"Shh-h-h," we told one another.

"2,001, 2,002, 2,003,...." A gravelly voice counted behind the door.

"I'm scared," whimpered Sally.

"Me, too," echoed Pee Wee.

I didn't know what to do. We had entered a hideaway, not knowing if we could find our way back out. I bolstered my courage and gave a firm rap on the door. Chills went up and down our backs as we waited. The voice stopped, but metal still clinked. We waited. At once, all was silent. We waited some more, expecting the door to be yanked open. The door did not move.

Slowly I turned the doorknob, which silently unlatched. I could easily push it open. Warm air from the barrel stove in the room rushed against us and felt so good. Then, we saw him in a far corner, a tiny man with white whiskers and blue-striped stocking cap, sitting cross-legged on top of a wooden table, counting stacks of coins. "2,050, 2,051, 2,052," his eyes never left the coins, nor did his head turn in our direction.

I stopped for a moment, trying to figure out where to go next in this story. Chris's brown eyes nearly bugged out of his face. Ruth had wrapped her coat around herself as if to protect herself or hide. The children sat trance-like without moving.

I'd become so engrossed by my own storytelling, that story time lasted more than the usual 15 minutes, and until I heard my stomach growling. How would I end the story?

"Oh, it's lunch time!" I announced.

The children blinked their eyes. Without their usual noisiness, they left the classroom to go home for lunch. I didn't know how the story would end, and actually, I didn't want it to end since I was having so much fun fabricating the wild tale.

On the way out the door, Chris said, "I hope I don't get the Automatic Flu. I don't want to miss out on *The Story*."

I walked home past the medical complex. Mary Ellen, a hospital employee's wife, stuck her head out of her duplex door and called to me, "How is that story going to end?" Apparently, the children retold *The Story* to their parents and neighbors, and they, too, contemplated the end.

ABC

Waiting for more children to be present for *The Story's* conclusion was only one complication of the flu epidemic. Halloween was nearing and Florence and I wondered how many students would be healthy enough to attend the party. We'd ordered a box of apples especially for the occasion and planned to make donuts. Fresh fruit was a rarity, so both these refreshments would make the event extraspecial. With our limited school budget, we used our own money for these treats, just as I used my own money for modeling clay, vinyl records, and word game anagrams.

The Thursday before Halloween, I awoke feeling as if someone had pulled the plug on my reserve of exuberance. Since the school Halloween party was to commence at 2:00 p.m. I needed to be in tip-top shape. The night before, Florence had stirred up cake donut batter and I'd fried all 150 of the puffy rings. As I'd stood over the hot stove, I became aware of a tightening in my throat. Next, I noticed how very tired I was, certainly an odd feeling since I was usually full of vim and vitality.

I can't get the flu now, I'd told myself. *The children have chattered endlessly about this party and I can't let them down.* After what seemed like forever, the last donut was extracted from the hot oil, set on paper, and rolled in sugar. This traditional Halloween fare waited in readiness.

After lunch on the party day, the excited boys and girls rushed in the door dressed in costumes. Some children had the good fortune of interested parents to help, and others, left on their own, had pulled paper sacks over their heads with holes cut out for their eyes.

"Your biscuits are good, Miss Bortel," Freddie said, reaching for his third donut. The white sugar sparkled on the rambunctious first grader's face. "How do you get the holes in the middle?"

"Thank you, Freddie," I responded. "These are called donuts." I didn't have the oomph to explain about the holes in the middle.

I'd asked Alfred Grant to bring his guitar and sing at the party. He knew the songs since he'd eavesdropped on our music lessons. I was extra glad I'd invited him since I didn't think I could sing a note in my current condition. His style was western-cowboy and he made the children laugh with songs such as "On Top of Old Smoky," and "Oh! Susanna."

In most cases, I looked forward to party times with children, but this afternoon, I kept glancing at the clock. The minute hand seemed frozen. Fortunately, the children were helpful guests and cleaned up the party litter before they grabbed a last donutand scurried out the door.

"Anna, you don't look like yourself," said Florence, ceasing her vigorous floor sweeping, and tapping her broom in from of me. "Now bundle up and go right home to bed. I'll finish the cleanup."

ABC

Too bad I no longer resided in the teacherage. After a month of living with Florence, I had moved to a fabulous upstairs two-bedroom apartment in the CAA complex. It was complete with foam rubber frieze-covered furniture, Venetian blinds, bed sheets, vacuum sweeper, steam iron, and electric coffee percolator. Forced air from an oil furnace kept me toasty, no matter what the temperature outside. There were six buildings on the complex with seven families, and I had the same amenities and privileges as the CAA people: use of the laundry facilities, a walk-in freezer locker, and ordering frozen food and meat from the commissary in Anchorage. I couldn't believe this bonus when I'd anticipated living in a small trailer on the hospital site. The apartment cost $50 a month, including utilities, but the renters in my Valdez house paid me $57, so my housing expense was covered.

I ventured out in the sub-zero air and stumbled toward my apartment, a half-mile away. My feet felt like clumsy blocks of ice. I bent down my head and groaned, "I think I can, I think I can."

After what seemed like an eternity, I dragged myself up the stairs. The can of chicken noodle soup I opened didn't taste like the homemade variety Florence made; in fact, it really didn't taste very good at all. I gave up eating, pulled on my flannel pajamas, and tugged my bed covers over me. I turned from side to side, but couldn't find a comfortable position. Finally, I dozed off, but at 1:30 a.m., I awakened with the chills. Even with the electric blanket turned to high, I shook. An hour went by, and abruptly, not only did I warm up, but I broke out in a sweat. I couldn't get the covers off quickly enough. Then, every joint began to ache.

Arvid would tell me that I have the Automatic Flu.

The next morning, I fought to focus my eyes on my bedside clock.

I must tell Florence that I can't teach.

She, like most of the village, did not have a phone; however, CAA had its own system, and could reach the hospital. The operator there would be able to get a message to Florence. My mind was foggy, and I fought hard to think. I didn't have the mental or physical strength to remember the phone number or to lift a finger to the rotary phone. *I need to go downstairs and tell Peggy Harris to call.*

Peggy and Adrian lived below me with their two boys. They were a friendly couple and Peggy was always up for exchanging news or hearing about my day. They invited me often to share a meal, and I'd always contribute, too. It felt a bit like family to have their nearby relationship.

I tried to move, but my body didn't respond. I knew I couldn't get out of bed. After drifting in and out of a fitful sleep, I gathered every ounce of energy and rolled over to face the wall. That effort left me breathless. Mustering all my strength, I pounded the wall.

Peggy was busy flipping pancakes. When she heard the commotion, she checked on her boys and when she found they weren't the culprits, she came bounding up the steps. I never locked my door, so she was able to come right in. How grateful I was to see her face in the dim room.

Peggy broadcast a call of alarm. Her husband, called the CAA station, and the operator on duty contacted Florence and Dr. Gaede. Florence obtained a substitute, Coleman Inge, who later told me he wasn't sure who had learned more, him or the students. Doc showed up at my door for a house call. At first he thought it was strep throat, but later he came back with the diagnosis of Asiatic Flu.

"Anna, it will take more than soup to get you back on the road to recovery," he said. "Penicillin is probably your best ticket."

Florence made me *real* soup, Margie brought over custard, CAA neighbors shared canned fruit, and Peggy scooped up my dirty clothes and brought them back clean, folded, and pressed.

Thanks to the miracle drug of penicillin, three days later I returned to direct my students in making papier-mâché' turtles.

ABC

"Will you finish *The Story* now?" begged Chris.

Only one child was absent, so I reviewed where I'd left off, and reminded them that we had been standing in the room with the strange little man and his coin counting.

> Suddenly, we glanced at our hands. Our fingers felt strange. We looked at each other, but dared not make a sound. We bumped into each other, but without making noise, backed out of the room. I pulled the door shut.
>
> I'd left open the door that led to this underground tunnel and now we could see that light filtering down to show us the way back. Just as before, we crouched down and dipped our hands into the numbing substance. Our speed increased and we seemed to fly up out of the doorway. The trek back was not nearly as difficult as the trip across, and together we held our hands in front of us as our mittens dangled by our sides from their harnesses. Strangely, our hands stayed warm, even though

we didn't wear our mittens. What was this peculiar covering on our hands?

This time, I'd watched the clock and knew when story time was over. The children implored me to continue, but I hadn't figured out what would happen next; instead, I called together the reading groups.

"We'd better hope she doesn't get the second Automatic Flu," said Arvid sad-eyed. "Or, we'll never hear the end."

The flu raged throughout Tanana, and in all the villages along the Yukon. Dr. Gaede shared in Sunday School Class that the day before, a call had come in on the two-way radio from Rampart. The entire village needed medical help. Even though his own children were ill and it was his day off, as soon as the reluctant winter sun provided enough light for takeoff, he and a nurse answered Rampart's pleas and flew up river in Dr. Gaede's small J-3 airplane. The doctor-nurse team walked from cabin to cabin. In one cabin they found all 11 members of the family stricken. The father and mother were still in their sleeping bags and unable to care for their children. Of the 15 children in the village, only one had made it to school the previous day.

ABC

In November, Margie and I asked the Joy Clubbers what they had to be thankful for. After comments about parents, puppies, new crayons, and fresh moose to eat, Arvid's hand waved like a flag. "The Automatic Flu is gone now."

He had heralded its arrival, and hopefully, he was an accurate predictor of its departure. One question remained, one that I'd now have to answer, "How will *The Story* end?" On Monday morning after recess, the children pleaded for the rest of *The Story*.

Huffing and puffing, we arrived at our classroom. We quietly shut the door behind us, and then looked down at our hands. The strange feeling grew stronger. Then slowly, oh so slowly, our hands began to glitter. As the light from the hanging fixture shone on them, we could see they were covered with gold.

"It's Golden Nectar!" I exclaimed.

When we shook our hands, the gold leaves slipped silently onto the floor. We flexed our fingers and stared in amazement. While we were temporarily immobilized, Edward and Linda found a box and gathered our treasure.

"Miss Bortel, what will we do now?" whispered Edward. It seemed as though this should be a secret and we didn't want the other class to hear any unusual commotion.

"Let me get a scale," I replied.

After carefully balancing the treasure chest on the scale and calculating the weight in dollars, I announced, "Boys and girls, we have enough money to fly to Fairbanks!" Everyone hopped around and hugged one another.

I'd scarcely finished telling *The Story*, when the children insisted I tell it again. At some point, I'd most likely repeat the tale, but I hoped not to repeat the Automatic flu.

NO DOUBT ABOUT IT–
WINTER IS HERE!

"Marjorie, don't you so enjoy the fragrance of smoke from wood stoves?" I asked. We were plowing through ankle-deep snow down Back Street, and it just seemed to me that the frigid mid-November temperatures intensified this marvelous aroma Daylight slipped into dusk around 3:30 p.m. It was nearly that time now, yet I was determined to get out and take a Sunday-afternoon stroll. Lamplight from the cabin windows cast a cheerful glow on the freshly fallen snow. Smoke spiraled against a night sky that was slowly breaking out with stars. The huskies seemed unusually subdued, and only the sound of someone splitting wood interrupted the serene setting.

"Why don't the villagers chop wood in the summer when it's warmer?" Marjorie wondered aloud. "Why do they wait until right when they need it?"

I searched my mind. I'd heard they believed that if they chopped too much wood ahead of time, they might die, and then all their efforts would be in vain. Florence had told me another reason. If other villagers see an ample supply of chopped wood, they might want to borrow it. The best way to avoid problems was to chop it as needed.

I burst out laughing, not at the reasons the villagers didn't chop wood, but at the memory of helping one of the Native women with her heating supply. Ruby and I had visited an older Native woman who we affectionately called "Grandma Elia." She was making moose skin slippers with decorated beaded tops for Ruby.

When we approached Grandma Elia's cabin, we spotted her sawing wood. Feeling sorry for her, we suggested she go inside while we sawed the wood. It was our first experience with a cross-cut saw and what a sight we two novices must have been! I got the giggles and soon Grandma Elia, who had been watching out the window, came out with instructions to help *us* as we struggled to help her.

Marjorie and I reached the end of Back Street and turned to go toward Front Street. "Do you feel guilty when you see how hard these folks have it, while we live nearby with furnaces and running water?" I asked.

"Yes," she replied. "There is such a contrast." In winter, the Natives hitched up their dog teams, traveled miles to cut the wood, hauled it back, unloaded it, and then split it. In the summer, they went out in their boats, snagged the driftwood, pulled it back to shore, and split it."

Arriving at the riverbank, I surveyed the Yukon. The river that had thrashed about all summer was still. Several weeks earlier I'd watched massive chunks of ice bobbing together as the freezing water thickened. Ice forms first on the edges of a river, where the water is more shallow. On November 3, the river ground to a halt, at least that which was visible to the eye. I'd been told the river wouldn't flow again until breakup, sometime between the end of April and early May.

The villagers chopped through the ice to get water and lifted wooden yokes onto their shoulders with five gallon Blazo gas cans attached to each side. In this fashion, they carried the water back from the river. This process was referred to as *packing* water. Hard work. Margie Gronning told me that Roy used a long heavy iron pole to keep his water hole open; sometimes that meant going down five to six feet. The Gronning's lifestyle replicated that of the other villagers.

I'd looked forward to the freezing of the river and wanted to venture to the island. I would see if my fantasies in *The Story* were in any way true.

ABC

Thanksgiving drew near and I wrote a skit with songs and choral readings for my first and second graders. The Native children would be the Pilgrims, and the non-Native children would become the Indians. I called Ruby for assistance in designing costumes and together we came up with a design.

I felt a kinship to Ruby, a farm-girl-turned-doctor's-wife. Even though she was married with children, and I was single, there was a growing bond; more so than with any of the other women. Maybe it was her make-do pioneer spirit and the way she not only accepted life as it was in the Bush, but exhibited spunky creativity that melded with mine. Or perhaps it was her desire to grow deeper in her faith, which reflected my own yearning.

The day of the program arrived. Florence and I opened the double doors between our two classrooms and proud parents crowded into the makeshift auditorium. I hoped the sagging floor would sustain all the additional weight. Although it was 25 degrees below outside, I noticed some of the children's and parent's foreheads glistening with sweat.

Thanksgiving Play practice. (Bottom left) Ruth Gaede, Naomi Gaede, Marie Sommers.

Dark-skinned Pilgrims stood together. The pale Indians shook their heads back and forth making their colored construction-paper feathers wave. The students enthusiastically said their lines and proudly showed off their gradually slipping headgear. I'd written a song about the Yukon River which they sang with gusto. As they solemnly completed the final Thanksgiving song, "Father we Thank Thee," I kept my eye on Edward, my ornery little pill. He looked so angelic in his black Pilgrim hat that tilted slightly to one side.

ABC

On Thanksgiving Day, Roy Gronning led a service at the Chapel. After the brief devotional, he suggested we sing. When Roy and Margie had discovered I could play the piano, Margie took a break from autoharp playing, and asked me to be the accompanist on piano instead.

Even thought the door was snugly closed between the chapel area and the Gronning's living quarters, the mouth-watering aroma of baking turkey crept out to the congregation. The Gronnings had invited a number of us to stay afterwards and the guest list included the Gaedes, Marjorie, Alice, and the Johnsons. Harold and Vera Johnson, who operated the booster station for CAA, 35 miles down-river at Birches, had flown in for the occasion. Birches was not really a village, but a spot along the river with their house and some out-buildings; otherwise, their family lived completely alone. Vera said they loved it. Whenever the weather allowed, Harold flew them into Tanana for a church service. Grandpa Sam Joseph hung back when the rest of the congregation left the chapel. Margie reminded him he was included on the guest list. His brown, wrinkled face turned into a happy grin and he joined the rest of us.

The Gronning's house was compact. The main area served as the living room, dining room, and kitchen. Adjoining this room were two tiny, and cold, bedrooms. The bathroom was an outhouse behind the chapel. Certainly one did not dawdle when tending to such business! Just like many of the other villagers, the Gronnings did not have electricity and lit kerosene lamps for light. The large barrel stove which provided heat, and had a flat piece of metal welded to the top so that a tea pot or bucket of water could be warmed. I couldn't imagine having two small children, diapers, 50 degrees below, and depending on this wood stove for heat, warm bath water, hot dishwater, and boiled water for drinking. Roy joined the other men who went out in boats and snagged driftwood for firewood.

We all bustled about with chores. Roy carved the 23 pound turkey he'd specially ordered from Fairbanks and had squeezed into the tiny propane oven at 4:30 a.m. Margie mashed an enormous pot of potatoes. I re-warmed my sweet potato casserole and other women spread out cranberry Jell-O salad, canned peas, and additional fixings. Ruby brought freshly-baked crescent rolls and pecan pie. Such a feast!

After eating our fill, we put our energy into games. I introduced the group to Scrabble, a new game. Naomi slid into a chair to join us. By this time in our flourishing relationships, Dr. Elmer Gaede had become "Doc" to all of us. Now Doc invited Harold to throw darts at the board. It didn't take long for Harold to figure out that Doc couldn't bear to lose and used this trait to cajole him into a lively match. Chris Gronning and Mark clung to their father's knees, raised their hands, and whined to be lifted up to pull out the darts.

Daylight had departed several hours before, and guests thought it was the polite time to go home; yet the conversation, game playing, and circle of friendship felt so cozy that I didn't want to go home and spend Thanksgiving evening alone. I also thought that if I played just one more game of Scrabble, I could beat Roy, who managed to make high- scoring words out of every group of letters he selected.

"You know what?" I whispered to Ruby. "I'm going to stay for supper and eat leftovers."

Ruby leaned toward me and lowered her voice, "Do you think we should?

Margie overheard our hushed conversation and encouraged us to stay. She returned the leftovers to the barrel stove to reheat, and soon we picked back tin foil covers and helped ourselves to a second round of Thanksgiving fare.

Roy nudged me and in a stage whisper and said, "Hey, Anna, do you want to try to beat me now?"

I was thinking through my strategy, when Margie placed a pan of hot water on the wood stove to make her prize-winning mint hot cocoa.

Roy brought in more logs and stoked the fire until it crackled loudly. Before he shut the stove door, some of the smoke escaped, bringing with it that remarkable fragrance. Now what could I spell with the letters z, q, and k?

CHRISTMAS TIME
IN TANANA

"Jimmy, cover your face, especially your nose, with your parka ruff," I said to a tall, brown-eyed first grader on our way to the Community Hall for a Christmas program practice. "Your nose is turning white."

No matter how cold the temperatures, the children bolted out the door for recess. Conveniently, their soft tanned moose-skin mittens were always with them, tied together by a colorful braided yarn harness that slipped over their heads. When not in use, they flipped the mittens around to their backs, twisted the yarn straps together and the mittens were out of the way, yet handy. This method also worked for adults. One could only imagine if someone was mushing a dogsled and dropped a mitten on the trail about 20 miles out in deadly cold weather. The mittens, although essential and functional were also a piece of artwork. Colorful beads bordered their backsides and rabbit fur bordered the top openings.

"Miss Bortel, your nose is white, too," said Jimmy, who had just inspected his classmates' faces behind their fur parka ruffs.

That was very possible. I'd always worn dresses or skirts for teaching. In late fall, I'd started pulling on winter boots for my walk to Tanana Day School. Once there, I exchanged my comfortable boots for shoes that matched my skirts and sweaters. But as temperatures plummeted, I found myself slipping into slacks with long-johns and hose beneath. In doing so, I relinquished my desire for style and fashion.

The Native people wore mukluks. The Athabascan style was above-the-ankle, home-sewn boots with pliable moose skin soles and coarse fur, such as beaver, on the sides. Rabbit fur adorned the corduroy casing around the top, which contained a tie with tasseled yarn ends. Narrow moose-skin ties were attached in the back, by the heel, and then brought forward to crisscross at the ankle before being pulled back again behind the heel and secured. Many of us added wool felt insoles and it was like walking barefoot in the snow. I wondered what my family in Ohio would think if they saw me wearing slacks and mukluks, not only for teaching school, but attending the chapel on a Sunday morning!

Jimmy was sticking close to me and interrupted my thoughts, "Miss Bortel, can I pull the curtain for the practice?"

"*May I* pull the curtain," I corrected him.

With the success of the Thanksgiving program, I'd formulated plans for the school Christmas program. Florence said that we would present it in the Community Hall, which would allow ample space to invite the entire village. Now with the anticipation of an even bigger program, the children had difficulty concentrating on their regular school work.

I really couldn't blame them. My mind centered on Christmas as well. I'd written a gift list to Millie: "*Could you buy and send a pick for my ukulele, a diary, a half-dozen centers for my record, and a half-dozen double-edged razor blades?*" I didn't know when I'd get out of the Bush. This was a problem. I wanted to send gifts to my family and friends; yet, my desire was thwarted by the lack of places to shop. I finally ordered gifts from the Alaska Native Crafts Clearing House in Juneau and from the John Plain Catalogue which mailed gifts from Chicago.

This year I was buying myself a present, a combination Hi-Fi radio and record player, which I ordered from a catalog. I didn't miss a newspaper anymore, but I longed for the sound of my vinyl records. What would Christmas be without carols? In addition, I needed a smaller record player. A record player had been standard equipment in the classroom, except for here. I decided to use my own money to buy one.

When the record player arrived, everyone clustered around it. I was surprised that most of the children had never seen such a contraption. As one would expect, I had many volunteers to turn the records. Some of the lyrics made no sense to the village children, but for several of the CAA children and to Naomi and Ruth, who had experienced life elsewhere, the songs evoked memories of Christmases past.

"I love the *city sidewalks* one," Naomi said wistfully. "Could you play it just one more time?" The only sidewalks in Tanana were the ones running within the hospital compound, or the wood slats that jutted out in front of several other village structures.

In the afternoons, the children energetically practiced their speaking parts and songs. At the moment, the Community Hall accommodated easily the 25 children, but with 200 to 250 people expected the night of the performance, I could already feel bodies pressed together with little breathing space.

Florence made colorful garments for her upper-grades class, and I rummaged about in my stored boxes to find the white capes and big red bows I'd used for my kindergarten graduates in Valdez. Without the convenience of department, fabric, or craft stores, one learned quickly to save everything and to see the potential in anything. Ruby and I traced the white capes for a pattern and sewed red capes for the boys. White bows pinned at their necks would be the final touch.

ABC

The big day arrived and the concluding dress rehearsal went well. I let the children out early and walked home in high spirits anticipating the Christmas Eve Program that evening. When I entered my bedroom to hang up my sweater, it suddenly struck me—with all the program preparation, I'd forgotten to consider my own attire. I couldn't wear mukluks and slacks to the Christmas Program—even if the temperatures warranted it. I selected a black-and-white dress, and probed my dark closet trying to locate the knee-high city dress boots. I found them, creased in folds from lack of use. My but they were tight after the roomy comfort of my flat-footed mukluks.

I stepped gingerly out the door in my slick bottomed boots and wool dress. My exposed legs felt the biting cold acutely, and I wished for my long johns. I shivered noticeably and pulled my parka hood closer. Anticipating the warmth of the Community Hall, I tried to hurry; all the while sliding from the snow build-up on the boot soles. The door swung open just as I reached the building and the cold air hit the warm air, surrounding me in a sensation of walking through a cloud.

A festive Christmas spirit greeted me. The suspended bare light bulbs illuminated our handmade decorations including red and green crepe paper streamers that swooped across the room. Florence's older students had strung a heavy wire across the front of the elevated make-do stage, on which curtains were attached. The curtain-pullers had clear instructions on when to do their task. The children glowed with expectancy and when they weren't squirming and messing up each other's costumes, they were trying to straighten out bows and capes. This was *the* event of the year, and anticipation had built to a crescendo throughout the school and community.

People entered in puffs of frosty air and the background din increased with the growing hubbub. Some parents sat on the wood benches that lined the perimeter of the room, and others found places on semi-rusted metal folding chairs. Younger siblings ran about trying to find their brothers and sisters behind the stage. The odor of smoked dried fish, stale cigarette smoke, and warm bodies became more noticeable as the fur-clad villagers packed themselves into the room.

Florence welcomed the audience and the voices quieted. Even the babies stopped their crying and the students' twittering behind the stage subsided. I liked to encourage my students to stretch their abilities, so I'd asked Willard, who had a good sense of rhythm, to direct the Christmas rhythm band. He'd replied with a grin and a twinkle in his eye, "Sure, Miss Bortel."

With all the gusto he could muster and with his little baton, he beat out the rhythm to "Jingle Bells," "Rudolph the Red-Nosed Reindeer," and other songs. Never once did he lose his tall red hat which nearly bounced off his head. The children sang the words first, and then played their triangles, sticks, and clackers. Willard bowed proudly after each round of applause—tipping his hat in response.

A number of children had speaking parts, and I'd tried to match their personalities with their parts.

Next, the upper grades presented their play of the Christmas story. Everything was going as planned and the students basked in the applause that filled the hall. Then it happened. On the grand finale the homemade curtain fell. I looked up from playing the portable pump organ to see what had caused the commotion. There, on his head, with his feet in the air was my little Freddie. Fidgeting about, he had slipped, grabbed the white sheet curtain, and toppled head first off the stage. The curtain followed him down and now only two flailing legs remained visible. The wire, which had supported the curtain, had been pulled down and was strung at nose level with the students remaining on stage. A row of eyes stared out above it.

Cameras clicked. The audience, and myself included, couldn't help but be amused by this unexpected entertainment! I forced myself to keep a straight face, but the audience snickered and some of the preschoolers unreservedly laughed out-loud.

Florence, did not see any humor in the interruption of a nearly perfect performance. She stood with her jaw set firmly, eyes glaring. The late hours she had labored on the costumes, the responsibilities she carried as head teacher, plus being in the throes of menopause, did not equip her to deal with this comedy. She stood on the stage, turning back and forth, glowering at the students; yet struggling to remain poised. The children put their hands over their mouths in surprise and tried to avoid their austere teacher's glare. They glanced at me for some clue as to what to do next. I hid behind my sheet music and attempted to fill in the awkwardness with "Joy to the World." In the background, cameras clicked and suppressed chuckles broke into hearty laughter. The humidity in the room stretched out the crepe paper streamers, which sagged down to head level. Florence pulled out a hanky and dabbed at her forehead, all the while alternately frowning at the streamers and forcing a closed lip smile at the audience.

Trying to communicate to the children that they were not at fault, I smiled brightly and vigorously pumped out the initial chords to our final number. Their panic subsided and they focused on the words to "We wish you a Merry Christmas." Florence thanked everyone for coming and the audience clapped heartily.

As much as I appreciated and admired Florence, I was glad I'd be leaving for my own CAA apartment that night and not the teacherage!

Christmas Day, I woke up with a silly grin, recalling the not-so-silent night of the Christmas program. I hadn't known what to expect for my first Christmas in Tanana, but so far it was truly jolly and joyous.

1958
POTLATCH CELEBRATION

Potlatches signified a special occasion, such as a successful hunt, important recognition of a person, or a funeral. Alfred Grant, our school janitor, had just been re-elected village chief for the New Year and that called for a potlatch. It would be a fantastic opportunity to get acquainted with the people and their traditions.

I made my way through the Community Hall's narrow corrugated tin entry, and spotted the Gaedes and the Gronnings sitting together on a corner section of narrow wooden benches that lined the room. The smell of wet moose-skin mukluks and cigarette smoke blended together with that of heating soup. I exchanged greetings, maneuvered around people, and sidestepped boxes of food set on a raised section in the middle of the room. In keeping with their custom, I'd brought my own bowl, a pie tin for meat, and eating utensils.

Potlatch at the Tanana Community Hall. (Center) Sally Woods, (Rt. Side) Ruby Gaede, Florence Feldkirchner, Roy Gronning. (In front of Roy) Naomi Gaede, Ruth Gaede.

Sally Woods, one of my second graders, took my hand, "Miss Bortel, I want to sit with you."

I would have adopted this beautiful, pleasant child if I could have. In class, she never forgot to raise her hand and consistently produced excellent worksheets. What a pleasure to have a student like her. Chris and his little sister, Judy, waved from nearby. Those two red-haired children were precious to me, too.

On the splintery, wooden floor, in front of the benches was a five-foot-wide yellow and red print oilcloth runner. Children and late-comers sat on the edges, facing the folks on the benches. On both sides, adults and children placed their eating utensils on the border of the oil cloth. I assumed this runner would serve as a tablecloth, so I was startled to see men making their way down the center of the cloth. It was if they were walking *on* the table. They carried sawed off five-gallon Blazo cans filled with steaming soup that sloshed back and forth. Carefully they stopped along the way, ladling soup into the waiting bowls. The clamor decreased as children stopped beating on their bowls and people no longer had to shout to be heard. Depending on a hunter's success, the meat and soup stock would typically be either moose or caribou. Several days before, Doc had bagged a moose. Added to the broth were varying kinds of canned vegetables and always macaroni.

Margie reached over and nudged my arm. "Here, I brought some salt along. This helps the flavor."

I'd noticed the taste was flat, although not unappetizing. Picking out a few moose hair, I added this seasoning which did improve its appeal. I glanced up to see a man with his back to me, carrying a cardboard box, and distributing large chunks of cooked meat that had been used for the soup stock. It appeared that he scrutinized each recipient before finding a custom-selected piece. I caught a glimpse of his face and realized it was Harper, the man we'd asked to paint my classroom in late summer, but who had refused, claiming he could not work on Labor Day weekend. He pulled out an enormous knuckle with meat and handed it to me. I was speechless.

The trophy-sized portion rocked back and forth on my pie plate. I wondered why I'd been singled out for this selective generosity.

"Hey, why are you so special?" teased Margie.

"Did you notice that no one else received such a prize piece?" kidded Roy.

Margie had instructed me to bring along a paring knife to cut off the meat into bite-sized chunks. After watching the Natives skillfully slice their meat, I tackled mine with positive results.

Again, the servers shuffled by, this time with Pilot Boy crackers and butter. At the Northern Commercial Store I'd purchased a long rectangle box with white sailor boys skipping across the blue papers box. Ship pilots used them at sea when they couldn't get bread, hence the term *pilot* bread. For all of their dull flavor, these saltless, four-inch round, thick crackers served a number of purposes: emergency gear for hunters or for bush pilots, after-school snacks with peanut butter, and teething crackers for babies. They seemed to be consistently stale yet never too old to use. No one minded, and everyone had a reserve of these rations.[9]

There was a lull in the activities and as we waited to see what would happen next, Doc asked, "Anna, are you and Ruby starting the census this Saturday?" He said this more as a reminder than a question. The census was not a formal, government census, but Doc wanted to get an idea of the village demographics and use the information for medical purposes, such as assessing how many people had tuberculosis. The census was for Natives and Whites alike.

Ruby and I set a time to start the census-taking the following Saturday morning. We welcomed the task that would put us into the Native's homes, but knew on weekends many villagers stayed out late and drank heavily.

Our conversation was interrupted by distribution of more food. Although people leaned back in contentment, the servers came with canned fruit, cigarettes for the adults, and gum for the children.

After awhile, the individuals in charge started to roll up the oilcloths and prepare the room for dancing. The Gaedes, Gronnings, and I decided to leave. None of us danced, and we knew that alcohol would come out, which would change the tone of the evening, and more so as the night went on. Besides, Mark Gaede and Chris Gronning were starting to pick on each other, which wasn't fun for anyone around them. We pulled on our parkas and collected our eating utensils. Students grabbed for my hand as I stepped over and around them. Eventually, I made it out the door. The raw air smelled startling fresh and burned my face.

Grandma Maggie Elia in front of her cabin holding a water fowl. (1958)

ABC

Census-taking proved to be a story in itself; although incomplete and leaving us wanting another *chapter.* Take for example, Grandma Maggie Elia. She had crossed eyes, and talked in subdued tones, as if someone might overhear us.

Ruby asked her where she was born. Grandma peered seriously up at our faces, "Mammie said I was born in the woooods."

"When were you born?" I asked.

She hesitated, then whispered, "Mammie said it was when the days get longer."

We subdued our amusement, hugged her goodbye and walked off wondering what else this winsome woman's life story held.

At another cabin, we heard music blaring through the thick logs. We moved closer to one another and slowed our pace. Hesitantly, we rapped on the door. Unruly laughter accompanied the sound of chairs scraping on the floor. The door flew open and before us staggered three Native men. Even without smelling their breath and seeing beer bottles on the table we knew we'd interrupted their party. They leaned towards us in an overly-friendly manner and gestured for us to come inside. Dubiously we entered but stayed beside the door.

"Who are you?" the bleary-eyed spokesman asked.

I explained that I was the school teacher and that Ruby was the doctor's wife.

"Who are you?" he asked again, latching on to my hand.

I described our roles and Ruby started asking the census questions which, surprisingly, he comprehended and answered. Furthermore, he yelled above the blasting radio and acquired the information from the other two. All the time he held my hand, which I struggled to pull free.

Terrified, but trying to remain calm, I said in a firm voice, "We need to leave."

His grip tightened and with a yellow-toothed grin asked again, "Who are you?"

I looked to Ruby for help. Bewildered, she pulled on the door handle. Suddenly, the man teetered backwards, and let go of my hand to balance himself. With loudly-beating hearts we hurried out.

ABC

The year ended with the Natives celebrating a new chief and me celebrating the completion of my first semester in Tanana, Alaska. The year began with my introduction to a potlatch and to Back Street on a Saturday morning.

ORDINARY VILLAGE LIFE

Like a firecracker, the New Year had started with a bang. But now, several weeks later, the days fizzled into the ordinary, each one hemmed in by the bleakness of the arctic terrain and the sameness of daily routines. Days drifted into weeks of 40 degrees below with only four hours of feeble midday grayness. When the mercury pulled itself upwards, ice fog habitually developed, dimming the already insufficient sunshine. When the sun did elbow through, the effect of the ice fog was dazzling. White-etched tree branches and buildings were glazed as if by an artist's brush. These rare moments were winter-time gifts.

The oppressively-low skies silenced the welcome buzz of airplanes, our primary link with the outside world. Sporadic mail delivery increased the sense of isolation. I read and reread letters, and opened packages slowly to prolong the satisfaction. Darkness, cold, indoor living, and lack of human communication easily festered into cabin fever. The sound of music could fill in the murky recesses of our days, and those of us who had the luxury of record players exchanged records and requested them from our families Outside.

I'd succumbed to the Asiatic Flu, but not cabin fever. I hadn't tired of popcorn and gabfests with women friends, slumber parties with Ruby when Doc was on a medical field trip, or mooseburger tacos at the Gronnings. I found mental stimulation through books and discussions. The discussion these days was about the world's first explorations beyond the earth.

In October 1957, the Russians shocked the world by hanging Sputnik 1 in space. How could such a second-rate scientific and technological power accomplish this feat before other more advanced countries? As if this maneuver wasn't stunning enough, the Soviet Union promptly shot up Sputnik 2 which orbited the earth with a dog on board. Political and scientific institutions in the United States fell under criticism

I'd written my parents that I could witness this amazing sight in the northern skies of Tanana; unfortunately, they were too far south to see the light zipping across the dark heavens. Paying attention to Sputnik wasn't a mere diversion; it linked our tiny village with all of humanity.

ABC

Second semester brought with it medical examinations, psychological testing, and achievement tests. Florence's impatience with achievement tests was evident in her grumpiness. In contrast, I found the results useful and thought-provoking. Usually, I could guess how test scores would turn out, but every now and then I'd find myself saying, "Hmmm," when a student who did poorly on daily worksheets, demonstrated through tests that he or she really had learned a concept.

Doc's medical examinations offered clues about children's behavior. One boy, who never paid attention, was discovered to be nearly deaf. This diagnosis explained why he interrupted me and his classmates, failed to follow verbal instruction, and flunked spelling exams.

On a rare day of favorable flying, the clinical psychologist from Anchorage slipped into the village. Originally from Estonia, I suspected that curiosity brought him to this bush school, as much as a sense of professional obligation. Dr. Kuusk, originally from Estonia, was a tall man with an overgrown blond mustache on his narrow face. Florence assumed he was analyzing her every remark so avoided him. I viewed him as an ally to better work with and instruct my students. I felt as though we in the village had rehashed every subject possible and pounced on this opportunity for fresh dialog

Winter daylight hours put brackets around airplane take-offs and landings, and most visitors were constrained to remain overnight. I took advantage of the situation and after school made coffee for the two of us. We sat in my classroom and he considerately translated theories into practical guidelines. I hoped to gain psychological insight into the *why* and also the *what to do*.

"Just call me Yuri," he said, when I continued to address him formally.

Pee Wee had performed for him by cracking nuts with her teeth and scattering shells all over the floor. The area around her desk looked like a squirrel lived in a nest in a tree above. I would have been embarrassed, had it not distressed and perplexed me so much. In spite of her bizarre gnawing fixation, I couldn't let her have a different set of rules than the other students, and made her clean up the mess. In spite of my frustration, Yuri pointed out that I was a firm disciplinarian, which was a positive characteristic, and even more so when conducted in a framework of love. "You are doing a fine job," he encouraged.

My mind stored every comment for future rumination. This was the most mental stimulation I'd had for awhile. We talked until he politely excused himself. "I'm sorry I'll have to end our time together, but the Gaedes have invited me for an early dinner."

"That will be a treat!" I replied. I could smell the yeasty fresh rolls that were probably just out of the oven now.

After tidying my desk, and checking for any stray nutshells on the floor, I zipped up my parka, and stepped out into the early evening. The moon couldn't penetrate the darkness and I switched on my flashlight. Fat snowflakes drifted down, and familiar buildings, like lighthouse beacons, guided me home.

I'd expected to eat dinner downstairs with Peggy and Adrian Harris, but as soon as I walked through the shared entry door, Peggy popped out with a message. "Anna, Wick phoned and wants you to go to the hospital immediately."

I couldn't figure out why Wick, the nurses' supervisor would need me, but I backtracked to the hospital, wondering if there was a crisis. *How can I be of any help in a medical emergency?* I paced through the hospital waiting room to inquire about Wick's whereabouts. Of all places, I was sent to the kitchen.

"What's the problem?" I inquired anxiously.

"Well, it's not exactly a problem," said Wick, slipping an apron over her nurse's uniform. Wick was noted for her tall erect posture and now she stood straight with her back to me while she scrambled eggs.

"Here, sit down and have some bacon and eggs–and then just stay for awhile," she said over her shoulder.

Several nurses walked in and sat down. They asked me about my day and then pulled out the word game Spill and Spell. The game was the new rage and anytime there was leisure moment, someone was sure to be rattling a can with the dice-size letter cubes. I was hungry, so it wasn't difficult to comply with Wick's command to eat, and I did love word games; but I was baffled whenever I questioned about the *medical emergency*, and someone would adroitly change the subject. Eventually, I got to the bottom of the subterfuge. Just like Florence, they felt uncomfortable in the presence of the psychologist, who had been assigned to their social care. Therefore, they'd maneuvered me into the position of social activities director for when he completed his meal at the Gaedes. Their logic? "Anna, you're good at conversation."

When Dr. Kuusk did appear, the group made uneasy small talk with numerous awkward pauses.

"Oh, why don't we play a game?" Wick acted as though she'd just thought up this idea.

His eyes lit up, he took off his sports jacket, and rolled up his sleeves. We glanced at one another warily. He seemed much too willing. The letters spilled out and he lined them up into words. After awhile, even I lost interest since his linguistic expertise gave him the edge on the rest of us. Besides, by this time, the nurses had gotten past their stereotypes about psychologists and found him more appealing to talk to than to spell with. Frankly, it didn't matter *who* the visitor was. Any newcomer to the village was entertaining, merely because he or she brought outside news and fresh topics. In the case of the psychologist, he also brought refreshing humor.

"You know, Anna would make such a good wife," Yuri said, playfully cocking his head toward Rose, the nurse nearest him, pretending I couldn't hear. "I watched her with those children and I can just see her with four or five of her own."

Before Rose could respond, Wick said, "That's true." Carefully avoiding my eyes, she continued convincingly, "Anna is getting married this summer."

Before I knew it, she had him believing an elaborately-constructed tale of my engagement and upcoming wedding. No matter how vehemently I denied the fabrication, he was convinced.

ABC

Unknown to this bunch, there *was* a man with whom I was exchanging letters. When my downstairs neighbor, Adrian, was attending a CAA training seminar in Anchorage, my name had entered a conversation with a man, Hugh, from Iliamna. Adrian had encouraged him to write me. "Anna, he is kind, patient, and attractive." Since this latter attribute was based on one man's description of another, I wasn't sure what it really meant. Did that mean he was a patient hunter? Kind to his mother? Attractive to employers because he was a responsible worker, or to wolves because he had plenty of meat on his bones?

"I told him that you don't smoke or drink, and that you are interested in religious work," added Adrian.

Between ice fog and sunshine, a letter arrived. I learned that prior to Hugh's CAA work, he had taught Vocational Agriculture School. Disliking dealing with the discipline problems, he had turned to this recent career in aeronautics.

Hugh's vantage point of Alaska differed from mine. I liked that. Lake Iliamna was 500 miles south of Tanana, and his enlightening letters opened a portal into a dissimilar section of Alaska. He lived beside the largest lake in Alaska and had at his disposal 1,150 square miles of ice skating, if so inclined, and ice fishing. Reading between the lines, his enthusiasm for the Last Frontier seemed to be waning. He related how getting into even rudimentary civilization required a three-mile walk. He mentioned alcoholic school teachers and the all too frequent murders and suicides in the village. In contrast, my experiences in Tanana were largely positive.

Hugh didn't conceal the fact that receiving my letters provided enormous pleasure. I couldn't argue. I felt the same. In the cold, dark winter months, it was like a ray of heartening sunlight to find an interesting letter from him in my mailbox. And my heart did skip a beat when he sent me a Valentine's Day card! It wasn't as though there were many opportunities here in the Bush for a single woman to meet a potential male companion. All the same, I cautioned myself. I didn't want another relationship like the one I'd had with Al. As the months went by, I asked him if there was an Arctic Missions there. He confirmed there was, but evidently he wasn't attending services. I took this as a chance to share my spiritual values.

ABC

January passed and my calendar showed variety in the usual schedule and events to look forward to. I red-penciled a heart on each day there was a Valentine party, of which there were three.

As the day neared for the classroom party, the children began making Valentines out of red, pink, and white construction paper, lacy white paper doilies, silver sparkles, and thick white paste. By the time school was out their cherub faces were sparkling, too, and dried peeling paste stuck to their fingers. After school, Josephine Roberts, a student's mother, slipped in the door and presented me with a box of chocolates. She was such a dear woman and her ongoing kindness meant a lot—both personally and as a teacher.

I volunteered to help the nurses put on a Valentine's party at the hospital. I stirred up cherry cupcakes and beat up creamy pink frosting. Cranberry punch was both a Christmas *and* a Valentine beverage, and could be enjoyed either simmering hot, or chilled with ice cubes. Someone came up with an idea for a relay race that involved passing a paper plate from chin-to-chin. We hooted and hollered. Thinking of word games came naturally to me, and after the plate game, the room got quiet as everyone tried to make as many words as possible from VALENTINE. I felt good that my food and games made a hit.

"I'm really glad you put this together," said Wick, pulling me out of ear-shot from the others. "You wouldn't believe all the bickering that's been going on. Everyone has a bad case of cabin fever and is sick of seeing the same people and the same inside walls all day. This should help us all."

ABC

About 9:30 a.m. I heard snickering and commotion outside my apartment door.

"Wake up, wake up," the voices shouted in unison.

Wick's voice gave her away and I suspected that she was the lead dog in this pack.

"Anna, let's hike across the river," Wick said as she and three other women pushed open the door.

I layered on the necessary clothes and we were out the door, and tromping down the riverbank. Before us lay a diamond-studded playground. Six inches of fluffy snow made the river crossing appear smooth, but the going was rough in areas where jagged planks of ice had awkwardly jammed up against each other in the freezing process, and rose at various angles, sometimes up to four feet in height. On the smooth surfaces, we rubbed away the snow to look down into the indigo ice depths. The ice appeared to be fractured, and cut lines ran throughout the polished thickness. The temperature, hovering around zero, felt comfortable after the weeks of inhospitable minus-degrees of cold, and the exertion of wading through soft powder warmed us enough to push back our parka hoods. All in all, it was a joyous feeling of new life and vitality

About three-quarter of a mile away, we looked back at Tanana: Green roofs, red roofs, shiny tin-roofs, and smoke spirals. I took a deep breath of not-so-cold-air. Wick stretched her arms wide as if to embrace the broad blue sky. We reveled in the expansiveness and luxuriated in escaping our confines on the riverbank. Simply walking across the river afforded a sense of vacation, that of getting *out* of the village and away from everyday life. Euphorically, we wandered up and down the riverbank, noticing game trails, poking our heads into the woods, and finding scratchy shrew tracks on top of the snow. A yelping dog team mushed somewhere in the distance.

We'd needed this. We started the hike back home, leaving behind stale attitudes and rejuvenated with a feeling of coming out of hibernation.

AN UNCERTAIN FUTURE

I lay in bed and squinted, trying to figure out what had changed. Something was distinctly different. Then, seeing sunlight painting the wall, I realized the glorious sun had returned, not for a brief winter mid-day visit, but to awaken us earlier and earlier each day, and then hang around later and later each night.

Even though I was not a morning person, I climbed out of bed and moved into my Saturday. After coffee and a bowl of Cheerios, I went outside and breathed deeply. Although the air was still chilly, there was no need to grab for my coat zipper or parka hood. I stood soaking in the unmistakable re-awakening of God's creation. I walked down the road and discovered another transformation. The snow didn't crunch. Instead, the mushy consistency clung to my mukluks and dampened the soles. I waded into the soggy snow and pushed my nose into the fuzzy pungent buds of pussy willows. At last, spring had returned to coax life back into thin winter-logged branches. A bird song broke the silence.

The next morning, instead of automatically reaching for wool slacks, I decided the time had come to reacquaint myself with skirts. With this option, it was as if I'd acquired an entirely new wardrobe! For the first time in months, I jubilantly walked to church with my legs meeting the air and liking it. Although winter temperatures had *only* plummeted to 51 degrees below, the 30 degrees *above* zero felt like a heat wave.

At school, the children were unusually restless. Energy coursed through their veins, just like spring sap rising in trees. A couple of weeks before Easter I asked, "How would you like to make an egg tree to decorate our room for Easter?"

Blank stares met the question. Part of the fun of teaching in the North was so many concepts were entirely unknown to these children. I was amused to see their heads crook to one side at the mysterious question.

"Who will bring in a bare birch or aspen branch?" I asked. I spread my arms about three feet apart to give them an idea of the size.

Many hands shot up. I didn't want to disappoint any, but I knew who the follow-throughers would be. "Walter and Chris, will you see what you can find and bring back by next Monday?"

The boys' faces glowed with this prestigious assignment and they nodded their heads dynamically.

"Now for all of you, we will need many eggs."

Obtaining real eggs in this north country was a feat rarely attempted. In their long journey from the mid-west farm lands, the eggs would break, freeze, or the typically sunny yellow yokes would congeal into an unappetizing and questionable dark orange. Most people used powdered eggs. Not only was the egg tree unprecedented, it was asking for the impossible. The most likely source for real eggs was to put in a special request to the NCC store, or to bargain with the hospital cooking staff.

The tree branch arrived as scheduled and among the students, Ruby, and myself we procured just enough eggs.

"We will blow-out the insides of the eggs, color the shells, and hang them on the branch," I told the students. "Gather around me and I'll show you how."

Boys and girls crowded near me, watching attentively as I demonstrated how to carefully puncture holes with a needle on either end of the raw egg and blow out the contents into a bowl. Some children plunged right in; others held back in trepidation, afraid their efforts would only result in crushed eggs. Regardless of their response, every child was completely absorbed in the project. A number completed the egg blowing and moved on to painting their eggs with food coloring and onion skin dye. Others relied on their proficient friends, or on me, to get past the initial stages. All these fragile eggs were hung by thread on the tree branch. The children were so pleased with the delicately decorated tree branch that they begged their parents to stop in to view their object of art and other handiwork—pastel Easter baskets with colorful artificial grass, papier-mâché eggs, and construction paper bunnies and chicks.

ABC

The Teacher's Conference in Anchorage opened another door to springtime. I hadn't left the village since my initial arrival in late August, and while I was packing my suitcase and preparing for the flight out, I realized how much I'd become accustomed to life in the Bush. Now, in March, I hunted for my handbag and wallet, which I had little use for here. Finally, I found them stacked high on a closet shelf. Choosing clothes to wear into Anchorage was another ordeal. Remembering my flight into Tanana with my less-than-practical suit, I chose a fuller skirt.

In Anchorage, the topic among women teachers, especially those from the bush, was the loose-fitting waistless chemise dress that was in vogue. We agreed that regardless of the styles, that warm underwear took precedence when it was 50 degrees below zero.

Getting out of the village reminded me that cars, sidewalks, hamburgers with tomatoes and lettuce, and newspapers still existed. When we went out to eat, I read through the entire menu; not because I couldn't make a decision, but because I just wanted to see the possibilities. Window shopping reacquainted me with home décor, popular colors in clothes, and clever gifts.

My mother and Millie, ever hopeful about changing my single status, had written about the possibility of me meeting Hugh there. I wrote back,

He did ask about the dates of the conference, but, I do believe I scared him off by my last letter, which he probably interpreted as 'too religious.'

My intuition was apparently right. He wasn't at the conference, and I didn't hear from him again.

ABC

The village shook off the winter doldrums and celebrated the rites of spring with a Spring Carnival during the same time as Easter. People spilled over the river banks in front of the Northern Commercial Store onto the snow-covered Yukon. Even though the snow was mushy, the river would remain solid until sometime in May when it would *break up* and move out to the Bering Sea. For several days before Good Friday, school let out early every afternoon for such daily events as sled dog races and snow shoeing competitions. None of the sled dog races were very long and there was constant activity with sleds coming and going, and other contests mixed in. Men, women, and children competed on different days. One morning, after listening to the children's recount of the previous day's races, a thought popped into my head.

"Boys and girls," I said, clapping my hands to get their attention. "Let's write a song about the dog races!"

Together, we worked on the words and the tune. The children bounced excitedly in their seats as we came up with names for the husky dogs; of course, they chose names of their own dogs.

"The Sled Dog Song"
Music and lyrics by Anna Bortel

We'll hitch the huskies to the sled and o'er the trail we'll go,
We'll bring our wood and water in then ride out o'er the snow.
Mush along, mush along, oh mush along my sled dogs.
The lead dog's name is Sandy. The swing dogs, Sugar and Pal,

Along comes Blackie and Sparkie, And Smoky with the long gray tail.
Mush along, mush along, oh mush along my sled dogs.

On Friday, I loaded my movie camera with film and enthusiastically made my way down the riverbank. The sun had eroded the worn-out snow on the southern exposure, allowing patches of mud to show through. This was a day off so I'd put on a pair of worn blue jeans, my old between-seasons rubber boots, and a wool head scarf. The boots came in handy for the mud-mix.

Onlookers laughed, joked, snapped pictures, and waited for the mushers to take off. The spring-loaded dogs jumped about impatiently as they yelped and whined in anticipation. At the signal, they shot off the starting line. All the while, kids chased husky pups, slid down the dirty river bank, and played tag. Young and old, newcomers and villagers, shared in this marker event of the year.

Amidst the cheering and yelling, I noticed Coleman Inge pause on the river bank and survey the river-turned-stadium. His hand shaded his eyes. Purposefully he moved down to the river. I thought he was just coming to join in the festivities, but then I realized he was making his way toward me. It took him awhile. Finally, he stood in front of me, a little out of breath, and asked politely, "Miss Bortel, we are in need of someone to play the organ for the Good Friday service that will commence in 15 minutes, at 3:00 p.m. Would you be able to help us out?"

I laughed nervously, pointed to my dirty boots and mud-splotched clothes, and pushed my hair back behind my scarf, wishing for an Easter bonnet.

"Coleman," I replied, "I look awful with these boots and old clothes, but if I can come as I am, I'll be glad to do it for you."

He sighed with relief, patted my arm, and expressed his appreciation for this last minute favor. As I made my way up the riverbank, the church bells rang out their invitation for the Easter service. By the time I'd reached the church on Front Street, much to my embarrassment, I'd collected more muck. I hoped that at least my face was still clean. I tried to inconspicuously move up the center aisle to the pump organ; but in the small congregation, many villagers recognized me as they settled into the pews. I felt better seeing that they too were wearing just-off-the-river attire.

ABC

In the middle of these welcome rites of spring, the State Department of Education (the Territory) sent me a contract to sign for the following school year. A contract was good, but uncertainty lurked in the details. The Territory would be taking over the school system at Tanana, rather than sharing it with the BIA, for whom Florence worked; and a new school was to be built, with two more teachers hired. At first glance, this all seemed marvelous. Then, some very unsettling questions surfaced, one of which stemmed from my need for housing since the CAA needed my apartment for their own personnel and the teacherage in which I'd stayed with Florence was in the same building as the classrooms, thus, closed with the school. *What if the school was not completed by fall? Where would I stay? Where would the additional teachers stay? Would I need to store my belongings during the summer when I returned home to Ohio? What would happen to Florence who worked for the BIA?*

A communiqué from the head office in Juneau requested that I ask Florence if she would like to teach for the Territory. My inquiry elicited a sober look of determination and I recognized that her resolute jaw meant there would be no further discussion. She had invested too many years in government work to consider leaving the BIA. Her reply of never," set the tone of our relationship for the rest of the year.

At the teachers' conference, I'd listened with rapt attention to tales of teaching in more primitive conditions than I faced here in Tanana. I felt the tug to go even further north. But, could I haul in my own wood for fuel? Could I bring in water for cooking and bathing? During this time, a letter from the Glennallen school principal urged me to reconsider their teaching offer, which would be inland, about two-thirds of the way toward Valdez from Fairbanks.

ABC

At 6:30 a.m. my apartment started to shake and roll. I awoke with a jolt, confused as to my whereabouts. When my mind cleared I become conscious that the cracking and groaning was an earthquake. Instead of decreasing in intensity, it increased, as did my heart rate. I hoped this pattern wouldn't recur, but a half an hour later it did. This tumult developed into *the* topic of conversation throughout the village. I chuckled when Margie told me she'd thought it was just Roy rolling over in bed! The earthquakes continued with alarming frequency, about four to six tremors per day. The Natives told us they'd never experienced so many before, which was no comfort to the rest of us. Someone in the village made radio contact to Fairbanks and learned that near the center, Mt. McKinley, the earth had broken into a crack forty feet wide and one mile long.

I wondered about the effect on the school building. Not surprisingly, a few days later, three BIA men flew into the village and inspected the structure.

"Send the children home if the wind blows too hard," one fatherly-looking man told me seriously.

Prior to this order, I'd noticed a cloud of dust floating down on windy days or during earthquake tremors. Sometimes it would glint in the sunlight, other times it appeared as a subtle haze between the front and back of the room. I'd dismissed it as normal in such a worn-out structure. I didn't think much of the BIA conversation until one Friday noon when I was working at my desk. Usually, Florence and I ate lunch in her quarters, but on this day, Mr. Windsor the BIA supervisor, had flown into the village. I expected he and she needed privacy for conducting business. Florence's crisp footsteps on the wood floor put a halt to my ponderings.

"Miss Bortel, would you please come into my living quarters," she requested formally. "I think you'll be interested in what Mr. Windsor has to say."

As abruptly as she'd entered, she turned on her heel, and walked back into the teacherage. Her face gave no clue and my mind drew a blank as to what the significance of this summons might be. When I entered the kitchen, Florence had a strange look on her face. Without any preliminary chatter, Mr. Windsor stood up, shook my hand, and tersely announce, "The school is condemned and therefore closed."

I stared at Florence in disbelief. Neither of us could utter a word. Everything seemed in slow motion. I replayed Mr. Windsor's words filling in the meaning: *School closed. No more school. Only mid-April. Yet, six more weeks of lessons.*

Everyone knew that the antiquated building needed foundation repairs, but how could we close on such short notice? Florence regained her composure before I did. She replied firmly, "We cannot close school this quickly. We must have school on Monday so we can pass out grade cards."

Mr. Windsor shrugged, "The children may take their textbooks with them." Then without any emotion he turned to me, "I will call your supervisor in Juneau tonight and he will wire or write you as to what to do next."

Florence and I remained paralyzed as he exited the teacherage. The enormity of this development nearly pressed the breath out of me. Not only was the reduction of our present semester by six weeks a blow, but a new school building could not be completed by the fall semester. Without the use of the current facility, the children in Tanana had no place to meet for school until sometime much later the next year.

This change affected Florence only short-term, due to her allegiance to the BIA, but for me it was a stunning blow with long-term consequences. I shook myself out of my stupor, and ran to the chief's house, beat on his door, and blurted out the news. I thought perhaps he and the village council could negotiate with Mr. Windsor before he left the village. Nothing, however, transpired with their meeting. I was left to muddle about in my bog of questions.

All weekend, I worked on grade cards, with intervals of relating the catastrophic dilemma to my friends. I rehearsed what to tell my dear students. Two of the CAA mothers offered to bring in cupcakes in an attempt to alleviate the dismal and hasty end of the school year.

Monday arrived. In childish innocence, the children scrambled into their seats, celebrated the end of school work, devoured the cupcakes, and capered out the door with their reports. But now looking around at crumbs, the egg tree, and vestiges of simple arithmetic problems on the chalkboard, I fought back tears. I'd maintained a facade of confidence, even though I realized that this very likely marked my last formal interaction with them.

I never knew what the mail would bring. The commissioner wrote that he didn't know the school had been closed so unexpectedly. He assured me the Territorial Department of Education would protect me and that I'd still be paid for the final six weeks. A letter from the certification supervisor followed with this information:

> At a recent supervisory meeting the closing of the Tanana Day School and your reassignment for the coming year were discussed. We have recently received notification of a vacancy at the Bettles Field School. Because of the new building which is to be constructed this summer, with a one bedroom school apartment, this is considered a choice assignment. The building is scheduled to be completed by October 1. There will be an approximate enrollment of 17. If you accept this assignment, please let us know as soon as possible and an amended contract will be made for you.

I knew that $98,000 had been appropriated for the Bettles School, on the Koyukuk (KOY-yuh-kuck) River, and just into the Arctic Circle. The new venture was enticing, yet, I had lingering reservations.

In the interim, I received more correspondence:

> Although we are not sure when the new school will be ready at Tanana, we would like you to fill out two copies of the inventory and requisition form which are enclosed.
>
> I have discussed the matter of school supplies with the BIA and they will probably transfer anything that they have on hand to us and there are undoubtedly quite a few things that we can

use. However, I am particularly concerned about textbooks as they may not be using the same series that we do.

I would also like information on the style of desks and condition of the quarters, furniture, and whether you believe we should order complete new equipment for the school or plan to use some of the aforementioned items.

Although you are not the head teacher, you are our only direct representative and consequently we will be channeling almost all of our requests of this nature directly to you; however, I would appreciate your working very closely with Miss Feldkirchner as getting the equipment list is a difficult job and will require the utmost cooperation between the teachers and our respective agencies. Final plans will be ready within a week or so

I was caught in the cross-fire between the BIA and Territory. Eventually, the Territory would supersede the BIA. I knew Florence would oppose any cooperation with the Territorial Department of Education, and just as I dreaded, she responded with outbursts such as, "There is talk that the books should be tossed out in the middle of the river before breakup. *That* should settle this fracas."

In general, Florence did not cope well with change. She liked predictability, order, and schedules. Every Friday after school, she cleaned the teacherage. Weather-permitting on these days, she opened the front door to invite in fresh air. There was a day to wash clothes and a way to hang up her coat. Her lesson plans never varied. Now, with this upheaval in Alaska's educational system, she was pushed over the edge. But rather than sitting down to cry or talk, or to check out the facts, she struck out at those nearest, which was me. Granted, unlike me, she didn't know where she would be stationed next, which must have been terrifying given her pessimistic nature. She functioned as a pawn for the BIA, and she had no idea what might become of her welfare. At least I had some choice in my future. Even though I understood Florence's mood, the thought of books traveling out to sea made me shudder.

Florence stubbornly refused to consent to *my* inventorying of the supplies and equipment, but ironically accepted my offer to type up *her* inventory for the BIA since she did not have a typewriter.

Now that school was over, I kept busy sorting and packing my personal belongings. With each box, I wondered if I would return to my belongings in Tanana, or reopen them in some other location.

ABC

The chapel group planned a farewell dinner for me at the Gaedes. Nurses sent a special delivery letter to Fairbanks for a 20 pound rib roast. CAA and White Alice people brought in casseroles, scalloped potatoes, and salads made of Jell-O and canned fruit. Ruby created a layered chocolate and white cake with "God Bless You, Anna" on the top, surrounded by yellow frosting roses. Roy hand-cranked homemade ice cream.

"Anna, we have a special gift for you so you don't ever forget Tanana," said Ruby, wiping her eyes.

I unwrapped the box. Lying in the tissue wrap I found an Indian doll dressed in moose hide, fur, and beads. My dear Indian neighbor, Lucy Kalloch, had made it.

My friends' outpouring of love moved me deeply and tears streamed down my face. I felt so mixed up. Over the year, we'd bonded and now I stood surrounded by their love, but still, I wondered if the party was a little premature. True, the future appeared uncertain, and I had no contract to stay. But I believed in miracles.

A few days later, I heard via the grapevine, that Mr. Isaac would be arriving in Tanana. Secrets had a short life-span in this small village, even without a dependable telephone system. All morning, I listened for the drone of a plane. Finally, I heard it. The noisy speck in the sky took shape, circled over the river, and landed. Since the airstrip road traveled past the CAA station and turned into Front Street, I managed to catch sight of Mr. Isaac walking rapidly toward the hospital. He appeared to be on a mission, but I wasn't sure his exact destination. The authority in the village rested primarily on the shoulders of the chief and the village council, but also included the CAA manager, and the Public Health Officer, who was Dr. Gaede.

It wasn't long before I heard footsteps coming up to my door, then a knock.

"Anna, let's go find some temporary living quarters for next year's teachers and school," said Mr. Isaac with a controlled but friendly look on his face.

We walked back to the hospital dining room to discuss with Doc the difficult situation. I tried to participate in the brainstorming, but felt so dejected I contributed little.

"It seems our only possibilities for temporary school facilities are the Episcopal parish house and the Community Hall—both less than ideal, but workable," summarized Mr. Isaac. Then putting down his coffee cup, he leaned forward and put his elbows on the table and asked, "Anna, would you like to teach here next year?"

I looked sideways at Doc who avoided my eyes. I suspected he and Roy Wall from the CAA had conspired and that this was the fruition of their behind-the-scenes work.

"Oh yes," I blurted out, afraid to believe the possibility existed– even though I'd prayed for a miracle.

In bewilderment, I told him, "But the Juneau office offered me the Bettles Field School…"

He paused. "I didn't know that." Then he added, "I will investigate this decision and send you a telegram as soon as I return to Juneau."

I should have expected as much. He was truly unflappable. Even if he had a plan out-lined, and now got side-swiped, he held his course.

"And, I'll need a place to live," I added.

"Since Dr. Gaede insists that you return to Tanana, it will be up to him and the CAA manager to provide housing for you," he informed me, giving a quick look at Doc.

I felt as confused as my student Pee Wee, who, when she'd run into me the day before, had wrapped her arms around me and asked, "Are you gone yet?"

ABC

Whatever happened, I welcomed the prospect of flying home to Ohio. Perhaps I'd just take off my decision-making hat for awhile and let Mother, Daddy, and Millie tell me what to do. On Thursday, as the plane lifted off and we flew over the semi-thawed Yukon, I realized that the only aspect of spring breakup I hadn't witnessed was the breakup of the Yukon River. Otherwise, the earthquakes, school closure, contradictory contracts, and conflicts with Florence, had broken me up enough. I'd gladly wait until next spring for any more breakups.

"Tanana"

Music and lyrics by Anna Bortel

Alaska has its forests
Its lakes and rivers, too;
The mountains and the animals
Including caribou.
But of its many villages,
There's one above the rest,
To thee, Oh Tanana,
We love you the best!
Tanana, Oh Tanana,
Beside the Yukon waters
You stand for home and all.
We'll cherish you in memory,
We'll honor you in fame,
We'll be the kind of citizens
Who's proud of Tanana.

THE GOING GETS TOUGH

What a mess! I stood with hands on hips surveying the school grounds at Tanana, in late August. With my back to the river, the retired schoolhouse lay before me like a faithful, but tired, old dog. To its left, the new school, started in July, was framed, and outlined a future dream. The temporary quarters for the school sprawled to the right and resembled a campground more than a school yard.

Over the summer, Dr. Gaede and others in the village had persistently pursued the possibilities for a school facility and discovered that the Quonset huts, which functioned as barracks for the White Alice workers, would be available. The windowless 20 by 18 feet, khaki colored, semi-cylindrical shelters had doors at each end. Five of these road-wide structures had been transported down from the hill and positioned on the vacant lot between the school and the neighboring Kalloch's house. All this had torn-up the ground and dust kicked up around my feet. The vague afternoon light on the cloudy day didn't enhance the strengths of this potential school campus. When I entered one of the buildings for further inspection, I started a mental list. *We need some steps into these. There's no wiring. No plumbing. No heat. I'll need to see who's available for hire.*

Before I'd left Tanana in May, a telegram had arrived from Mr. Isaac, suggesting I stop in Juneau on my way Outside. At Juneau, he offered me the position of Head Teacher for the Tanana School with the responsibility to hire two more teachers. He also showed me the architectural plans for the new school and asked for input. Before leaving, I met Miss Morey, my educational supervisor and together we ordered school equipment and supplies.

As Head Teacher the package included increased pay and increased responsibilities, including organizing this unusual fleet of buildings into a school.

A shadow darkened the door and Mr. Isaac joined me, bringing with him the faint smell of pipe smoke.

"Looks like you'll need some help getting these Quonsets into shape," he said, stating the obvious. "I'll send out a carpenter. Could you motivate the community to join you in this cause?"

I hoped that the villagers' elation would carry beyond their initial welcome-back fanfare. I'd expected my friends, and some of the parents, to shower me with enthusiasm, but it was the usually-restrained Natives who surprised me with their demonstrations of affection and handshakes.

Silence weighted down the air. *How could school start in ten days when as yet the tent portions of the Quonsets weren't fastened to the floorboards?*

"Anna, start school when you are ready," Mr. Isaac remarked gravely.

He was the perfect person for dealing with bush teachers, bush life, and the unforeseen that happened in village schools. I felt he understood the circumstances and would back me when necessary; not in a forceful manner, but steadfastly. I expected the going would be tough this coming year, and that bush teaching was about to take on a whole new meaning.

I put up notices in the post office and at the Northern Commercial store asking for volunteers. My pleas for assistance spurred the villagers to rally and support the men from the hospital, CAA, and White Alice site, who were already committed to the task. This project became the focus of the village and people buzzed about in participation; even children hung around offering their aid and grinning about "school starting soon." Ruby baked cupcakes and oatmeal cookies, and I stirred up cocoa and made sandwiches.

Men and women helped in whatever way they could. We didn't have electrical fixtures or light bulbs and neither did Northern Commercial. Since the hospital maintained close involvement with this project, Alice Peters, who was flying into Fairbanks, volunteered to go shopping for us. While she was gone, the CAA personnel connected electrical lines from the hospital, which was the source of electricity for the village. Men used their muscle and an available truck to haul up over 175 barrels of heating oil from a recent barge delivery.

Fortunately, the Quonset-hut setting didn't daunt my new, very young, co-teachers, and with humor and vigor they pitched in to clean and organize. Harriet Amundson was a fresh-faced, robust farm girl from Minnesota. She brought along an impressive informal resume of mechanical and other fix-it skills. Herman, a slim, quiet Yupik (YOO-pik) Eskimo from Bethel, sported a short crewcut and black framed glasses. He seemed a bit lost in the hubbub, but unreservedly carried out any instructions I sent his way. Children swarmed around him—good credentials for someone entering the teaching business.

Herman Romer in Tanana, Alaska

I'd allotted one shelter well each, or *hut*, as we frequently referred to the Quonsets, to Harriet and Herman for teaching. Harriet's hut was for third and fourth grades, and Herman's was for grades five through eight. I requested that two shelter wells be joined together for my first and second graders, with one end for my office with school equipment and supplies. This super-sized tent was stationed in the center of our camp. Once cleaned up and in livable condition, another shelter would become home for Harriet and me. Until that time, the Gaedes had kindly offered us their basement.

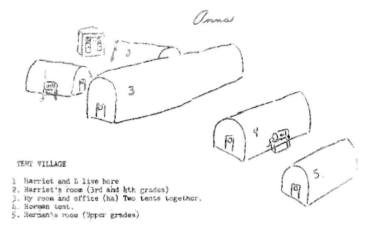

TENT VILLAGE

1 Harriet and I live here
2. Harriet's room (3rd and 4th grades)
3. My room and office (ha) Two tents together.
4. Herman tent.
5. Herman's room (Upper grades)

Quonset Hut School Camp in Tanana, Alaska (Winter 1958)

When we'd scrubbed and transformed the shelter well into a cozy domicile, Naomi, came over with her blonde-haired doll and small suitcase. "Betty and I want to live with you," she informed me. "We won't take up much room, maybe just space enough for one of those army cots my daddy has. It would fold up for the daytime."

"Oh, Naomi!" I said, bending down slightly and putting my arm around her. "I'm so happy you like my new home, and I will miss living with your family, but I think all your other dolls and all those stuff animals in your bed will miss you."

For a moment she looked disappointed, but then she pulled the turquoise corduroy parka hood over her Betty doll's pig-tails, and said, "Okay," and skipped out the door.

Initially, Herman stayed in the condemned school. Later, I had another Quonset brought down for his quarters.

The long days merged together. We teachers swept and mopped wood floors, then hauled boxes from storage and attempted to create an educational atmosphere. To fashion a school was challenging enough, but to create living quarters was overwhelming. In village style, we used what we could find. The stove and refrigerator for the future teacherage arrived on the barge, but rather than store these appliances for their modern home, we incorporated them into our primitive conditions—an odd contrast. At moments, I feared my two capable team members would desert me in the midst of the disarray, but they never slacked in their commitment.

"Hey, everyone," I said one evening as the rain pelted the shelter wells and punctuated the fact that we were actually in tents, "Let's initiate this stove and have a tea party!"

I pulled out cups and saucers which seemed completely incongruent with this backdrop. We invited in the remaining evening workers. For some reason, as I looked at my new coworkers, I thought of Florence.

"Miss Feldkirchner wrote me and she's very unhappy with her assignment in Barrow," I shared with the group. "If you can imagine, she says she wishes she could still be teaching here in Tanana."

Everyone laughed loudly, in a kind of comic-relief, and made comments about our disaster site. Harriet moved across the plywood floor, vibrating the makeshift table. Tea sloshed out of my cup and into my saucer.

"Oh, I guess when we sit down to eat, we're really going to have to stay seated," she observed wryly.

ABC

I faced daily to-do lists. It seemed that whenever I crossed off one item, another one wrote itself in. In spite of this, one morning, I stopped to acknowledge the autumn chill in the air and the warning that winter would soon over-ride the opportunities for berry picking. I figured this activity could be explained as part of initiating Harriet to Alaska. Ruby's love of the outdoors made her decision easy and we found containers for gathering blueberries and low-bush cranberries, or at least that's everyone else called the small tart berries. Technically they were lingonberries. Ruth and Naomi joined us and we all took turns pulling Mark in a red wagon until our destination took us off road to a boggy area where Ruby and I had found success before.

We'd praised the joys of berry-picking to Harriet, but after stumbling among the humps of wet moss and searching *just a bit further*, all we'd accomplished was getting our socks and shoes soaked.

"So, what if we have a wiener roast?" suggested Ruby. That was her solution for about everything, whether celebratory or disappointing.

Our spirits lifted as we anticipated the warmth and liveliness of a small fire on the river shore. Regardless of what we did on this sunny autumn day, it was a respite from the dust and residue of insulation in the shelter wells.

ABC

The day before the opening of school, Philip Kennedy, the Department of Education carpenter, found us in our shelter wells, and offered us another reprieve.

"How would you teachers like to go on a boat ride?" he asked. As diligent as he worked on the school, he was never frantic, and now balanced work with play. A flat pencil was balanced behind one ear and sawdust clung to his green and black wool jacket. He jiggled nails in his pocket.

"When do we go?" queried Herman.

"The sooner the better," Harriet answered for us all.

"I've hired Carl to take us on his boat upriver," Philip replied. "We'll meet him down on the riverbank in front of the hospital at 4:00 p.m."

"Don't worry," said Harriet. "We'll be there on time."

I couldn't believe this. Someone had taken the time to consider our pleasure, and offered us a break from our pressure.

Raring for a diversion, we arrived on the riverbank before our tour master. Above us, ducks and geese headed south in large V's. Already, I'd noticed golden birch leaves releasing their grasp on summer and falling to the ground. Carl opened up the throttle and we sped away from the shoreline; the sharp wind cut through my jacket and I wished for another sweater. *I don't remember it being this cold so early last fall,* I thought.

The shelter wells diminished and then disappeared altogether. About two miles upriver, Carl brought the boat back toward the shore, where our tour commenced with an up-close view of a fish wheel. It was securely lashed to the riverbank. The river's current dragged around the two enormous wooden-edged screened scoops wherein spawning salmon heading up stream were caught. The scoops then sent the salmon down a trough into the fish box. Fish lay there gleaming and flopping all about. Later, the owner of the fish wheel would collect his prizes and take them home to dry on fish racks, to be used for food for his family and sled dogs.

Fish Wheel on the Yukon River

Often times, typical village experiences turned themselves into songs in my mind, and this was no exception. I found myself humming and working with word rhymes as we completed our five miles upriver to a sand bar, and then back to the village. I'd have to refine my *Fish Wheel* song and teach it to my students this year.

"The Fish Wheel"
Music and lyrics by Anna Bortel
The fish wheel goes around and makes a queer, queer sound.
Sw—i—sh, sw—i—sh I caught a nice big fish.

ABC

School started on time. A miracle. That first morning, Harriet and I climbed up the stairs from our basement room in the Gaede's house to find Ruby preparing sourdough pancakes and moose sausage. The aroma of coffee mingled with that of fried grease, and small glasses of Real Gold canned orange juice waited at our place settings. Doc had already left for the hospital. Naomi and Ruth sat at the table in matching dresses, with the variation that Naomi's was blue, and Ruth's was pink. Mark had somehow tangled with a syrup bottle and licked his fingers. Mishal cried out intermittently from her crib in the bedroom. The Gaedes had adopted this beautiful half-Inupiat (In-OO-pee-at) Eskimo baby in February.

How we appreciated this family's undergirding of a place to sleep, prepared meals, and tangible support in creating a place to hold classes. We bowed our heads and Ruby prayed for us as we started the school year.

"Well, I bet we'll have some stories to tell after today," I said as Harriet and I left for the shelter wells-turned-schoolrooms.

Even in these dire circumstances, I felt exhilarated about the first day of school. I did a last minute check of lesson plans, textbooks, wide-lined paper, sharpened pencils, and waxy smelling crayons, and then took my time crossing to the bell at the old schoolhouse. Some of the children trailed behind me, begging to ring the bell. I reached up to the rope and prepared for a hefty pull. Much to my surprise and that of the children, the soft weather-worn rope plopped right down upon us. We stared down at the tattered rope with frayed end.

"I guess this rope retired, too," I sighed.

The children laughed and then asked what I'd do without a rope. I looked around and saw some long two by four inch boards near the school construction. Probably most of the children had already arrived and if I'd only clap my hands they would line up. But it didn't seem right. We couldn't start the year off without the opening exercise of the bell ringing. Balancing the board in the air, I beat on the bell. The usual clank sounded more like a clunk, but the children recognized its significance and hopped about until they formed the necessary lines to enter their classrooms. I heard Herman call his students to order and noticed that this quiet-spoken teacher could be a firm disciplinarian. Just because these classrooms were primitive didn't mean the children could forego structured behavior.

Those first days, the unusual setting distracted some of the boys and girls. One thing they had carried with them from the old school was their memory of *The Story* about the golden nectar. Somewhere in the daily scramble, I managed to write home to request the drink mix I'd noticed in the stores over the summer, which, of all things, carried the name, *Golden Nectar.*

ABC

When Harriet and I moved out from the Gaede's and into our Quonset, we had multiple headaches. For one thing, cold crept up beneath the flooring and I wasn't sure that even thicker felt liners in my mukluks would keep my feet from being permanently frosted. With Ruby's assistance, Harriet and I nailed old roofing sheets around the bottom of all five huts. Both Ruby and Harriet brought their farm girl capabilities and paused only long enough to pick up another nail before wielding their hammers. Philip Kennedy brought over his payloader and banked the sealed off airspace with mud.

Harriet and I hated trekking out to the privy at night. Once again using her carpentry skills, she sawed a hole in a wooden box and placed it over an improvised indoor potty. After wiping up the floor a number of times, we decided that we needed a sanitary engineer to improve the design.

I would have liked a sanitary engineer for other matters, too; those of which Florence had done the previous year. Without her around, latrine duty fell to me; this meant every week I needed to lime the school outhouse.[10] This worked fine until the subzero temperatures arrived and the privy contents never melted down. For some reason, the person who had constructed the privy left a board across the middle of the two-hole opening. In the dead of winter, the pile on the board grew higher and higher. One Saturday, I went out to check the toilets.

"How could this happen!" I gagged. The pile was higher than the seat. *Now what college educational course had explained how to handle this?!*

I had no choice but to take a hatchet and chip away until I was certain it was low enough to use for another week.

Even though we lacked plumbing in our shelter wells, we did have access to the orphaned BIA washing machine in the old school. I stretched clotheslines the length of my previous classroom and turned the heat up so my clothes dried nicely.

On September 30, enormous white flakes fell from the sky and didn't stop for five days, by which time the temperatures had dropped to four degrees below zero. At the same time, the space-heater stove in Herman's quarters refused to work. Every night after school, we teachers worked on the stove, and every night, Herman wished for even a campfire. We summoned the hospital maintenance man and the men who were working on the new school in hopes they might lend some expertise. No success. In desperation, we tried another heater. It didn't work either. Being nearly inseparable anyway, we invited Herman to eat meals with us; otherwise, I shared my one-burner Coleman with him for his own cooking. Truly this was camping out! Finally, the CAA mechanic heard of our plight and worked on the obstinate stove until it produced heat once again.

The previous year, Florence had persuaded me to start a school newspaper, which would be the only newspaper for the village. Her older students edited the paper and there were reporters for the hospital, CAA, and village. The efforts had been successful, so I resumed that responsibility of *The Northern Lights*. The October 1958 issue documented our efforts when the student writer, Larry Grant introduced the teachers:

"Meet the Teachers"

Miss Harriet Amundson is from McGregor, Minnesota and is a graduate of Greenville College, Greenville, Illinois. She made her first trip to Alaska when she came to Tanana August 30. She thinks winters here will be like winters in Minn. She teaches third and fourth grades during the day and works on the school stoves in the evening.

Mr. Herman Romer is from Bethel, Alaska. Last year he taught in Naknek. Mr. Romer attended school in Texas and is a graduate of the University of Alaska. Mr. Romer teaches the upper grades during the day and works on school stoves in the evenings.

Miss Anna Bortel is from Bowling Green, Ohio. She has taught in Ohio and Illinois. She taught in Valdez, Alaska before coming to Tanana last year. Miss Bortel teaches first and second grades, is the Head Teacher, and works on school stoves in the evening.

Ice cakes floated down the river and grew thicker every day. Winter boldly advanced ahead of schedule, and I hoped I'd sewn enough wool slacks for the winter that already intimidated us. If this was only the end of September, what would January and February deliver?

Exiting my dark hut, which we could have dubbed the *mole hole*, I checked out the school progress: acoustical tile on the ceiling and large spaces cut out for windows. The men were working frantically to get the structure closed in before the weather worsened. I looked in amazement at what would be a skylight in the utility room. No more darkness. In the kitchen, I could see where cabinets would be hung. No more Blazo boxes for dishes and canned goods. I made a wish to be in our new habitat by Christmas.

ABC

By October, we'd conquered most of our daily obstacles.

"Well, what can we do now for some excitement?" I asked Herman and Harriet one night as we sat together grading papers, eating fudge and popcorn, and listening to records.

"Maybe something for the community," suggested Herman.

"All there is to do is go to shows and dances at the Community Hall," moaned Harriet.

"What about a Talent Show?" I asked.

Herman and Harriet reacted with such enthusiasm that the needle on the record bounced out of sequence.

We could raise school funds by charging," declared Harriet. In further discussions we decided that 25¢ would be reasonable.

Like a barking husky grapevine, word traveled around the village. When the time arrived, the Community Hall could barely contain the villagers and the increased population of construction workers. Our planning and recruiting paid off. We teachers performed musical numbers and skits with our students. Two Native men played guitars and another man his harmonica. Our Tanana Sewing Club slipped on aprons and used kitchen utensils to accompany our rendition of two humorous songs. Doc played his accordion. People cheered and laughed. The Show strengthened community bonds and in addition, we counted out $36.50.

I reflected on how much I'd seen the Natives, old-timers, CAA, hospital personnel, and others grow closer together during the short time I'd been in Tanana. One day over a cup of tea at Ruby's, I shared a dream that would benefit everyone.

"Ruby, since last year I've considered starting a library for our village." I waited for her comment.

"Oh, you know how so many of us enjoy books and how that helps get us through the winters," she replied.

"How will we do this and who will help?" I asked.

"I'd love to … and I know there's a need, but I'm not sure I have the time…. ," she said.

The conversation stopped, but when I returned to my shelter well I detoured into the school and talked with the contractor.

"So you need some boards for shelves … hmm … I think I can help you out," he said, pointing a work-gloved hand toward a stack of lumber.

The next day, Ruth brought me a note from Ruby. *We're coming over Friday night to help with the library. I've asked Olga Neufeld, Wally, and some others to come along.*

Ruby had recruited a new nurse and the lab technician to help me achieve my dream. I asked Wally Hanson, the hospital lab technician, to drag over the boards for shelving. He was six-feet-tall and thin as a two by four. The divorced man had empty space in his afterhours and was hungry for companionship. Harriet volunteered to show him the woodpile. The two of them haggled about the design and eventually pulled out hammer and nails for their task. In whatever manner they figured it out was fine with me. I just wanted the job done.

Olga Voth Neufeld, an R.N. from California, looked for ways to use her time when off duty. With their common denominator of Mennonite background, she and Ruby had already found much to talk about. She was soft-spoken and precise, and the *precise* made her a perfect partner in our team. Olga, Ruby, and I wrote *Tanana Public Library* in the books we'd personally donated or accumulated, and then glued on library card envelopes with inserted check-out cards. Olga mentioned the need for a Dewey Decimal System, but after a brief discussion, we agreed that we weren't that sophisticated. As we worked, we brainstormed about places to solicit more books and how we would urge people in the village to donate, too. Much to our appreciation, books were donated by the Daughters of the American

Revolution (DAR) in Fairbanks, and there was talk of a traveling library stopping in as well.

After achieving our goals for the evening, we enjoyed pizza and appraised our endeavors.

"Trying to put books in a bookshelf with a curved wall behind it isn't easy," commented Wally.

"This is only one peculiarity of this village school," quipped Harriet.

The fledgling library filled me with satisfaction, not only for my own gratification, but as a service to the community, and in hopes of genuinely establishing relationships among the diversity of people. True, the going got tough with the many inconveniences, but many of us were tough people, who stuck together and who knew how to work hard, play often, and pray much.

ABC

"A Day at School"
Performed at the Talent Show with Tanana School teachers and students.

Mr. Romer: Miss Bortel, I can't stand that tent! I woke up choking with fumes from the stove at 4:00 this morning and there was soot all over the place.

Miss Bortel: We'll have to work on the stove after school, Mr. Romer. It's time for the bell.

Miss Bortel: Good morning, children! My, you look nice this morning. You must have gone to bed early last night and had lots of sleep. Did you all come to school with clean hands this morning?

Freda: I took a bath last night, teacher.

Miss Bortel: Good.

Miss Bortel: It is time for arithmetic. Shall we have a flash card drill, first? (Flashes one card. Knock on door.)

Edward Kennedy: Miss Bortel, we are out of drinking cups in our room.

Miss Bortel: (Gets cups. Flashes another card. Knock on door.)

Tom Swenson: I'm from the Yutana Barge and we just delivered the school supplies.

Would you please sign this paper, Miss?

Miss Bortel: We are so glad our supplies are coming in. We were afraid they might not arrive before freeze-up.

Tom: You'll have to get someone to come down and haul them up.

Miss Bortel: Oh dear, who should I ask this time to help us out: CAA, Hospital,

Morrison-Knudson? (Flashes another card, knock on door.)

Andrew Kennedy: I am a Morrison-Knudsen man from up at the site and I hear you need some wiring done.

Miss Bortel: We do, but I think Mr. Upickson is over wiring it now, but you can go and check. We certainly appreciate your offer to help, though.

Miss Amundsen: (Appears just as man leaves.) Miss Bortel, the fire went out in my schoolroom stove and the kids are cold. I told them to put on their coats—and they even need their mittens. Should I send them home?

Miss Bortel: No, oh dear. What next? Do you suppose the (fuel) barrels are empty?

Maybe we had better check.

Mr. Romer: (Brings in box of tests.) Miss Bortel, I just started to give the tests and the

Department of Education only sent 14 tests and I have 17 students. What should I do?

Miss Bortel: First, let's send for Pete Miller.

Mr. Romer: Pete Miller? Why Pete Miller? He doesn't have the tests I need.

Miss Bortel: Yes, Mr. Romer—I'm sending for Pete Miller from hospital maintenance to fix Miss Amundson's stove. Now about the tests—I'll have to write the Anchorage office for more. You will have to postpone the tests for another week—just have your regular classes today. (Harriet and Herman leave as nurse comes in.)

Shirley: Miss Bortel, the upper grade boys were to come to clinic for their physicals at ten o'clock. The doctor is waiting to check them. Were you planning to send them?

Miss Bortel: I'm so sorry. We'll get them over immediately. (Sends Judy to Mr. Romer's room.)

Joyce: She pinched me, Miss Bortel!

Miss Bortel: Couldn't you children please be my helpers when I am so busy? Oh, Freda, you were to go to the dentist's 15 minutes ago. Put on your coat and run over fast. Tell him

I'm sorry you are late. Children, it's recess time. We'll finish our arithmetic after recess.

Naomi and Ruth Gaede in the Quonset Hut school camp (1958)

THE TOUGH GET TOUGHER

Snow swirled over our tent city until it resembled an igloo encampment. In fact, by November, the snowfall equaled the previous year's total and visions of Valdez danced in my head. Piles of snow provided excellent insulation around the huts, but plummeting temperatures meant an ongoing battle to keep our fickle oil stoves working.

One evening, Herman, Harriet, and I welcomed the invitation to see nature films at the hospital. The other two teachers rowdily gathered their outdoor gear for the short walk in the 43 degree below zero dark night and begged me to hurry with my preparations. They'd completely forgotten our stove vigil.

Inadequately designed narrow three-fourths inch copper tubing carried the oil from the outdoor tanks into the huts and to the stoves. With these polar temperatures, the oil thickened and would eventually slog to a stop. We'd be doomed.

"We can't leave or the stoves will freeze up," I exclaimed in frustration.

My colleagues stared at me incredulously.

"We'll have to tap the lines to keep the oil flowing," I reminded them. "Let's work on all five lines before we leave, and then one of us can run back in a few hours to go through the same procedure all over again."

We plunged out into the powdery ice box to tackle the oil lines. The tapping rang out loudly in the crisp air. When we'd completed our task, we took our chilled bones to the embracing warmth of the dependable coal heated hospital building. For a short spell, we escaped our ever-consuming battle against winter.

The contrast between this environment and ours was jarring: bright lights that were not bare light bulbs hanging on a conduit, no drafts, a floor that didn't sag or bounce, water coming out of a faucet rather than a water bucket, and indoor toilets. There was plenty of room to move around and it was warm enough that I felt comfortable without my extra sweater. We sat back as if we didn't have a worry in the world and learned about crawly creatures in the Arizona desert. Ethel invited us for tea; simultaneously, Ruby asked us to stop by for cocoa. All three of us were night owls and we accepted both offers. Before going to Ethel's I returned to our encampment, made the rounds, and beat on the oil lines. When we progressed to Ruby's, I once again followed the same procedure.

While I beat on the pipes, I compared the comforts in the hospital, nursing quarters, and other medical residences, with the living conditions we teachers called work and home. I couldn't help but wonder why people seemed attracted to our crude one-room habitat. It really couldn't be the environment; it had to be something else. The hospital staff lived and worked together. What did they do when there was friction? Where else could they go? Attending one of the churches presented new faces, as did mingling with CAA families; nevertheless the steady stream of guests to our shelter well attested that the compass bearing for socializing and entertainment pointed to the straggly snowbound school compound.

At this moment, as the clanging of a metal wrench on the metal pipe rang out in the frozen air, I would have traded places.

"It just feels so good to come here," Ethel had told me when she curled up on my bed with a wholesale magazine, which was our version of window-shopping. Ethel Jenkins, the Head Nurse, was from Arizona and of Indian descent; this made for interesting conversations about the comparisons to the Alaska Natives. We hit it off right away and I enjoyed her sense of humor and friendship.

Oftentimes, the nurses stopped in after Sunday night chapel services and joined us in listening to *Unshackled.* In those days, and especially in Alaska, we clung to any radio program available. This program told dramatic true stories of men on skid row who had found new life. Other times, a group gathered for a catalog party where we pored over Sears & Roebuck and other mail-order magazines, and placed orders. Questions of, "What are you getting?" and "What color do think would look best?" were sprinkled into our shopping forays; which culminated in writing in item numbers and colors, then calculating postage.

I made them Salmon Belly Chowder, but my own get-away was to eat steaks, coconut pie and other out-of-my-ordinary cooking at the hospital dining hall, or sip tea with Ruby.

I stopped beating on the pipe and stood in the darkness. The only sound was my heart beating in my ears after the exertion. I expected that my team-mates weren't just drinking hot cocoa with floating marshmallows, but nibbling on something freshly baked at the Gaedes. I was ready to sit and join them. I walked toward the welcoming light in the duplex window.

"Another one"? Harriet policed Herman, just as I called a "hello" and opened the door. I untied my mukluks and padded to the table in heavy wool socks.

The Gaede children were running around in pajamas and slippers, and Ruby had warmed homemade cinnamon rolls. Herman spread a layer of thick frosting on his second roll. Conversation changed to the movies we'd just watched.

When there was a lull, I said to Harriet and Herman. "Kid's I hate to suggest this, but it appears we're going to have to babysit the stoves tonight." This exercise had not been included in our *Fundamentals of Teaching* book, either.

Harriet yawned widely, but when I volunteered for the 2:00 a.m. shift, she volunteered for 4 a.m. and Herman agreed to 6:00 a.m. I knew that after completing my duty, I'd burrowed beneath my covers, grateful that the next alarm I'd hear, and the ensuing banging, would be made by my loyal coworkers.

ABC

We weren't alone in our midnight madness. Usually the Natives showed movies at the Community Hall only on weekends, but for some reason, they started showing them on weeknights as well. The children accompanied the adults and as a result, the children would fall asleep at their desks or stare into space.

"Boys and girls, it is very important for you to get enough sleep so your minds will work when you come to school," I exhorted, as did the other teachers.

The students looked at me with glazed expressions. I wasn't sure I'd conveyed the seriousness of the situation until one day after school when a mother stopped in my hut. "I thought my boy was joking. He says he don't want to go to show last night. He wants to spend show money at the store."

Rest may have been our Fourth *R* but in addition, we emphasized the importance of cleanliness. As time progressed, little Freddy, who looked like a street urchin, would have won the prize for the most improved. He loved school and took my admonitions to heart. Soap and water, impetigo treatments, and a good night's rest transformed him into a dapper young man.

A girl in the community related to me, "Freddy is such a changed person. He is clean and has more manners. Can you believe he makes his mother let him go to bed early? Then he wakes up at 4:30 and wants to go to school!"

Freddy's grades improved, too, and his misbehavior diminished. I needed this encouragement, but it had its drawbacks. On Saturdays, the one morning I could sleep in, he'd come knocking on my hut door at 7 a.m. in winter darkness.

"Who's there?" I'd call out.

"It's me, Freddy," he'd answer in a cheerful little voice, "I came to see you."

"Freddy, I'm not up yet." I'd say in an annoyed *and* amused chuckle. "Please come back at nine o'clock, okay?"

With a meek "yes," he'd leave, only to return in 15 minutes when the conversation would be replayed. After several Saturdays of attempting to arouse his teacher, he quit coming.

Health education continued with a visit from the Public Health dentist, Dr. Tom McQueen, and his assistant, Ada Jakes, who flew into the village to examine and treat the Native children. I couldn't believe the children were raring to go for their appointments. Whenever a student returned and I referred to my check-list, I looked up to see every eye glued to me and every pencil laid down. As soon as I announced a name, that boy or girl would scoot out the door as if going to a fire. At recess, children circled around the classmates who had been treated, and listened to their stories and stared at their gauze-packed mouths and holes from pulled teeth. When the Novocain wore off, the quiet classroom would be interrupted with a shout, "It's waking up! It's waking up!" I'd never before witnessed children who took so much pleasure in dental visits.

The minus 40 degrees continued with occasional bouts of *only* minus 20 degrees. On these *warm* nights, we welcomed undisturbed sleep without night duty. Each time temperatures dipped to minus 35 degrees, Harriet or I would put our potatoes, onions, and eggs on the opened oven door and keep the oven on low heat. Even then, there were times when this precious commodity succumbed to frostbite. To obtain fresh produce was tough enough, but to preserve it was even more difficult. We'd sent an order with one of the nurses flying to Fairbanks, but at some point, the celery and lettuce froze. Earlier in the fall, a care package from Harriet's mom fared better. She'd filled a box marked "*Fragile, Eggs, Special Handling*," with fresh produce from her farm. We were ecstatic to find potatoes, turnips, cabbage, and eggs all in good, not-frozen, condition. We'd been using potato flakes and now we savored every mouthful of *real* mashed potatoes.

Understandably, food played an important role in our lives. "Where did you get this, Anna?" someone would ask, and in the same breath want to know, "Can I get it, too"? Over the summer, in Ohio, I'd discovered boxed whipped topping, Dream Whip. At a chapel party, I'd put dollops of the imitation whipped cream on pumpkin pie. "Mmmm" was the consensus. Women made requests for packages and I wrote Mother to send me two big boxes.

Culinary skills were not limited to women. "Grandpa's cooking a pork chop dinner for us tonight," announced Harriet, using her after-school nickname for Herman. Unlike us, Herman splurged at the Northern Commercial store. How could we chide him for this luxury when he presented us with delicacies such as non-wild meat cooked on the one-burner and a salad of canned shrimp added to a can of mixed vegetables. From time to time, he'd show up on our doorstep with spice cake batter and the request to bake it in our oven.

Inside Arctic Missions' Chapel. (Front row) Ruth Gaede, (Second Row) Linda Byrd, Naomi Gaede, (Third row) Byrd sister, (Fourth row) Harriet Amundson, (Fifth row, second from aisle) Dr. Elmer Gaede, (Sixth row) Wally Hanson, (Standing in back, L to R), unknown man, Anna Bortel, Margie Gronning, Herman Romer, Mishal Gaede in high chair.

ABC

The interminable cold interrupted our sleep and our school schedule, but not our social life. "How would you teachers like to come to the hospital wiener roast and skating party on Friday night?" asked Ethel. In these temperatures our noses would drip, eyes water, and fingers tingle. I didn't know about the others, but I was a clumsy skater. We accepted. The temperatures chilled neither our enthusiasm nor a romantic attraction. Harriet shared matter-of-factly that a hospital employee had asked her to the party. She assumed he would come to the hut and they'd walk together to the skating site on the river. This being the case, Herman and I bundled up and left her in her flutterng anticipation.

The hospital maintenance man had rumbled out on the ice with his CAT (Caterpillar bulldozer) to clear the snow and the frost heaves to make a smooth skating surface. Large bonfires lit up the night beneath the starry sky, and reflected off the glare ice. Metal skate blades flashed. Small flares leaped about in the blackness as people's flashlights showed them the way to the party. Shouting, teasing, and laughter filled the evening.

I didn't expect that one of the first people I'd spot would be Harriet's Romeo. "Herman, isn't that the guy Harriet told us about?" I pointed to a fellow in an olive-green army surplus parka who was zig-zagging through the expanding crowd. Every now and then his parka hood flew back exposing thick black hair. He greeted other skaters and appeared to be having a very good time.

"Why is he so nonchalantly skating about on his own?" I said. "Poor Harriet."

After awhile, he skated toward me.

"Where's Harriet?" he asked, puffing.

"Waiting for you!" I answered perturbed.

He gasped. Stumbling about he unlaced his skates, and in stocking feet, fled up the bank and down the road. Soon he returned with Harriet beside him. I wasn't sure if her face was rosy from the exertion, the icy air, or the attention of suitor. Throughout the evening,

Harriet never strayed far from her escort's side, although she and Herman played crack-the-whip with the children. The two of them were excellent skaters and acted like kids themselves. Lines of exuberant children linked themselves together with hands on the parka waists of the person in front of them. The first in each line grabbed either Harriet's or Herman's waist and off they went in two swinging circles. At some point, the tail-ends would go so fast around a corner that the caboose would lose hold individually, or drag with them the coupling in front of them. Away they slid on their knees or behinds. Everyone hollered in terror and glee.

Eventually Harriet wore down and caught her breath beside a bonfire, where she ate browned hot dogs, cast furtive glances at her suitor, and overall appeared quite captivated. The night held its magic; however, the would-be romance began and ended all within that succinct span.

ABC

Ongoing battles between the brutal cold and the stoves continued. On December 13, the school construction crew left Tanana. A Native man was hired to keep watch over the old and new school, and I attempted to help him. When the furnace in the old school gave up the ghost, I sought help from the CAA mechanic who serviced it. But then that night, it went out again, and before we knew it, the water pipes froze and burst! We turned off the water, but the damage was done. As if the mess wasn't discouraging enough, it meant that we would have to carry water over from the hospital for our use in the huts—bathing, dishwashing, and cooking. Ironically, the damage left a display of glorious shimmering stalactites and stalagmites. Fortunately, Herman had moved into his own Quonset.

During this time the electricity switched off sporadically in our school compound. One midnight, the stack blower on our stove chimney stopped whirring, indicating a power outage. I knew this silence meant the furnaces had ceased functioning in the new school. Overcome with weariness, I sat in my bed with tears streaming down my face. I was tough, but these circumstances seemed tougher. How could I fight so many uphill battles? If it wasn't the huts, it was the old school; if it wasn't either of these, it was the new school. I sobbed until I could hardly catch my breath, and then wiped the moisture off my face before braving the icy blast between my hut and the school. I dragged myself through the drifting snow to reset the starter on the furnace.

Amidst the frustrations, the joyous season of Christmas pressed closer. After my children left in the afternoon, I assisted Herman in teaching his upper grades two-part harmony for "Christmas Night" and "Angels We Have Heard on High." Each rendition sounded like the winter wind whistling around the corners of the dilapidated schoolhouse, but I reconciled myself that their lack of precision didn't matter. Their fervor would make this a joyful experience for their parents.

I'd ordered Christmas candy from the Sears catalog. To my disappointment, I received word that it would be back-ordered and unavailable for Christmas. We adapted. Homemade fudge and popcorn balls were substituted for red and green ribbon candy and chocolate-covered peanut clusters. Creating holiday happiness didn't rest solely on me, though. Someone else had caught the spirit of the season.

"Do any of you know why Donald isn't here this morning?" I asked my students.

They looked quizzically at each other, but said nothing. After I dismissed the class for lunch, along came Donald, peering out from under his parka hood, pulling a bedraggled Christmas tree. He had spent the morning hunting for it, chopping it down, and pulling it to school. How could I reprimand this exhausted little boy, when with hopeful eyes, he looked up at me and said, "How do you like it, Miss Bortel?"

Our dark schoolroom brightened with this and other artistic touches. We put up Donald's tree at one end of our hut. Besides decorating the tree, the children cut and pasted colorful bells and Santas which they strung from the hut framework. Holiday music on the record player added to the atmosphere and the children vibrated with pleasure.

The day of the Christmas program arrived. The children filed into the classroom and as usual, detoured to the Christmas tree before taking their seats. All at once, they rushed over to me. With terrified eyes and trembling bodies they blurted out, "Come here, teacher! There is someone in our room." They clutched my arms and huddled around me. "Are you scared?" one little boy's voice quavered.

I couldn't imagine what had frightened them. There beneath the Christmas tree was a young Native man, curled up, and sleeping off his night of alcohol. I'd wondered about a strange odor when I'd entered the room, and now I saw the pool of urine. Nudging him, I called his name. No response. The children turned their faces up to me with confidence that I could handle this situation. Again I called his name. No response. By this time, word had spread through the other classes and Herman poked his head through the door. "Mr. Romer, could you please stay here while I go to the hospital for help?" The hospital served as an emergency source for any village crisis.

Jerking open the hospital door, I found Alice in the reception area and explained the situation. Recovering from my shock, I joked, "He doesn't have a tag or a ribbon, so I don't want to keep the gift under the tree!"

Alice assured me someone would arrive to care for this unusual gift. I returned to my students, checked on the young man, who was still inert, and proceeded to restart the day with attendance-taking. Shortly, the all-purpose ambulance arrived and hauled away the Christmas boy.

That evening at the Christmas program, the children sang their best. I sighed with relief and with hope that the next year we would be in our wonderful, spacious school, rather than the crowded Community Hall.

The New Year did not start with a celebration, but with body-shaking tears. Following a New Years Eve party, I'd worked endlessly on our oil lines. Then, at 3 a.m., I collapsed in bed, chilled to the bone, and utterly worn out. I had reached the end of my rope and had no reserve to cope with one more minute of this pioneer life. Harriet, the hardy Minnesota girl, struggled numbly with the lines at 4:00 a.m. Temperatures were freezing outdoors and now sunk lower inside our Quonset. She desperately fought to restore some heat. Herman quietly carried our potatoes and onions to his place to keep them from freezing. Our fortitude was freezing to a standstill in the winter battle.

January 1959. Fifty degrees below zero. Four hours of daylight. No running water. No heat. Construction on the school halted due to the unavailability of windows.[11] I'd left the model school in Pekin, Illinois for this? The going was indeed very tough.

Salmon Chowder

- 1 lb. Fresh salmon poached, (or 1 14 ½ oz can salmon)
- 2 T. butter or margarine
- 1 med. onion
- ½ C. celery, diced
- 1 T. flour plus 1–2 T. water
- 2 chicken bouillon cubes
- 2 C. water
- 2 C. diced potatoes
- 1 13 oz. can evaporated milk
- 1 t. dill weed
- ¼ t. basil leaves, crushed
- 1 15 ½ oz. can cream-style corn
- salt and pepper to taste

Drain salmon, reserve liquid. Sauté celery and onions in margarine. Add bouillon cubes, water, and potatoes. Cook slowly until potatoes are cooked. Mix flour with water to make thickening, add to potatoes, celery, onion mixture. Add salmon, reserved liquid, milk, dill weed, basil, corn, salt, and pepper. Heat thoroughly, but do not boil. Serve with cornbread or fresh rolls, and a salad. Invite your neighbors if you want to share.

1959
THE 49TH STATE

. . . .

1741	Russian navigators, Chirikov and Bering, discover Alaska
1784	First settlement on Kodiak Island
1867	Russia sold Alaska to the United States for $7,200,000
1848	1914 Gold strikes and rushes
1959	Statehood, January 3

"The windows are here and Alaska is a state!" I breathlessly ran in to the hut; the floor shook beneath my feet. Harriet steadied her cocoa. "Let's have a party!" I shouted. With all our tensions, we needed laughter—in large doses. I exited as quickly as I'd entered and went to spread the good news to the Gaedes, Wally, and Ethel.

Earlier in the day, I'd reviewed with my students the history of Alaska and the story behind our state flag. Together we stood and sang the Alaska State Song. I was proud to be a part of this state and of history-in-the-making. That evening, my friends and I celebrated in the old schoolhouse. When Herman had returned from the Christmas holidays, he'd brought smoked salmon strips, and mentioned that sometime I should try putting salmon on pizza. When I pulled out salmon pizza from the oven, he couldn't believe his eyes. Along with this uniquely Alaskan pizza, I combined crushed blueberries and cranberries and made a statehood beverage. After viewing slides that several of us had taken, we turned to view the dirty dishes. Since the water pipes had broken in the old school house, during a recent dip to minus 50 degrees, our next door water use had ended. Wally volunteered to carry the washable items back to his duplex, which was the other half of the Gaede's building; therefore, nearby. The following day, when Harriet and I went to reclaim our dishes, we found clean pots, pans, dishes, and water glasses stacked toward the ceiling in his kitchen: a balancing act and a work of art!

My focus returned to the new school. Mr. Lundgren, the school construction foreman, found me after class. "Anna, I know how anxious you have been about the windows. I want to ease your mind: the windows made it in and are installed."

I sighed and said a prayer of thanks. Even once the windows had arrived in Alaska, getting them *to* Tanana was still a challenge. They had to be flown at a low altitude so the thermopane wouldn't break, which required perfect weather.

"Come see how they look, and then I'd like your janitor to watch how to operate the furnace." He took his time speaking and I got the feeling he knew how emotionally fragile I was at this point. Nothing he said made me feel weak or silly, but his words came out wrapped in gentleness.

Remembering the exasperating episodes with the stubborn furnace in the old school, and how Elias Dick, the janitor, had difficulty understanding our choleric oil stoves, I felt dark foreboding. Our future apartment was attached to the school, and I would be depending on that furnace to maintain heat in my living quarters and to keep the sewer system functioning. It went without saying that I was highly motivated to learn the ins and outs of not freezing to death in this Frontier.

Mr. Lundgren put a hand on my shoulder. "I agree with your concerns," he said in a paternal manner. "Let me show you how it works, and, I promise to leave instruction books."

I took a deep breath of hope. We would soon occupy the new building and say goodbye to the huts. In anticipation of moving day, we started to pack books and supplies. Our wave of relief was a bit premature. The final sprint into our modern facility was not without road bumps. The soap dispensers called for liquid soap, but we'd been supplied with powdered. We had roll toilet paper, but the containers required flat, folded sheets. These minor concerns could be overlooked, but another could not. No fire extinguishers had been ordered. I sent a letter to Mr. Isaac informing him of this dilemma; at the same time, I let him know we still needed curtains and curtain rods for our living quarters. Thankfully, by the time Inspection Day arrived, all permit-denying issues had been resolved.

ABC

I stood in wonder in our living quarters. Our picture window opened toward Back Street and could have been a real-life movie screen. A yelping dogsled mushed nearby. Further back, a buzzing airplane climbed to a higher altitude. I was euphoric about double sinks, Formica countertops, a floor that was level and solid, real cupboards, and a utility room with a washer and dryer *and* a skylight!

That evening, the Gaedes, Tom McQueen, and Wally arrived to help us carry our belongings from the tent camp to the teacherage heaven. The following day, February 2, 1959, the children carried their school supplies from the dark, dusty tents to their never-before-used school desks in the modern school. They walked silently into the school and stood awestruck as they appraised their spacious, tall-ceiling, airy classrooms.

Herman, Harriet, and I each had our own room with windows across one side and a blackboard with bulletin boards stretching across the other. The rooms were joined end-to-end. Herman's and Harriet's were connected by accordion-folded partitions which, when pulled back, transformed their classrooms into an auditorium. Across the hall, the boys and girls each had their own *indoor* bathrooms. I had my own office and would no longer share a teaching space with office supplies and files. I compared these luxuries with those in my Pekin school and decided I'd rather be here—now that I was out of the huts.

Parents were jubilant, too. Some ordered shoes for their children to wear in school, rather than their moosehide mukluks. A few of the little girls even showed up in frilly nylon dresses and looked like pastel butterflies; although later they resumed wearing more practical, warm clothes. Everywhere a grateful and triumphant spirit reigned.

In *The Northern Lights*, a reporter surveyed responses to the school:

> Diane: Our room is pretty and our stoves don't go out.
> Clarence: The blackboards are bigger.
> Gary: It's nice and warm.
> Frieda: It was dark in the tents, but it's nice and light in here.
> Edward: We don't have to go out to the bathroom any more.
> Miss Anna Bortel: It's a dream come true! I'm tired of oil stoves.

New Tanana School (Fall 1960)

Most of the community turned out for the school dedication, on February 15, 1959. Everyone had worked hard and celebrated the culmination of their efforts. Third-graders, Chris Sommer and Sally Woods carried in the Alaska and the United States flags, after which the Pledge of Allegiance was recited. Coleman Inge gave the invocation. The Girls Chorus sang "Tanana Song," which I had written, and "Going over Jordan." Marshall Smith, one of the older students who had won the writing contest, read his essay "How Can I Help Make Tanana School a Good School?" He stood tall and proud throughout his short presentation, and again when the essay was published in the February *Northern Lights.*

I'd talked with several old-timers and then discovered some tattered books and papers in the dusty old schoolhouse attic. The adults and even the children seemed to enjoy my presentation of Tanana School History.

April 8, 1921: The matter of the school remaining in the Barracks Bldg. at Ft. Gibbon Post was discussed. Directors Kay and Cook were in favor of not moving the school back to Tanana until the end of the school term of nine months ending in June. Director Howard was in favor of moving the school without delay back into the town within the Territorial School District as the question of defective lights was no further a matter of consideration, it now being all daylight and especially as the spring thaw would surround the barracks building with swamps and mosquitoes and no adequate sidewalks leading up to the building.

Dec. 7, 1921: Director Kay notified the Trustees that the Tanana Public School would be moved to the new barracks at Fort Gibbon. Gasoline lights used. Man hired for 50¢ a week to bring in drinking water.

Nov. 24, 1924 to Jan. 5, 1925: School closed to curtail expenses and relieve the children from attending school during the short days of winter.

Nov. 6, 1926: School Board Meeting called for the purpose of finding out just what was really allowed as school supplies, as a bill had come in from Joseph Ancick with a pair of canvas gloves charged. Miss Hengst, janitor and teacher, explained that it was necessary to have canvas gloves for the purpose of firing the stove as she always burns her fingers on account of the fender being too close to the stove. The School Board agrees to allow canvas gloves and allows the bill to go through to Bureau to Juneau.

1940s: The Mission site school shut down due to epidemics. No longer were there two schools in the area, only the Tanana Day School.

April 1958: The Tanana Day School condemned.

September 1958: School held in the Quonset huts.

January 26, 1959: New school inspected.

February 2, 1959: Moved into the new school

I underscored the similarities between the 1921 school situation and ours, 30 years later. We too, had been in barracks. We too, carried water.

Alfred Grant read a greeting he'd written on a red Big Chief tablet. Whereas I had spoken on "Looking Back," Roy Gronning preached on "Looking Forward." The program concluded with the Girls Chorus singing "We would be Building," and the benediction by Coleman Ingle.

The audience applauded.

Children grabbed their parents' hands to show them the blackboards, bathrooms, and drinking fountains. Several women, including Ruby, had put together beautiful serving tables with yellow plastic roses and lace tablecloths. I was determined to make this event as classy as any in the other states. The menacing temperatures and plain village setting would not stand in my way. Parents brought cookies and the White Alice baker sent down 14 dozen brownies.

My stalwart co-teachers and I had endured. They'd never left my side and had taken the crushing hardships in stride. Now we were in one of the most up-to-date schools in the new State of Alaska. But, of all the luxuries that were now ours, running water and reliable heat were all I asked.

ABC

Years later, on August 10, 1996, the Tanana School would be dedicated to and renamed *Maudrey J. Sommer School.* Maudrey Sommer was the mother of my students, Marie, Chris, and Judy.

ABC

The new school was only one component in growing community pride. Prior to the dedication, a January issue of the *Tanana Council News* emphasized the accomplishments and attractiveness of the village: 300 people; 20 miles of roads in and around Tanana; a 4,400 ft. airstrip; CAA (which had recently evolved into the Federal Aviation Agency, or FAA); a Public Health Hospital; 3 churches; a post office; a Northern Commercial Store; 14 privately-owned cars and trucks—in addition to the CAA/FAA and hospital vehicles. Furthermore, plans had been approved for garbage removal and for telephones placed around the community for inter-village emergency use. Discussion had begun regarding installing electricity throughout the village.

Alaska State Flag

In 1926, the state flag was designed by 13 year old Benny Benson, an Aleut student who entered his design in a territorial contest. The contest was open to all Alaska school children. Out of 142 submittals, Benny's was chosen. Below his design he wrote: *The blue field is for the Alaska sky and the forget-me-not, an Alaskan flower. The North Star is for the future state of Alaska, the most northerly of the union. The dipper is for the Great Bear, symbolizing strength.*

Alaska State Song (adopted in 1955.) The lyrics, written by Marie Drake in 1935, originally appeared in poem form. Several years later, Elinor Dusenbury wrote the accompanying music.

FURTHER NORTH?

Daylight extended midway into suppertime, and temperatures hovered around the minus 25 degrees mark with occasional dips to minus 40 degrees. Spring only mocked us. Herman and I decided to check out the new airport coffee shop. Although not officially open, FAA personnel, Pete and Joan Myberg, served us coffee and cherry pie. Just the thought that we were eating out enhanced the flavor.

"Herman, I'll make you salmon pizza or moose roast any time, if you treat me to the coffee shop," I announced.

We looked forward to the future possibilities of chili dogs, cheeseburgers, tuna salad, and Danish pastries. Who said we lived in the sticks? We almost had a restaurant.

This latest village amenity, propped up our depleted spirits, but it wasn't enough. When information about the upcoming teachers' conference in Fairbanks arrived in the mail, I ripped open the envelope. I'd already determined that this year, I'd most certainly go. I invited Harriet and Herman to join me, and they jumped on the band wagon. We had fresh fodder for our conversations and we discussed, debated, and changed our minds about which sessions to attend.

Daily duties seemed a little bit easier with our great escape just around the corner, and I decided there was no better time than the present to form a Parent Teacher Association. Although parents and teachers already worked well together informally, having an official

PTA would streamline our efforts. On March 8, 1959, the first PTA group for the Tanana School met. The agenda consisted of parliamentary procedure, discussion about raising funds for playground equipment, and a film on tuberculosis.

Herman's Room Mothers provided refreshments. One dessert in particular caught my eye: a 9 inch by 13 inch sheet cake with purple frosting. I'd never seen anything quite like it. After a tentative sampling, I guessed she must have added grape Kool-aid mix to the powdered sugar frosting, before spreading it on the chocolate cake. Different, but not a bad combination.

At last, it was time for the conference. Doc had sold his Piper J-3 two-seater and now owned a four-place Piper PA-14, which he referred to as the "Family Cruiser." He planned to fly to Fairbanks and pick up a missionary couple. The timing was perfect for us all to catch a ride one way with him. Herman, however, was raring to get out of town, and decided to leave two days earlier to attend the dog races.

During my stay in Fairbanks I shopped for an organ at the Music Mart. Earlier, I'd made up my mind either to take a summer trip to Europe or to purchase an organ. Now, with the opportunity in front of me, I leaned toward an organ. The musical instrument could not be just any organ; it had to be one that could withstand the jarring transportation into the village. And, I wanted the organ for my apartment, but also for school events, so portability was a factor, too. It wasn't as though Fairbanks had a plethora of organ stores, but finally I found a Hammond spinet. The salesman assured me he could ship it safely by air—without any shipping charges. He didn't have the mahogany-finish I wanted in stock, so it would have to be ordered. I didn't like waiting, but the first *real* organ along the Yukon would have to arrive by its own time-table.

ABC

After I returned to Tanana, Mary Ann Burroughs, the new Director of Nurses, who replaced Ethel Jenkins when she resigned, brought guests to see me. It was beyond me why Mary Ann had chosen Tanana, Alaska. She'd traded her job of nursing movie stars at a Beverly Hills Hospital in Los Angeles, for this primitive spot on the globe. From what I understood, she was originally from Hawaii. She was high-energy and looked so cute with her long dark hair piled on top of her head. When she topped it off with a silk head scarf and sunglasses, she looked just like a movie star herself.

Several times a week, I could count on someone from the hospital staff hauling over visiting health-care professionals or newcomers to our apartment. At least, with the Mybergs opening the Airport Coffee House, *Anna's Coffee House* wasn't the only place for coffee and meeting.

On this occasion, Mary Ann introduced me to Barbara Reid, the new Public Health Nurse, who, along with her supervisor, Fran, traveled among the villages. Whether healthcare workers or educators, we were all concerned about the welfare of the children in the villages.

Fran vividly described her experiences in Alaska. She could have been overwhelmed by the medical needs, poverty, alcoholism, and lack of conveniences, but she took in stride the culture. She neither pitied the Natives, nor had an attitude of superiority, but was grateful for the skills she'd acquired that could be put to use.

Ever since I'd come to Alaska, I'd wondered what lay further north. At first *further north* meant north of Valdez; now *further north* meant up to where Eskimos lived. Fran told me about Anaktuvuk (An-ak-TU-vuk) Pass, smack dab in the middle of the Arctic Circle. Her gleaned information came from proposals for medical research of those peoples. Apparently, there were several nomadic groups, totaling around 100 Nunamiut (NOON-a-mute) Eskimos, who followed migrating caribou herds in the pass. These inland people had only been discovered recently, during the war years, and were unique because the majority of Eskimos lived along the coast.

From what I gathered, the landscape was barren—no trees or much vegetation. Fran wasn't sure if the people lived in sod huts or if there was any type of other construction materials. There was no school, but some of the children had been sent to a boarding school in Wrangell, in southeastern Alaska. After witnessing how homesick their children became, and how vulnerable they were to outside influences, such as alcohol, the parents stopped sending them away for education. They desired their own school. Even though there were numerous unknowns, these details and images stirred my imagination.

"Why are you so interested?" asked Fran. "I mean, are you really considering going up there?"

"Well, the children need a teacher—and after living in the shelter wells—and surviving, I think I can probably manage about anything!" I asserted boldly, and then wondered if I'd been too confident.

"Well, why don't you ask Dr. Gaede if you can accompany him on his upcoming medical field trip there," she said. "You could offer to cook."

"Oh!" I burst out, in surprise and anticipation. "Do you think I could?"

"Sure, he almost always takes his own plane when he does these kinds of things."

My mind swirled with images of a barren mountain pass, and little children learning how to hold pencils and raising their hands with questions. I had many questions of my own. *What does a sod house look like and how is it constructed? Can it have more than one room? I'd ordered a year's supply of food and it chugged down the Yukon to find me. Without a river or a real landing strip, how do they get anything?*

After she left, I asked Doc about the possibility.

"Sure! Just think what an adventure it would be." That pretty well summed up how he framed everything in life.

I mused on the coincidence that I'd only recently heard about Anaktuvuk Pass and now would see it. When I requested a leave of absence, Mr. Isaac granted it with a telegram.

Administrative leave authorized; Employ substitute if possible. Please submit report on number, names, ages, grades of pupils available for a school in Anaktuvuk Pass. Also any information pertinent to starting a school.

ABC

Besides the hospital personnel making their way to our quarters, Miss Morey, my supervisor was scheduled to arrive. I'd met her on another occasion when we'd ordered equipment and supplies for the new school. She stood nearly six feet tall, was 18 years my senior, and left no doubt in anyone's mind that she was in control. I obsessed about everything that could go wrong, from the appearance of my bulletin boards, to the manner I related to Harriet and Herman, to the way I kept school records. In trepidation of her five day visit, I developed a hive on my upper lip. Doc took one look at me and had me come into the lab where Wally drew blood and checked my white count. All was well, even though I felt miserable.

I watched her step off the airplane. The high-powered, practical woman wore her brown hair pulled back tightly and was dressed in slacks. She greeted me and quickly turned to business at hand. I could have used opening remarks such as, "How are things going in the new school? "What an ordeal getting to this point." "We really appreciate your stamina and resiliency." Not a word.

The first days, I had little contact with her. I taught my classes and cooked her meals while she and the janitor sorted the tools in the old school.

"Anna, I need to talk to you," she said one afternoon.

I knew my time had come and I could feel my jaw tense. I expected she'd observe my teaching style or assess my classroom environment, but she informed me that on Saturday she and I would compile an inventory list. The job was tedious and anxiety hovered like a thunder cloud, but that was the worst of it all. She never paid attention to the new worksheets I'd developed or the way the student's sat quietly in their reading circles.

After I waved her off at the airstrip, I returned to my apartment, disregarded papers to grade, deflated like a balloon on my couch, and closed my eyes with a long sigh. My breath trailed out as if I'd held it for five days.

While I waited for the calendar days to move through April, my much-anticipated Hammond organ arrived. The students swarmed around, curiously watched my feet move across the smooth wood foot pedals, and reveled at this outlandish village contraption.

"I'd rather have this than anything else!" I gushed. Perhaps I *had* been in the Bush too long, but making music revived my spirit and nourished my soul.

ABC

Finally, April 21 arrived, the day to fly further north, in fact, 180 miles north of the Arctic Circle. I bundled up and carried a compact bag of personal items, and met Doc at his red Family Cruiser on skis. He stood awkwardly, with most of his weight on his right leg, and shoved a pair of crutches behind the back seat. He'd been plagued with sciatic nerve flare-ups and had struggled to simply maintain a normal work week at the hospital. Ruby was there as well, with worry lines all over her face.

"Doc, how are you going to fly with your pain?" I asked.

"I guess you'll have to take-over if there's a problem," he forced a grin and tried to minimize the seriousness of the situation.

To get any relief, he had to lie completely prone. Now, he'd be scrunched into a seated position. He turned away from us and painfully lifted his left leg into the plane. The white felt, army-issued bunny boot didn't make things easier. I couldn't fathom how he'd walk in snow with crutches. Ruby and I turned to each other. Under her breath she uttered something in her native tongue of Platt-deutsch. I didn't need to understand it, but I could tell by her tone of voice that she was irritated he'd even considered taking this trip. She and I watched wordlessly as Doc popped a pill into his mouth and tossed back his head as he swallowed.

We flew to Bettles Field, approximately 125 miles directly north. Here Doc refueled and checked on weather conditions at Anaktu-vuk. My heart beat a little faster. This well-kept-secret, Anaktuvuk

Pass village, was supposed to show up in only 100 miles. Now I'd find out what was further north.

From Bettles, we followed the meandering John River north to the entry of the Brooks Range, which opened to a several-mile-wide valley.[12] Granite mountains with icy peaks rose off the valley floor on either side. Trees disappeared and all that remained were shadowy patches of willows. I'd lived surrounded by the Chugach mountains in Valdez, which had become familiar and comforting. These Arctic Circle mountains were different. Perhaps it was their white and gray nakedness, with no spruce to cover them or soften their contours. The Brooks Range testified to Alaska's untamed wildness.

About 10:30 a.m. Doc dipped the plane wing and circled a cluster of snowy mounds. "I think we've found our village," he said. "Now we just need to find a place to land."

The only noticeable signs of life were smoke spirals coming from what looked like softened igloos. The spirals blew decidedly to the south and functioned as wind socks. "Wind from the north," commented Doc. He made a low pass of 200 feet over the settlement and opened the throttle; people popped out everywhere.

"See them waving and pointing?" said Doc. "The landing area must be over there ... the lake."

The plane covered the mile distance quickly and Doc peered out a side window. "Looks like some hard drifts ... it could get rough." I was too excited to be afraid. The wings waved back-and-forth as the gusts pummeled the plane, but then touched down smoothly; and after a sharp bounce or two, slid to a stop on the hard-packed snow.

Adults and children arrived in staggered groups, each subset panting, yet smiling. Their cheeks were crimson and their brown eyes sparkled. The Eskimo women were a dazzling contrast against the white snow with many hues of cloth coverings over their parkas.

Doc opened the door and I pulled myself out first. Then, I turned to see if I could assist him. I could hardly bear to watch him maneuver tentatively out of the airplane. He sucked in his breath several times, but, once on the ground, he brought out his likable smile that invited the small group toward him.

"I am Doctor Gaede," he pronounced the words slowly. "This is Anna Bortel."

I hefted out his medical bag and other supplies. Two men and an older boy reached forward to carry the boxes. Behind me, the red aircraft shuddered in the gusts and Doc pulled out tie-down ropes.

"Hello," I called through the wind to the several women and small herd of children. I pointed to myself, "Miss Bortel. Teacher." The little children grinned back and then raced around the airplane in a silly game of chase, always turning to see if I was still watching.

We followed our welcoming committee to a nearby Quonset hut which had been erected by the Air Force Medics. How they achieved this feat, I had no idea. There were no roads, or a river or landing area adequate to accommodate a transport-vehicle for such large materials.

A generator produced uneven light from the bulbs hanging from the ceiling, and pushed out only tepid heat from a space heater; as in the school huts, walking on the floor resembled balancing on a boat at sea. Although the temperature was above freezing, by no means could the interior be referred to as warm.

Fran and Beverly, who had arrived earlier, had already given skin tests for tuberculosis. Fran stood a head above many of the villagers and was taller than Doc, but with indifference to her height, she wore winter boots with a short heel. Her pretty smile, graceful movements, and gentleness let everyone know she was a lady at heart—a tough lady in a wild country.

If I had to guess I would have said Beverly had grown up with brothers. She was a bit rough-and-tumble, with her auburn hair pulled back into two stubby pig-tails, which flung around as she moved abruptly; this made patients laugh.

Even though there were backless benches near the rounded walls, some patients seemed more comfortable on the floor. They passed the time watching us closely, with softly spoken comments in Eskimo. Fran and Beverly prepared to administer polio shots. Doc got busy behind an area partitioned with a hanging blanket. I had promised to do the cooking and dish washing, so tried to figure out what resources were available. Already a pot of water boiled on a Coleman camp stove. Doc could have lived on bologna and bread, so it was no surprise to find that Ruby had packed both. She'd added cinnamon rolls, canned chicken and rice soup, powdered milk, and canned fruit. The nurses had other canned and small boxed goods.

One older Eskimo woman, Mae Kakinya (Kaa-KIN-yah), and her husband, Elijah, who lived further north, heard the doctor was coming, and traveled miles by dog sled for a medical examination. Elijah spoke some English and explained this to us when they opened the door and stood stock-still.

"Hello," I said to Mae. "You've had a long trip."

She looked at me blankly, and then at her husband. Elijah spoke to her in Eskimo. Without hesitation, she pulled her heavy caribou parka over her head and sat down to wait. Beneath this outerwear, she had on a dark floral cotton dress open at the neck, most likely from a missionary barrel and brought in by some bush pilot. When her turn came to be examined, and she was asked to remove her dress to facilitate the examination, she stared uncomprehendingly, then took hold of either side of the neckline, and forcefully ripped the dress apart from top to bottom! Undergarments covered her body, but I kind of choked and then stood flabbergasted. Doc took it in stride and pressed his stethoscope to her chest. At the conclusion of her exam, I found several safety pins to refashion her dress, and she pulled her parka over her head and back in place. No one knew the difference when she stepped out from behind the curtain.

ABC

Pat O'Connell, the trader, invited Doc and I over for Irish stew. There was no way Doc and I could pass up the opportunity to see more of Anaktuvuk Pass, even if he had to limp and grimace to get here. "Of course it's made from caribou!" Pat O'Connell replied, laughing at our question.

Pat's one-room house was three-quarters of a mile south of the Quonset, and on the north edge of the village, just across a frozen creek. A kerosene lamp provided the only light in the small confinement and the corners of the room retreated into dimness. It was probably better that way since there were cardboard and Blazo boxes helter-skelter and spilling with ammunition, books, worn-out magazines, dirty clothes, and indiscernible items made of caribou. In spite of his housekeeping clutter, his cooking skills excelled, or at least the stew did with caribou, potatoes, and onions.

From what we'd observed, the short, sinewy sixty-some year-old trader from Canada, was the only white person living among these Eskimos. We savored every bite of the warm stew while he talked without stopping. He had a somewhat know-it-all attitude, but we listened raptly to his tales of survival of the fittest.

"And, that plane left Bettles and was never seen or heard of again." He left that information hanging in the air for a few seconds and got up. "Would you like some more coffee?"

Just listening to his stories left me trembling.

A noise outside his door startled me. It was Simon Paneak, the leader of the village. He pulled his glasses from his face and pushed back his heavily fur-ruffed park hood. The large-boned man moved straight toward me and held out a letter.

"You read," he said, then didn't say another word.

I read it aloud. The letter informed the village that there was no room for their children at the boarding school in Wrangell.

Simon Paneak looked at me and narrowed his eyes intently, "We have 20 to 30 children. No school. We want school. You tell Department of Education we want school. Maybe they listen then. Maybe you come teach?"

I sat stunned. *Could I make it in such an isolated village? And, how did he know ahead of time that I'd be accompanying the medical team—and that I was a school teacher?*

"We want school, our children need education," Simon said unwavering. He had a distinct presence and spoke with authority; not that he was argumentative, but I got the feeling he wouldn't back down either.

"Okay, Anna, you go write a report to the Department of Education, and I will build a schoolhouse," said Pat.

That night, I couldn't fall asleep and it wasn't only the unusual accommodations. Nor was it entirely because the uncomfortable army cots squeaked, or that we women slept with only blanket partitions between us and Doc, whose long, drawn out snores reverberated in the hollow hut, and startled me with intermittent snorts. These were only superficial disturbances that otherwise I could have put up with. What really bothered me was a string of thoughts and arguments I couldn't stop. *Why am I drawn to this village? I love Tanana and my friends there. But this village needs a school teacher and I'm acquainted with bush teaching—I'm even accustomed to crude conditions. I would be so alone here with no white women to share with. What if I got sick in this isolated place?* Near dawn, I relinquished my anxiety to the Almighty.

The next day while Dr. Gaede completed his work, I visited homes to obtain the requested educational information. Fran and Beverly had arranged for a chartered bush pilot to pick them up and we said goodbyes. Before departing, we wandered through the village and snapped pictures. A man invited us into his place. I'd thought the Tanana Native's cabins were bare, but this sod house had a lower ceiling, dirt floor with willow branches, and a pile of caribou skins, which we supposed were for sleeping. A small stove of sorts was the only upright furniture in the room.

I was convinced that a school was crucial. But, could I *teach* here? This settlement made Tanana look like a modern city. Here there were clumps of partially buried sod houses, small dog houses, and meat caches suspended on stilts. Pat's trading post randomly stocked rolled oats, flour, sugar, tea, coffee, Pilot Boy crackers, and canned milk; every now and then a jar of peanut butter or box of cornmeal showed up, or perhaps a jar of jam. There were no trees, no school, no FAA, no medical facilities. A home-based post office received and sent mail whenever a bush pilot showed up, which was not more than once-a-week. All the same, what Anaktuvuk Pass *did* have was a chapel, magnificent mountains, and people who were highly motivated to support my efforts.

Children trailed us back to Doc's PA-14. "You a teacher." "You a teacher!" they chanted. Even though I tried not to let my mind form future plans, I couldn't help but love these cheerful rosy-cheeked prospective students. I'd wanted to go north, but could I survive this far north?

BREAKUP

· ·

When I arrived back in Tanana I made a bee-line to my bathroom. I hadn't taken my clothes off in three days. Before I even finished luxuriating in the bathtub, the School Fair Committee arrived in my living room to complete plans for the Fair which would be held two days later. This was a premiere event and we were raising money for playground equipment.

My classroom turned into a movie room with Walt Disney cartoons and a popcorn stand outside the door. The folding doors between Harriet and Herman's rooms were opened and in that large space was a dart game, ring toss, White Elephant homemade items, fishing pond, and handcrafts. There was a refreshment booth with hot dogs, cake, cookies, and coffee. This village had never seen such a carnival and people hung around until 10:00 p.m. when we closed down the fun. We counted out a grand total of $368! We'd spent $100 on expenses, so that left us with a $268, which, without much debate, was allocated for a swing set and slide on the playground. I chalked this up to a smashing success on all accounts.

More first-time events continued through the end of the school year. I decided that there should be a graduation banquet in honor of the eighth graders—even if there were only two students. The seventh graders, who also attended, designed menu folders and nut cups. They had no idea what I was talking about when I'd made the suggestion, but once instructed, they worked busily folding and filling—sampling a mixed nut or two. When the task was completed, they stood back from the table and admired their accomplishment. All at once, a girl said in awe, "We have never had a graduation program before!"

I'd ordered frying chickens from Fairbanks for our entrée and after cutting the chickens into pieces, I dipped them in flour and started frying in oil the plump breasts, thighs, and drumsticks. The students set the table and chattered happily. "Mmm." That smells good, Miss Bortel." I wiped my flour-dusted hands on my apron and turned around. Watching their wonderment and pleasure made it worth the effort.

Graduation exercises completed the end-of-year finale, and the *firsts* for Tanana School. Tom McQueen and Wally pushed my organ into our classroom-auditorium so the graduates could walk down an aisle with a musical accompaniment. As in the school dedication, Rev. Coleman Inge spoke the invocation and the Girl's Chorus sang. Dr. Gaede titled his address, "The Practical Exam." Even though only Violet and John graduated, approximately 60 people celebrated the culmination of eighth grade. I celebrated the culmination of a tough year in Tanana and the survival of life in the huts!

The *firsts* were finished at school, but a *first* for me was the Yukon River breakup.

One Wednesday evening, Naomi and Ruth knocked on my door with a note from Ruby inviting Harriet and me to grill chicken along the riverbank. Doc was tied up at the hospital so our gathering would only include Ruby and her brood. With four children, she had her hands full, and then putting together a meal to eat outdoors required extra effort; yet, this doctor's wife would have been happy to fix picnics every night of the week. Within the hour we were stoking a fire and listening to sparks ignited by dripping chicken fat.

The river itself captured most of our attention. In fall, anchor ice initially formed along the shallower shoreline and snagged susceptible ice chunks floating down the river; eventually, the river froze from shore to shore. In spring, the melting snow and ice caused the river to expand. The water flooded above the anchor ice, popping it up, until a channel ran free where the anchor ice had held the solidified river intact. On this May evening, water lapped up along the edges of this channel, near our picnic spot.

"The ice went out at Nenana (Nee-NAN-uh) on the eighth, already six days ago," commented Ruby. "With all that pressure upriver, ours should go out here any day."

Each year, Alaskans place bets on when the Yukon will dramatically shake off winter and resume its summer form. The pivotal point is Nenana.

"I sure hope I don't miss it," I said.

"You won't. The hospital siren will go off," assured Ruby. "And, you'll probably hear the rumbling and cracking of the river breaking up, too."

I couldn't imagine mile-wide ice ripping apart and smashing its way down the river.

After we'd finished the tasty chicken and licked our fingers, we noticed how the water was creeping up.

Later, Harriet and I walked back to the riverbank. No signs of a campfire remained—only swirling muddy water.

At 3:00 a.m. the hospital siren jolted me from my dreams. I drowsily stumbled about trying to find my shoes and a coat. Harriet shouted for me to hurry, and we ran to the river's edge. We heard the crashing before we saw the colossal ice chunks thrashing about, heaving against one another, grating and grinding. Moonlight lit the drama. Nearby, the Gaedes ran out of their house in bathrobes and slippers. Along the riverbank we heard people yelling.

"Hey, let's get the ambulance and drive up to Picnic Point. We'll have a fantastic view from there," said Doc enthusiastically.

Along the way, we picked up several nurses and we were like giddy kids sneaking out to a party. It was worth the jolting ride it to witness the phenomenal overview of miles of warring Yukon struggling to break free. As we watched, we saw sparks of light flickering along the riverbank.

"Look, people are starting bonfires!" exclaimed Harriet.

The rite of spring engaged everyone's attention. We drove back and joined the villagers huddled around fires with coffee pots brewing on the glowing centerpieces. Socializers visited from fire to fire and we joined the dynamic procession.

I returned to bed for a few more hours of sleep and woke to find winter vanquished and summer's return. A mere 24 hours earlier, the Yukon had been helplessly ice-packed, and now, only hunks of ice remained on the shoreline, while the river victoriously raced out to the sea. Driftwood logs that had toppled from eroded banks or had become dislodged from sandbars sped down the river highway. Soon we'd hear *kicker-boats* chasing after the firewood. Now I understood why Alaskans seldom referred to *spring* but instead spoke of *breakup.*

With summer officially here, Harriet climbed onto a plane bound for her Wisconsin farm. Ruby invited Herman and me for pancakes and eggs before he also left for the summer. None of us teachers knew where the next school year would find us. We'd had our ups and downs working together and living closely, but we'd clung together as a tough trio. We said goodbyes with mixed emotions.

ABC

In 1917, a bunch of bored railroad workers started betting on the breakup of the Tanana River at Nenana. Each winter, a cable on a four-legged tripod is connected to a clock on shore. Participants purchase tickets for $2.50. The instant the ice moves, the line to the clock trips, marking the official breakup time, and announcing the end of winter. The earliest recorded breakup took place on April 20, 1940, and the latest occurred on May 20, 1964. Historically, the ice on the Tanana at Nenana, has most often broken-up on April 30. This Nenana Ice Classic is the only type of state lottery. Winners divide their rewards and other proceeds benefit the residents who help orchestrate the event. In 2010, the jackpot was $279,030. The pot is split by all winners.

A FEW MORE ALASKA EXPERIENCES

As head teacher, tying up loose ends fell to me; or in this case, tearing apart loose ends. The decrepit old school still held furniture and equipment that needed to be disposed of before the familiar landmark was torn down. Additionally, I needed to make arrangements for the Quonsets to be removed.

All the to-dos clogged my mind. And then Ruby asked me if I wanted to assist on a medical field trip to Nulato (New-LAT-o.) I flatly refused. She asked again. My response fell on deaf ears, hers and Doc's.

Doc wouldn't take "no" for an answer, "I'm going to hold clinic at Barbara's house—you know, the Public Health Nurse. We could use another hand."

I held my ground.

He cajoled me, "I won't be around next year to take you on these kinds of Alaskan experiences, so you should take advantage of the opportunity."

I relented.

We flew down the Yukon River. For Doc, this was as natural as getting into a car. He flew to medical emergencies, to hunt moose or caribou meat for his family's dinner table, and for the sheer pleasure of being in the air. Most certainly this mode of transportation was not without its hazards. He'd been forced down in a blizzard, following a polar bear hunt; risked landing on the frozen Yukon River amidst snow-camouflaged pressure ridges when oil leaked from his plane engine and splattered over his entire windshield; and put his plane into a thicket of trees when he underestimated what he thought was short vegetation. This physician would have been quick to admit that his prescription for adventure was hunting, flying, and providing healthcare in Alaska; not that he deliberately set out to live on the edge, but it just seemed to be a frequent outcome.

Ruby was not seeking a prescription for adventure—even though she thrived on living in Alaska. Just living in this environment brought with it occurrences that were unique. Just being a bush pilot doctor's wife had side-effects of adrenalin over-load.

The two hour flight gave me plenty of time to reflect on my own so-called adventures and in particular a new-for-me experience in Tanana.

An older Native lady had died. She was the first local person to die within a year, and I felt I should attend her funeral. The Episcopal Church was packed with people and Margie sat with me.

"I'll just stay for the service, and then work on reports," I whispered.

"No, Anna, you need to go out to the cemetery. You've never experienced this and I think you'll find it very interesting," Margie whispered back.

After the benediction, we followed the others outside. The hand-constructed coffin sat with the lid removed; the woman's body was wrapped in a simple bed blanket. People milled around, some smoked cigarettes, and when everyone had exited the church, several men pounded nails into the coffin lid and hoisted it onto the back of a pick-up. Family members climbed up beside the coffin. Two more pick-ups arrived and among all three vehicles, most of the crowd found a spot.

"Here Miss Bortel," one of the student's mothers reached out to pull me up. Legs hung over the tailgates, arms stretched over the sides, and faces looked over the cab. As jam-packed as we were, no one could have untangled themselves enough to fall overboard.

The cemetery was out by Mission Hill, some distance away. There was scarcely room for the width of a vehicle and branches slapped against anyone on the outside edges. The road, primarily a muddy trail, often sloped and had huge holes. Trucks took turns getting stuck and passengers unloaded and walked while the drivers and other men dug, grunted, and pushed until once again the vehicles could continue on their way.

At long last, the trucks, coffin, and all the entourage arrived. The body was buried among the short white fences that outlined previous gravesites. I was glad Margie had pulled me into this experience.

ABC

In spite of how the school year had ended the year before, with a rift generated by educational politics, Florence Feldkirchner, and I had re-established our friendship. Once we completed the business before us and she had the knowledge of where she'd teach next (which was Barrow), and the assurance that she'd continue to receive a paycheck, she had relaxed. A sign to me that all was well between us was when she invited me over for her "Feldkirchner" soup. After she relocated to Barrow, which hung onto the coast of the Arctic Ocean, at the most northerly point of Alaska, we exchanged letters often. She was hungry for news about her previous students and the village. When she invited me to visit her in Barrow, I'd accepted.

The flight provided a wide-angle view of the Brooks Range. The crystal mountain peaks shimmered in the sunlight. Further north, the mountains gave way to flat country and as far as the eye could see, semi-thawed lakes splotched the swamp land.

Just when it seemed we would fly right off over the ocean, and off to where steely water and gray sky met, the plane banked and we landed at the top-of-the-world village. Unless I climbed into a Native's skin boat, this was the farthest north I'd ever be.

I stepped out of the airplane and wind gusted across my face. I dug in my pocket for a headscarf. The skies drooped with wet clouds. The temperature must have been around 45 degrees. June in Barrow didn't offer a friendly reception.

"Anna, it's so good to see you," Florence said sincerely. Relinquishing her reserved manner, she warmly embraced me.

"Here's our ride," she motioned toward a truck with blankets spread in the back.

We lifted ourselves up on the tailgate, swung around our legs, and scooted so our backs would be against the cab. This offered slight protection from the sea breeze. The frozen ruts in the gravel kept us bouncing on the hard, metal floor. I was struck by the grayness—gravel, puddles, sky, and dirty snow piles. Even though the Barrow sun didn't rest between May 10 and Aug 2, it didn't provide much warmth. I couldn't imagine the winter when the limp sun didn't even rise between November 18 and January 24.

Florence maintained her work schedule, which with the BIA was year-around, but connected me with the dentist's wife and two nurses who readily served as tour guides. They had lived in Barrow several years. I'd only been here a few hours and decided this place would be at the bottom of my list of places to teach in Alaska, so in addition to asking questions about Barrow, I questioned them how they ever ended up here, and what they did to keep their sanity.

For one thing, there were more people, more businesses, and thus more opportunities for entertainment, recreation, and socializing than in other villages. Barrow claimed between 800 and 1,000 Eskimos, making it the largest Eskimo settlement in North America—and that was only Natives. Added to this population were school teachers, missionaries, medical employees, store owners, hotel and restaurant staff, and construction workers. In contrast to the population of 100 in Anaktuvuk Pass and 300 in Tanana, this was a city; a city of opportunities.

Most of the buildings stood on short piers. The number one reason was the permafrost which prevented foundations to be dug. Another factor was that if a building was constructed on top of the icy soil, the heat within the structure would eventually thaw the permafrost, destroying the firmness and stability of the base. This could be witnessed by the number of houses that dipped in a corner and heaved in another.

"We always wear water-proof boots here," mentioned the dentist's wife, Katherine. She was young, short-legged, and full of life. She jumped over the puddles as if she were playing hopscotch. "The ground can't absorb the moisture since it is frozen, so the only time the water puddles disappear is when they freeze into ice."

Along our walk, there was no tall purple-pink fireweed like I enjoyed in Tanana, or fragrant pink wild rose bushes. Occasionally I'd spot a tiny group of stubby pink or yellow flowers nested into the tundra. The latitude, soil, and weather defied plant life.

We headed to the shoreline and walked out on the ice to an open channel between floating ice-packs. The water startled me with its ominous blackness.

"This isn't friendly water," commented Jean, one of the nurses. She was more quiet than my other two guides, and serious, too. "It's scary to think what would happen if you'd slip in; I mean, not just freezing or drowning, but what if you were pulled beneath the ice-pack?"

"Well, I guess you'd just die no matter how it turned out," said her companion, JoAnn, breezily.

Walking helped stave off the chill, but I didn't mind when my tour guides suggested we go indoors to observe some Native dances. Not many tourists had an opportunity to enjoy this dramatic ritual of drumming, chanting, and movements that depicted a hunt.

My cheerful guides provided a comprehensive overview of Barrow both current and past, and I returned to Florence's with plenty of conversational material.

Over her trade-mark soup, which was just as heavily peppered as I'd remembered, Florence listened to my enjoyment of my episodes. In spite of the pleasure of new experiences and the broader exposure to Alaska, I couldn't get past the pervasively dreary atmosphere.

"Anna, I've taught in Alaska for many years," she said. "But this is the most depressing place of all."

I couldn't argue. Ever since I'd crossed the Alaska border, I'd been creeping farther north; after this experience, I knew without a doubt that my desire did not extend *this* far.

After five days, she bid me a sad good bye.

When I got back to Tanana, and even though I'd be seeing them in Ohio later in the summer, I wrote my parents:

> The Arctic Ocean was so foreboding … I could write and write about all the things I learned but if you ever have a chance to read "Fifty Years Below Zero" by Charles Brower—he was white man who whaled and trapped in the late 1880s; maybe you'll catch the spirit of the place. I met his son and daughter-in-law.

TAKING IT EASY

In late summer, I returned to Tanana and flew over the crazy-quilt of autumn red and gold tied into deep green spruce. A rainbow of magenta and indigo painted the rich blue sky. The muddy Yukon River seemed to know its time was limited and vigorously traveled along.

Over the summer there had been some changes. Gravel now covered the pit where the old school had been. Playground equipment would soon spring up in its place. The village atmosphere felt different too. Doc had taken an assignment on a Blackfeet (Blackfoot in Canada, Blackfeet in the U.S.) Indian reservation in Browning, Montana. I'd already received letters from Naomi, and she missed Tanana as much as her mother. Dr. Stanley Hadley was the new PHS Medical Officer in Charge. The Gronnings had returned home to Mishawaka, Indiana. These absences left empty holes in the community and in my friendship circle, even though Mel and Pat Jensen replaced the Gronnings at the Arctic Missons'chapel. Mel was nearly as tall as Roy, and already balding. His high energy demonstrated itself in his preaching, as well as gung-ho efforts to clean-up the area within the white picket fence around the house-chapel. Pat was slower to warm up and appeared physically fragile. I wasn't sure how she'd make it in this demanding environment. Their daughter, Naoma, was one of my first graders, and son, Tim, a year or so younger.

Harriet and Herman returned to complete my teaching team. To begin with, not only did Harriet live in the second bedroom of the attached school apartment, but Herman bedded down on the living room couch, until a cabin at the end of the village was completed for his use. We'd lived closely the previous year, but this semester, every time I turned around, I was face-to-face with either my co-teacher or my roommate. Trying to make decisions as simple as shared meals, could flare into hurt feelings, or a judgment that I had taken a side. Herman would want to eat at Myberg's Airport Café and Harriet would assemble hot dogs and potato salad for a picnic. Or, Mary Ann Burroughs would invite us to the hospital dining room for pork roast and Harriet jumped up at the chance while Herman slouched out the door. When Herman prepared dinner, I'd cluck my tongue over the prices he'd paid at Northern Commercial, but smacked my lips over the store-bought goodies. In summary, it was like a three-person marriage.

NORTHERN COMMERCIAL COMPANY

Cash-C.O.D.-CHG

Branch		Tanana	Date 10–10–59
Sold to Herman Romer			
Frying Chicken	2.20		
Shrimp	.85		
Cranberry Sauce	.45		
Qt. Ice cream	.90		

$4.40

During the day, I fulfilled my role as head-teacher, and they would be my subordinates; at night we'd stand in line to brush teeth. The mornings would begin with meeting one another in our robes at the coffee pot. Later I'd bump into them in the school hallway and deal with some teaching issue.

Instead of 29 students, 65 lined up in front of the classrooms. I couldn't imagine how we could have contained all the students if we hadn't constructed a larger school. In addition to our young, day-time students, Herman started an algebra class for adults one evening a week. The class drew a dozen people. From what I observed, Herman related well to this older age group, and his students were attentive and motivated by his lessons.

Notwithstanding the inter-teacher frictions, which weren't all that unusual given the proximity and role issues, I found teaching rewarding. Some of the rewards were very tangible. Nearly every day one of the students would present me with a bouquet of colorful sweet peas, orange nasturtiums, or sunshine yellow marigolds. How could I not smile?

Until the capricious frost determinedly came to stay, we were the appreciative recipients of cabbage, lettuce, and carrots from Lewis and Lucy Kalloch. In return, I helped the old-timers fill out Sears order forms for coats and socks, towels and fabric, and other necessities. The process of writing specific information on lines and making choices in boxes overwhelmed them. When Christmas rolled around, Lewis showed up on my doorstep and asked if I'd stop over to read two Christmas letters they'd received. It warmed my heart to do so.

By mid-September, temperatures averaged 30 degrees and six-inches of snow covered the ground. This year, however, we had nothing to fear. Our heating source ran of its own accord without vigilant pounding and repair.

What I did *pound* on were the bootleggers and villagers who ordered in and allowed alcohol in the village—even though Tanana had voted itself *dry* and liquor-free. One Sunday morning, a drunken villager staggered up and down the streets with a guitar, singing and falling down. Like a Carry Nation, I stormed over to the village commissioner to express my opinion, and then intercepted the plane at the airstrip that I knew was carrying the alcohol. Both parties listened to my preaching, nodded their heads in agreement, but once I left, business continued as usual.

While this was disturbing, our little village was becoming less detached from the outer world. The airport boasted the first telephone in Tanana which was not limited to the village. Prior to this, the telephone system linked only the FAA complex, the hospital, and the airport office. Now, if need be, an individual could go to the airport and call outside the village. For instance, the doctor could call ahead to Fairbanks or Anchorage for emergencies. Likewise, someone from the Lower 48 States could call the airport and request that a specific person be contacted. There were no private phones in home, but I guessed it would be a matter of time before we added that to our rapidly evolving civilization.

Radio contact improved too. A radio station that broadcast inter-village communication, could now reach into Tanana. During *Tundra Topics*,[13] a personal message broadcast, people tuned in and could hear when someone was flying in, or had a request for fish, and so on. Whenever someone overheard a message for another villager, he or she would contact that person. For example, one evening, I saw Mel Jensen's pickup in front of our picture window. Mel had come to notify me that he'd just heard a message. Mr. Gowan from the American Indian Mission in South Dakota was flying in on Wednesday to visit with us. I appreciated this advance notice.

The Gronnings had managed without running water, but Mel and Pat struggled with this inconvenience. I was happy to share the modern amenities of our apartment, and every Saturday, Pat, Naoma, and Tim, came over to take baths. Wally invited Mel to bathe at his duplex.

ABC

In December, when the mercury fell to 35 degrees below, frost engraved itself along the baseboard behind the daveno, and the thermopane windows grew hoary lichens. I wrote my folks, It's -44 degrees, but I have so much pep and never get sick. Our days are indeed short. Yesterday, the sun rose at 9:46 a.m. and set at 1:43 p.m.

I commented to Harriet, "We'd better not sleep too late on Saturdays or when we get up the sun will already have gone down!"

The semester ended peacefully. In Tanana tradition, we walked around to homes, greeted people and shared plates of home-made holiday cookies. Later in the day, Tom Tryland, the 80-year-old Norwegian prospector and Adam Minook, a Native grandfather, joined us for Christmas dinner. Tom presented us with a large and a small box of chocolates that he'd carefully wrapped in worn wax paper and some old cord, and then the old-timers bestowed upon us tales of yesteryear. Tom assured us that he still had his gold pan, and that it was just a matter of time before he'd strike it rich.

I did my share of visiting, too. I'd baked big batches of Christmas Sugar Cookies and when there was a lull at my own house, I packaged up red and green sprinkled cookies, bundled up, and knocked on doors. I knew stopping at Grandma Maggie Elia's would elicit tales of yore and amuse me to no end.

Maggie's perspective magnified the isolation of the older Natives' lives. During much of her lifetime, *getting out of the village* meant going to fish camp, checking traplines, or perhaps climbing into a boat and going downriver. She'd been flabbergasted when I told her that Anchorage was not a hospital, but a *large village.* It made sense. What she knew about Anchorage was friends and family going with a bush pilot to the Public Health Anchorage Native Hospital, to be hospitalized for tuberculosis.

Grandma was happy to see me. "Sit here, Anna. I have something special for you." I had no idea what it might be and she seemed in no hurry to deliver the surprise. I asked about her daughter, Jeanie. The older Indians referred to both men and women as *he,* which made for complicated listening. When she told me that, "He had done this or that for Christmas," I got all tangled up; it wasn't until a few more sentences that I pieced together the context, and that she was referring to Jeanie. We teachers had pretty well broken the students of this, but the older people would probably never change.

All at once, Grandma Elia remembered that she wanted to give me something special. I described this specialness in my Round Robiner letter:

> Grandma Elia wanted to treat me to Indian ice cream. I can usually eat anything, but THAT, I couldn't down. Another old Indian woman said, "That will make you sick!" I tried to eat and Grandma Elia said, "You like it?" I evaded the question. It must have been old moose and fish grease with some berries or fruit added. I watched my chance to dispose of it when other people came into the cabin. Later that night I went to the FAA station and visited, and had white man's ice cream. Now THAT was special.

All in all, though it was only mid-year, I felt relaxed and rested.

1960
CHANGES, CHICKENS, AND CONCLUSIONS

When I'd first come to Tanana, I expected the long dark winter evenings would drag on and on. I imagined munching popcorn, drinking steaming cocoa, and reading books to pass the time. This didn't happen. Granted the thermometer sunk to 58 degrees below for five days straight, and we let out school so the children wouldn't have to walk to school, but those five days didn't invite in boredom as an exchange. The children were unaffected by the cold and made use of their time-off by sledding down the riverbanks. We teachers decided to restart classes so at least they'd be some place warm, regardless if they thought they needed that respite or not.

In the spring of 1960, when the sun chased away the winter night, I was still trying to steal time for book-reading and even hoping for some boredom. Outdoors, I squinted in the dazzling rays that reflected off the snow. April birds twittered.

"Say, Anna, why don't I come over in the morning for waffles?" Wally called to me as I strolled down the springtime-muddy road past the hospital grounds. "I haven't had any since Ruby left."

The next morning, over waffles covered with warm syrup, Wally, Harriet, and I reviewed the last three years in Tanana.

"Before when we wanted *to eat out* that meant we had three choices—going to the hospital dining hall, friends' homes, or to a potlatch. Now we can have hamburgers and pie at the airport café," I started.

We went on to discuss transportation changes. Earlier in the year, three snowmachines buzzed into the village. The odd-looking caterpillar contraptions on skis carried individual drivers behind minimal plexi-glass windshields. They sat right out in the frigid air and had journeyed all the way upriver from Bethel.

"Do you think they'll replace dog sleds?" I asked Wally.

We speculated about the possibilities.

The conversation switched to statehood. Rather than counties, Alaska local government was emerging in the form of boroughs. These divisions were to provide services of education, land use planning, and tax assessment.

"Just imagine," I said, "We're making history as the youngest U.S. state."

At a very local and immediate level, history was in the making at school, where I intended to introduce the children, and villagers, to chickens—which some had never seen. I'd ordered some potential chicks from a teacher friend in Illinois. When the four fertilized eggs arrived, I nested them gently in a little improvised incubator with a light bulb for heat and hoped for an Easter emergence. I was ecstatic. Like a mother hen, I hovered over them. Like a flock of mother hens, the students headed to the incubator as soon as they'd hung up their coats and before finding their seats.

Teachers' Conference was around the corner, and I cornered Wally to chicken-sit for me. "Wally, you must guard them carefully and turn them daily. I will show you."

ABC

Air travel was changing. Climbing onto a low-wing airplane in a tight skirt was a thing of the past. Now when I flew out for the Teachers' Conference in Anchorage, there were short steps that folded out with the door, not rungs, *and* no longer did the pilot narrate sightseeing, and instruct us to let him know if we needed more cabin heat, or yell over the prop racket that in case of an emergency there was a fire extinguisher—behind someone's seat. Now we had stewardesses.

The conference was in Anchorage. From Fairbanks to Anchorage we flew on a large Alaska Airlines jet-plane with a *Gold Nugget* imprint on its tall tail. During the flight, a stewardess announced the showing of a film, which was an experiment for the airlines. I had no interest in films. I was occupied with searching through the clouds to find Mt. McKinley. I expected their experiment would fail from lack of passenger attention.

At the conference, teachers were all abuzz about the next year's placement. When they heard I'd been to Anaktuvuk Pass, they hounded me with questions: *Is there a school? Is there at least a Community Hall? No teacherage?* I responded in the negative to nearly everything, but added that there was a very small log chapel that had been offered to serve a dual purpose. At the end of January, I'd read in the *Fairbanks Daily News-Miner* that the state legislature had okayed appropriations for additional schools, with $90,000 appropriated for Anaktuvuk Pass. *Maybe my assessment had a part in that decision,* I'd reasoned. *I wonder when that project will start?* In spite of all the comments, ranging from, "That's a chance of a lifetime!" to, "I'd go there at a drop of the hat," Mr. Isaac informed me he doubted they'd find a teacher who was qualified, or who would last into the winter.

ABC

While I was gone, Wally had attentively followed my instructions, but then one morning when I checked the eggs, I scowled in alarm. *Was I imagining? Or, were they cool to the touch. What kind of mother was I?* I rearranged them and repositioned the light bulb. Later in the day, I took their temperature. They were *very* warm. *I think I've cooked my chickens!*

Easter neared. Nothing happened. No pecking sound from an egg shell. Then one morning the children and I discovered an egg had exploded and splattered its contents over the other eggs! Disappointment reigned in the classroom. Native children witnessing the birth of chicks was not to be.

ABC

Elias, the school janitor and the eighth grade boys decided that the school teachers needed to compete in a dog race. We were skeptical about our ability, but only temporarily resistant to the contest. It was agreed that the teachers would ride down river *in* the sleds and then exchange places with the experienced driver, the student, on the ride back.

We gathered below the riverbank in front of the hospital, where Doc had kept his airplane tied down.

"Miss Bortel, come, hang onto Blackie," Tom, one of the eighth-graders instructed me.

Somehow the dogs, which usually howled on top of their dog houses, or curled into tight ear-to-tail balls, had been transformed into powerful, raring beasts. They pulled and yelped as Tom tried to straighten out their harnesses. My heartbeat quickened as I sensed that this wasn't just a simple joy ride, but more like being tied to a rocket ship. Perhaps I should have stayed home and graded papers.

My instructor's final words were not reassuring. "No matter what, just hang on tight," he yelled. He grabbed the sled handle and shouted "Mush" to the dogs. For a moment he ran behind, letting the dogs pick up speed, and then he jumped onto the sled runners behind me.

I was too busy paying attention to my own dilemma to watch Herman or Harriet maneuvering into place. Before I felt prepared for this launch down the Yukon River, the straining dogs pitched forward and we were off. Away we flew. I screamed and hollered. The wind knocked back my parka hood, and a blast of cold air shot down my already tingling back. Tom laughed. I'd imagined a smooth gliding sensation. The river pathway, however, was a rugged trail of ice upheavals and wind-crusted drifts. I hung on. This was nothing like my *Sled Dog* song which merrily conveyed a sense of tranquility while enjoying the beauty of nature. I was petrified.

When we got to our turning-around point, Tom and I exchanged positions. Now I was suppose to have learned from him and be able to get the team back to the finish line in front of the village.

After only a few minutes, Harriet's team passed us and our two teams tangled in their harnesses.

"Hold the brake! Hold the brake!" the eighth-graders shouted.

I stepped down as hard as I could while Tom tended the dogs. Then he jumped back into the sled. "Mush, Miss Bortel!"

Forty minutes later, trailing behind Herman and Harriet, Tom and I straggled back to the finish line.

"What took you so long," joked Herman, the winner. He tossed his head in exaggerated pride.

"I think you had the advantage when our dogs tangled and you passed," I teased.

My heart pounded in my ears, but now that I'd arrived safely back at the finish line, I burst out, "I loved every minute of it! Even if I get an *F* in dog-mushing." From now on, watching dogsled races would be from a more appreciative perspective.

To thank the eighth grade boys for their wild and unusual graduation gift to us, a few days later, I made cherry pies, and we all sat around with pie and cocoa, reliving our sledding experiences. When we recounted the events, exaggerated twists and turns added to the humor and close-calls were turned into near-death possibilities. Harriet, Herman, and I dramatized our terror. The boys threw themselves back in their chairs and chortled uproariously. Regardless of the outcome, everyone had had an unforgettably good time.

ABC

My three years at Tanana drew to an end. I'd never grown deaf to the sweet children voices of, "You a teacher." Yes, I *was* a teacher and I couldn't deny a child the opportunity to write his or her own name, read, and gain skills and information that would improve his or her future. I'd decided to be *that* teacher who was qualified and could make it through the winter.

At a farewell party at the Community Hall, the evening was filled with cake and coffee, hugs and handshakes, gratitude from parents, smiles from the children, and anecdotes of "We'll never forget when you…" I held tightly to the happy moments and at the very end broke down in tears. I'd grown relationships with the parents and had watched children's faces when they'd caught onto a concept. I felt at home in this Athabascan Indian village. Leaving was harder than I expected.

My heart strings were pulled taut already, and then the next day, Herman brought over blueberry muffins he'd stirred up especially for my birthday. I made coffee. No matter our differences, we'd survived when other novices would have called it quits.

Herman had requested to stay at Tanana. Harriet was assigned the school at Huslia (HOOS-lee-uh), northwest of Tanana, on the Koyukuk River.

Within days of completing the Tanana school year, my plane took off for Anaktuvuk Pass. I looked below at the familiar roof tops. The major change between this final flight and my initial flight was the enormous flat-roofed school which symbolized my efforts in the small Native village that crouched along the muddy rushing Yukon River. Now, I was off to teach in a makeshift school facility and live in a tiny cabin. Except for brief acquaintances made during the medical visit with Doc Gaede, I didn't know a soul. I'd thought Tanana was remote, but I was heading further north and into one of the most desolate of all Alaskan areas.

Anna's Moose Chili

Brown:
- 1 lb. ground moose meat (or beef)
- 1 C. onions, chopped
- ¼ C. green pepper, chopped

Add and Cook:

- 1 can tomato soup
- 2 C. (16 oz.) canned, stewed tomatoes
- 1 can pinto beans
- 1 can kidney beans
- 1 t. vinegar
- 1 t. seasoned salt
- 1 scant teaspoon chili powder (more if desired)
- pinch of crumbled basil leaves

MORE PRESCRIPTIONS
FOR ADVENTURE

You just met Anna Bortel. This is only one of her adventure stories. Be sure and read *A is for Anaktuvuk Pass: Teacher to the Nunamiut Eskimos!*

Anna introduced you to the Gaedes—Doc, Ruby, Naomi, Ruth, Mark, and Mishal. You can find out *their* prescriptions for adventures, too.

From Kansas Wheat Fields to Alaska Tundra: A Mennonite Family Finds Home

Take one young Mennonite girl and transplant her from the flatland prairies of Kansas. Give her village potlatches, a school in a Quonset hut, the fragrance of wood smoke, Native friends, a doctor for a father who creates hunting tales and medical adventures with a bush plane, a mother who makes the tastiest moose roasts and has the grit to be a homesteader, and throw in a batch of siblings. Weave into her journey the perspectives of her family members and have them face the lack of conveniences, isolation from extended family, freezing temperatures, and unknown hardships. Mix all these together with an attitude of humor, ingenuity, optimism, and you'll get a sense of adventure! Find out who really finds home.

Alaska Bush Pilot Doctor

Fasten your seatbelt for bush flying crack-ups, fly-in house calls in 50 below temperatures, hunting adventures, and a psychotic woman climbing out of his small Piper aircraft at 2,000 feet above the Yukon River. Pack your sense of humor for his attempts to get Ruby out for her moose hunt. Hang on for the thrills and rigors of life in the Last Frontier.

What's next?

- Ruby tells *her* side of the story, how she met a farm boy and expected a peaceful life on the Kansas prairie and how her world got turned upside down when she discovered he preferred flying, medicine, and the Last Frontier to milking cows and harvesting wheat.
- Mark gives his humorous account of growing up in the backseat of his father's airplanes, carrying a gun bigger than he, and by age 12 shooting a moose, mountain goat, sheep, and caribou. Flying a plane before legal age come with the territory.
- The Gaede kids grow up and invite you to follow them as they try their hands at homesteading—with exasperation, surprises, and laughter.

To be the first to know about a new book in the Prescription for Adventure series, purchase a DVD of Anna Bortel Church recounting her remarkable stories, learn about the Alaska Unit Study for homeschoolers, download a free Reader's Guide, or request a speaking engagement, go to *http//:*www.prescriptionforadventure.com. Your comments and reviews are welcomed. Send to npenn@prescriptionforadventure.com.

GLOSSARY

Aleut–the Native people who have traditionally lived in south-western Alaska and the Aleutian Chain. This people group was nearly devastated by contact with the whites. Not only were they subject to unknown diseases, they were practically enslaved by Russian fur hunters and traders, and later by Americans who forced them to continue killing seals in the Pribilof Islands.

Alcan–the Alaska-Canada Highway.

Athabascan–Indians, who were traditionally nomadic, and lived in a vast area of Interior Alaska, and into Canada. They range from the shores of Cook Inlet, west to the Kuskikwim and Yukon Rivers, north as far as Arctic Village and ANWR, and west to the Canadian border and beyond. Their territory makes up the greater part of Alaska.

Bureau of Indian Affairs (BIA)–a federal agency which ran educational and health programs for the Natives starting in 1931. In 1954, that function was transferred to the U.S. Department of Health, Education and Welfare, now known as the Department of Health and Human Services, or the Indian Health Services (IHS).

Blazo—a brand of white gas. It came in five gallon cans packed in wooden creates. Both empty cans and crates were used for a variety of household purposes in remote towns and villages.

Breakup—the spectacular display of the river ice breaking loose from the river banks and wildly crunching and tearing its way out to sea. This event signals the end of the restraints of winter and the beginning of summer. In areas where no rivers exist, the term is used in conjunction with snow melting before the frozen ground is thawed and can absorb the flow; thus, resulting in mud bogs, water in basements, and standing water which freezes at nights and re-thaws each morning. Alaskans seldom talk about *spring time* rather they include *breakup* as the name of the fourth season.

Borough—Alaska is divided into boroughs, rather can counties or parishes.

Bunny boots large army issue boots, which in the 1950s and 60s had white felt exteriors and smooth, slick-bottomed soles. They were intended to keep a soldier's feet warm for four hours at minus 50 degrees.

Bush—any part of Alaska that is inaccessible by roads or rail and accessible only by boat, airplane, sled, or snowmachine.

CAT—Alaskan refer to any caterpillar or bulldozer piece of equipment as a CAT.

Cabin Fever—a psychological state characterized by depression, restlessness, and sometimes violence. This is credited to the effects of being both housebound and locked in the dark deep freeze of winter, and from the resulting deprivation of sensory variety, physical mobility, and physical activity.

Cheechako—newcomer or tenderfoot.

Daveno or davenport—a sofa or couch. Term used in the 1950s.

Dry village - not allowing the legal sale of alcoholic beverages in the village.

FAA–with the event of statehood, CAA (Civil Aeronautical Authority) changed its name to Federal Aviation Agency.

Frost heave–a rise or bump in the road caused by seasonal freezing and thawing of the ground, which expands and contracts the soil.

Inupiat–one of the two Eskimo groups in Alaska. Both live along the coast: the Yupik along the Bering Sea and the Inupiat along Arctic Ocean. Each differs from the other linguistically.

Kicker boats–what the Natives called boats with motors.

Longshoresman–someone who works on the waterfront docks, loading or unloading, or doing other such jobs.

Mush–an order used to start or to urge on a dog team. Sometimes the Natives would instruct their children to mush along (hurry).

Outside–anywhere outside of Alaska, most frequently used in reference to the Lower 48 States.

Payloader–any type of tractor, usually on wheels, sometimes on a track with a scoop or bucket. Otherwise known as a front-end loader.

Permafrost–ground that remains frozen for two or more years. Although the surface may thaw during warm periods, the ground below remains frozen, often to great depths.

Potlatch–a primarily Indian custom which commemorates major life events. Traditional foods are served and dances performed.

Skid Row–a rundown urban area consisting of bars, prostitutes, and vagrants.

Snowmachines–anything resembling a snowmobile.

Teacherage–name of the dwelling in which teachers lived; sometimes attached to a school building, usually near the school building. In the same way a parson lived in a parsonage, a teacher lived in a teacherage.

Tundra–a treeless area covered with low-lying vegetation (small flowers, mosses, and lichens), under which is permanently frozen sub-soil.

SUGGESTIONS FOR FURTHER READING

The *Alaska Almanac*. Portland, Oregon: Alaska Northwest Books, 1976–2010.

Alaska Geographic: The Kenai Peninsula. Anchorage, Alaska: Alaska Geographic Society, 1994.

Anderson, Andy and Jim Rearden. *Arctic Bush Pilot*. Kenmore, Washington: Epicenter Press, 2000.

Brower, Charles D. *Fifty Years Below Zero: A Lifetime of Adventure in the Far North*. New York: Dodd, Meade and Company, 1942.

Century of Faith, 1895–1995. Centennial Commemorative Episcopal Diocese of Alaska. Fairbanks, Alaska: Centennial Press, 1995.

Feyes, Claire. *Villagers: Athabaskan Indian Life Along the Yukon River*. New York: Random House, 1981.

Gaede-Penner, Naomi. *From Kansas Wheat Fields to Alaska Tundra: A Mennonite Family Finds Home*. Mustang, OK: Tate Publishing, 2011.

Gaede-Penner, Naomi. *Alaska Bush Pilot Doctor*. Mustang, OK: Tate Publishing, 2012.

Jacobs, Jane. *A Schoolteacher in Old Alaska: The Story of Hannah Breece*. New York: Vintage Press, 1995.

Madenwald, Abbie Morgan. *Arctic School Teacher: Kulukak, Alaska 1931–1933.* Norman, OK: University of Oklahoma Press, 1992.

Movius, Phyllis Demuth (ed.). *When the Geese Come: The Journals of a Moravian Missionary, Ella Mae Ervin Romig, 1889–1905, Southwest Alaska.* Fairbanks, Alaska: University of Alaska Press, 1997.

Persons, Jean. *From Dog Sleds to Float Planes: Alaskan Adventures in Medicine.* Eagle River, AK: Northbooks, 2007.

Rearden, Jim. *Fifty Years of Frontier Adventure.* Kenmore, WA: Epicenter Press, 2001.

Roberts, Josephine. *Tanana.* Fairbanks, AK: Spirit Mountain Press, 1983.

Schwalbe, Anna Buxbaum. *Dayspring on the Kuskokwim: The Story of Moravian Missions in Alaska.* Bethlehem, PA: Moravian Press, 1951.

The Mile Post. Anchorage, AK: Morris Communication Corp, 1949–2011 (printed annually.)

READER'S GUIDE

This guide is excellent for families, reading groups, and homeschooling students. For best results, read over the questions before starting the book. All questions are intended for individual reader response, followed by group discussion.

1. Select three of the most humorous incidences in the book. What made these amusing to you?

2. What did you learn about Alaska that you found most interesting?

3. What intrigued you about Anna's life choices as a woman, a single woman, a school teacher?

4. In both Valdez and Tanana, Anna was in a pivotal position of helping the community work together for the common good, regardless or ethnic, religious, or occupational differences. List five examples.

5. Compare and contrast the conveniences among the Natives' cabins, the Arctic Mission's house, the medical compound, the Quonset huts the teachers

lived in, and the new school apartment. What would distress you the most?

6. What kinds of people do you pay attention to? Explain your choice(s).

   a. Athletes

   b. Movie Stars

   c. Leaders in your areas of interest or profession

   d. Someone who has beat the odds

   e. Ordinary people who make a difference in their world

   f. People with a lot of money

   g. Unconventional people who aren't afraid to try something different

   h. Other _____

7. How would you describe a role model? Who is *your* role model for living life fully? What are his/her characteristics? What steps are you taking to be like that person?

8. How often do you reflect on the impact of your life on other people? What prompts this consideration? For whom are *you* a role model? What do you think a person would want to emulate in your life?

9. Has reading Anna's story made any difference in your attitudes, goals, values, choices, curiosities, or motivations? Explain.

10. Who do you know that would benefit from reading this book? Pass it along.

SONGS AND
SHEET MUSIC

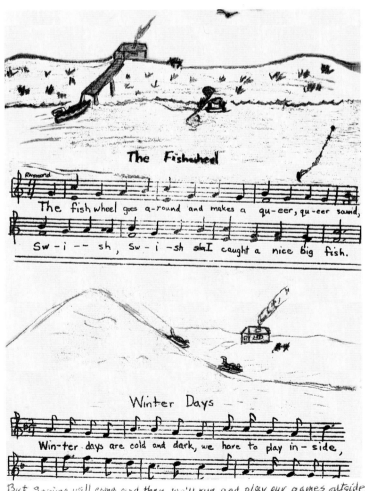

Tanana

Music and Lyrics
Anna Bortel Church

A - la-ska has its for-ests Its lakes and ri-vers, too,

The mountains and the an - i - mals in -clu-ding car-i-bou.

But of its man-y vil-lag-es, there's one above the rest,

To thee, Oh Ta - a - na, We love you the best.

Chorus

Ta - na-na, Oh Ta-na-na, Beside the Yu-kon waters.

You stand for home and all. We'll cherish you in memory

We'll hon-or you in fame, We'll be the kind

of cit - i - zens Who's proud of Ta-na-na.

The Sled Dog Song

Spirited

We'll hitch the hus-kies to the sled and o'er
The lead dog's name is Sa - n - dy, The swing

the trail we'll go, We'll bring our wood and wa-ter
dogs, Sugar and Tui, A - long comes Blackie and Spark-ie

Chorus

in then ride out o'er the snow. Mush a - long!
And Smo-ky with the long gray tail.

Mush a - long, Oh mush a-long my sled dogs

INDEX

Adak 64
Alaska-Canada Highway (Alcan). 18,46,47,40,82,83,122
Alaska State Flag 231, 237
Alaska State Song. 231
Aleut. 48,56,142, 237
Amundson, Harriet 23, 205, 212, 213, 216, 217
Anchorage 24, 41, 58, 60, 64, 83, 91, 95, 96, 98,
     100, 116. 135, 136, 147, 182, 185, 191, 217, 264, 265, 268, 269
Anderson, Carl 77,78,79
Anderson, Dorothy 77,78,79
Arctic Missions 143,144,147,224
Arvid 154, 159, 161
Asiatic Flu 154, 160, 181
Barney, Mr 91
Barrow 207, 257, 258
Bethel 205, 213, 268
Birches 166
Bortel, Clifford. 25
Bortel, David 28, 29
Bortel, Mildred (Millie) 28, 29, 91, 170, 192, 201
Bortel, Myrtle. 25
Burroughs R.N., Mary Ann 240, 241, 262

Butcher, Mr. 63, 65, 68
Bowling Green, Ohio 26, 38, 103, 213
Bowling Green State University 29, 32
Breakup 164, 198, 201, 251, 252, 253, 254
Brooks Range 62, 245, 257
Bureau of Indian Affairs 124, 125
Burnham, John 68, 69
Burnham, Ilene 68, 69
Cashen, Dean 124
Chitina 41, 59
Chugach mountains 137, 245
Community Hal 136, 169, 170, 171, 172, 173, 175,
200, 214, 222, 272 1
Coolidge, President Calvin 26
Cordova 97, 98, 99, 102
Crissey School 33
Crosby, Anna 26, 38
DC-3 . . . . 97, 98
Distance Early Warning system (DEW) 296
Dick, Elias 232
Dorcas Club 113, 114
Drake, Marie 237
Dusenbury, Elinor 237
Eagan, Govenor William (Bill) 92
Eckman, Rev. Leonard 102
Eckman, Wilda 102
Eisenhower, President Dwight 113
Elia, Jeannie 164
Elia, Maggie 164, 178, 265, 266
Elmendorf Air Force Base 58, 135
El Nathan Children's Home 56, 57, 65, 78, 116, 142
Fairbanks Daily News-Miner 269
Feldkirchner, Florence 126, 130, 131, 136, 137,
174, 175, 198, 207, 257

Fort Gibbon 141, 235
Free Methodist Church 40, 57, 63, 71, 75, 77, 95, 103
Gaede, Dr. Elmer 147, 166, 167, 210, 224
Gaede, Mark 147, 166, 167, 178, 208, 210
Gaede, Mishal 210, 224
Gaede, Naomi 147, 166, 208, 210
Gaede, Ruby 147, 166, 208, 210
Gaede, Ruth 147, 166, 208, 210
Gilson, George. 117
Gilson's Mercantile. 28, 117
Gowan, Mr. 264
Grant, Alfred 147, 158, 175, 236
Grant, Larry. 213
Greenville College 33, 213
Gronning, Chris 166, 167, 175, 178, 264
Gronning, Margie 140, 142, 143, 164, 166, 167, 224
Gronning, Rev. Roy 142, 143, 164, 166, 167, 175, 236, 261
Hanson, Wally 261
Harding, President Warren G.. 215, 224
Harrais, Margaret Keenan 57, 70, 92, 113
Harris, Adrian 159, 183
Harris, Tommy. 92
Harris, Peggy 159, 183
Inge, Rev. Coleman 131, 160, 193, 235
Isaac, Robert 24, 124, 125
Jacks, Ada. 223
Jenkins R.N., Ethel 220, 240
Jensen, Mel. 261, 264
Jensen, Naoma 264
Jensen, Pat 261, 264
Jensen, Tim. 264
Johnson, Harold 166, 167
Johnson, Vera 166
Joseph, Freddie 155, 158, 173

Joseph, Sam 143, 166
JOY Club 153, 154, 161
Keasling, Ernest 38
Kennedy, Philip 208, 211
Kokrine, Gregory 136, 142
Kokrine, Margaret 136, 142
Lake Iliamna 186
Lazy Mountain Children's Home 55, 142
Look, Donna 72
Look, Jan 72
Look, Ronald 72
Lower, Rev. Howard 95
Lower, Jessie 95
Lundgren, Mr. 232
Macomber R.N., Marjorie 149
McGregory, Al 82, 121
McGregory, Ruth 121
McQueen, Dr. Tom 223, 233, 252
Minook, Adam 265
Monclova School 33
Morey, Lois 204
Morrison-Knudson Contractors 217
Mt. Edgecumbe Vocational School 125
Mt. McKinley 47, 195, 269
Myberg's Airport Café 262
Myberg, Joan 239
Myberg, Pete 239
Nason, Blanche 239
Neufeld R.N., Ogla 215
Nuchalawoya 140
Nickerman, Ed 93
Nicolai, Joyce 72
Northern Commercial Company 134, 262
Novatney, Dr. Dorothy 64

Nulato. 255
Parent Teacher Association (PTA) 239
Pee Wee 148, 156, 183, 200
Peters, Alice 143, 205
Peterson, Aunt "Pedo" (Esther) 55, 56, 64
Pilot Boy Bread Crackers 177
Potlatch 136, 175, 179, 268, 275
Prevost, Rev. Jules. 140
Reid, Barbara 241
Richards, Supt. Don. 89. 90, 117
Roberts, Josephine 186
Rodli, Agnes. 121
Romer, Herman 23, 205, 212, 213, 216, 217, 224,
                                        225, 228, 229, 262, 263
St. James Episcopal Church 133, 134
Segerquist, Aunt Louise 55, 56, 58, 61, 64
Sommers, Chris 235
Spring Arbor Junior College 32
Spring Carnival 192
Sputnik. 182
Stein, Jay 40, 52, 71, 78, 106, 107
Stein, Wilson 40, 52, 70, 71, 78, 79, 106, 107
Tanana Spring Carnival 192
Tanana Public Library 215
Taylor, Andrew 52, 56, 57, 58, 59, 102
Taylor, James. 52
Taylor, Louela. 52, 56, 58
Taylor, Roy 52
This-Side-of-Heaven Children's Home. 142
Thomas, Mr.. . . . . 136, 137, 139, 140
Thompson, Hannah 72
Thompson Pass 45, 62, 100, 101
Tiekel Roadhouse. 84
Tryland, Tom 265

Tundra Topics. 299
Vaughn's Roadhouse. 295
Wall, Roy 200
White, Alice. 125, 135, 199, 203, 204, 236
Willard. 172, 173
Wilson School 33, 38
Windsor, Mr. 124, 125, 195, 196
Witt, Auburn 77
Witt, Bessie 77
Woods, Sally 16, 154, 175, 176, 235
Worthington Pass. 46
Wrangell. 242, 248
Yukon Barge. 126, 142, 143

ENDNOTES

∙∙

1   Oleo—Oleomargarine, now referred to as just margarine. A butter substitute, which when first introduced was subject to food administration alarm, regulation of color dyes, taxes, restricted sales, and competition with farmers who produced butter and were concerned their source of income would be destroyed. At one point, it was also relegated to "poor people's" spread, and there was cultural prejudice regarding who used what.

2   Tiekel Roadhouse was at Mile 52 of the Richardson Highway, or Mile 48 on the old trail. It had been established in 1904 by Frederick B. Vaughn, and designated "Vaughn's Roadhouse." Vaughn was the postmaster for the area from 1917 to 1919. Originally, the roadhouse complex consisted of six log buildings. The roadhouse itself could seat 30 people. Homegrown vegetables were a feature of its fine reputation. Later the name designated the area of the roadhouse, which was near the Tiekel River. In 1955, the only evidence of the roadhouse was about 100 feet off the highway; a simple log cabin in a clearing with a backdrop of heavy forest.

3   Several years went by and a letter arrived from Al's mother, who had become a friend of Anna's. Sad news. Ruth miscarried the baby she and Al so anticipated. Time passed and a more shocking letter arrived. Ruth's second childbirth ended in death for her and her baby. Following this, Al remarried, and after that failed marriage, remarried again. One day when Anna was reading the *Alaska Magazine*, she casually glanced at the "End of the Trail" obituaries. With disbelief and sorrow, she recognized Al's name. While on a business trip in southwestern Alaska, he had died of a brain hemorrhage.

4   Athabascan Indians occupy a vast area in interior Alaska; whereas Yupik and Inupiat Eskimos are settled more traditionally along the coastline.

5   CAA/FAA–Civil Aeronautical Authority, which in mid-1958 became Federal Aviation Agency (FAA).

6   The White Alice Communication System was a telecommunication system constructed in Alaska during the Cold War. It connected remote Air Force sites in Alaska, such as the Distant Early Warning (DEW) line, to command and control facilities. The station on the hill behind Tanana had large, flat antennas. This radar station, along with over 50 others in Canada and Alaska held up an invisible 3,000 mile barricade near the Arctic Circle to protect North America. Various stories were conjured as to the name choice: reference to the wife of someone in the defense industry, or perhaps a code word. The facts? *A*laska *I*ntegrated *C*ommunications and *E*lectronics.

7   "Tanana" means "River of Mountains." Old maps describe the approximately 250-mile-long river as the "River of Mountain Men"

8   *Division of Church Denominations in Alaska,* Research Paper presented for graduate credit in History of Alaska 541, by Phyllis Matheny and Anna Bortel, June 1963.

    The earliest attempts at missionary work in Alaska began in 1793, when Empress Catherine the Great of Russia issued an Imperial order that missionaries be sent to the American colonies. In accordance with the order, 11 monks sailed to Kodiak Island. From this point, their influence spread to the Aleutian Islands, to Cook Inlet and the mainland, and eventually to Southeastern Alaska. Due to these initial religious efforts, the Russian Orthodox Church remained the strongest single sect into the early 1900s.

    From the eastern side of Alaska, the Church of England sent pioneer missionaries from the Northwest Territories of Canada in 1847. Later, when the American Episcopal Church commenced its work in Alaska, the Church of Canada turned over its missions in the Yukon Valley to these Americans; consequently, the Episcopal influence was strong in Tanana and the Mission upriver of that village.

    In 1877, the Presbyterians were the first denomination from the United States to take on an assignment in Alaska. The inception of the Presbyterian undertaking was inseparable from the work of Dr. Sheldon Jackson, who balanced the roles of both missionary and general agent for education in Alaska.

    The Presbyterians recruited 17 school teachers for their mission-related school system of 500 students, and Congress provided the Alaskan territory with $25,000 for a school system to be administered by a general agent, Sheldon Jackson. During this era, missionary efforts resulted in the formation of schools and orphanages, although the Moravians, Methodists, Roman Catholics, and other denominations instigated these institutions. With no ill-feelings, many eventually relinquished their schools to the Presbyterians. As a result, for over ten years, church and state effectively worked together.

Next to the Russian Church, in 1894, the Presbyterians accounted for more missions in Alaska than any other group. In fact, for many years, the Presbyterian mission's interests were second only to the Alaska Commercial Company in directing the destiny of the Alaska Territory.

In 1880, in a superb example of inter-denominational cooperation, Sheldon Jackson met with church representatives to negotiate an informal division of mission areas in Alaska. Following the natural growth of the denominations, they mapped out areas for each denomination's concentration of effort. The Episcopal Church assumed responsibility for the Yukon River area and northward. The Methodists accepted the Shumagin and Aleutian Islands and the Alaska Peninsula. The Baptists undertook the development of Kodiak Island, the Cook Inlet and Prince William Sound regions. The Moravians concentrated on the valleys of the Kuskokowim and Nusagak Rivers. The Congregationalists focused on the Cape Prince of Wales area. The Presbyterians, already settled in Southeastern Alaska would stay there, but also agreed to commence work at Point Barrow.

The only practical way Sheldon Jackson could accomplish his goals of organizing schools in the remote parts of Alaska, was to allocate areas to the different denominations, and then attach the responsibility and expense of setting up and managing schools.

9   Pilot Boy Crackers (Sailor Boy Pilot Bread Crackers)—Ship pilots used these at sea when they couldn't get bread, hence the term *pilot* bread. These saltless four-inch round, thick crackers serve a number of purposes in Alaska: emergency gear for hunters or for bush pilots, after-school snacks with peanut butter, and teething crackers for babies. They seemed to be consistently stale yet *never too old* to use. No one minds and everyone has a reserve of these rations. They come in a long rectangle box with white sailor boys skipping across the

blue papers box, are in all rural stores in Alaska, as well as available for purchase at Costco in Anchorage, Alaska.

10   Powdered lime was used to increase the decay of excrement and decrease the odor.

11   The unavailability was due to a strike at the Libby Owens Glass Factory in Toledo, Ohio. Ironically, the strikers were the parents of students in the school where Anna's brother, David, was principal.

12   In 1980 this 8,500,000 acres became the Gates of the Arctic National Park.

13   *"Tundra Topics* was a program on Fairbank's KFAR radio station that was a life-line for people in remote areas. It communicated personal news, such as assuring someone that their loved one at the Tanana hospital was doing better; general news about a pilot arriving in the dark and needing someone to set up bonfire lights along the runway, or river, so he could see to land; information about weather or where a caribou herd was spotted for hunting; an individual's upcoming arrival in a village; or an emergency request for a bush pilot fly to take a person in to medical care. *Tundra Topics* is no longer in existence.

LIVE

listen|imagine|view|experience

AUDIO BOOK DOWNLOAD INCLUDED WITH THIS BOOK!

In your hands you hold a complete digital entertainment package. In addition to the paper version, you receive a free download of the audio version of this book. Simply use the code listed below when visiting our website. Once downloaded to your computer, you can listen to the book through your computer's speakers, burn it to an audio CD or save the file to your portable music device (such as Apple's popular iPod) and listen on the go!

How to get your free audio book digital download:

1. Visit www.tatepublishing.com and click on the e|LIVE logo on the home page.
2. Enter the following coupon code:
   cb2f-46a4-5d0b-37ab-67df-4665-6971-ed29
3. Download the audio book from your e|LIVE digital locker and begin enjoying your new digital entertainment package today!